Industrial Policies for Growth and Competitiveness: Volume II

Industrial Policies for Growth and Competitiveness: Volume II

Empirical Studies

Edited by
F. Gerard Adams
University of Pennsylvania

Lexington Books
D.C. Heath and Company/Lexington, Massachusetts/Toronto

Library of Congress Cataloging in Publication Data
(Revised for volume 2)
Main entry under title:
  Industrial policies for growth and competitiveness.

  (The Wharton econometric studies series. Industrial
policy studies)
  Includes bibliographies and indexes.
  Vol. 2 lacks series statement.
  Contents: [1] An economic perspective—v. 2.
Empirical studies.
  1. Industry and state—Addresses, essays, lectures.
I. Adams, F. Gerard (Francis Gerard), 1929–   .
II. Klein, Lawrence Robert.   III.   Series.
HD3611.I38   1983   338.9   81–48557
ISBN 0–669–05421–7 (v. 1)
ISBN 0–669–09593–1 (v. 2: alk. paper)

Published simultaneously in Canada
Printed in the United States of America on acid-free paper
International Standard Book Number: 0–669–09593–1
Library of Congress Catalog Card Number: 84–48529

Contents

Preface and Acknowledgments   ix

1 **Empirical Analysis of Industrial Policies: The Challenges   1**
   F. *Gerard Adams*

   The Concept of Industrial Policy   2
   Evaluating the Success of Industrial Policy   6
   The Methodology of Policy Simulation   8
   Outline of This Book   11

2 **International Interactions of Industrial Policy: Simulations of the World Economy, 1982–1990   15**
   Lawrence R. Klein, Andrea Bollino, and *Shah Fardoust*

   Theoretical Framework   17
   Scenario Assumptions   18
   Empirical Results   21

3 **General versus Industry-Specific Industrial Policies: Quantifying the National and Sectoral Impacts   31**
   F. *Gerard Adams* and *Vijaya G. Duggal*

   Industry Policy Simulations   33
   Comparison of Policy Instruments   34
   Industrial Impacts of Incentive Policies   35
   Macroeconomic Impacts of Incentive Policies   36
   Evaluating the Costs and Benefits   44

4 **Regionalized Analysis of Industrial Policy   49**
   John A. Del Roccili and *Priscilla Luce*

   The Structure of the Regional Model   50
   Alternative Simulations of Regional Growth   54
   Conclusions   65

5 The Effects of Foreign Export-Promotion Policies on the United States: Macro Model Simulations 67
F. Gerard Adams, Lawrence R. Klein, and *Vijaya G. Duggal*

International Aspects of Industrial Policy 67
The Impact of Foreign Industrial Policies 69
U.S. Foreign Industrial-Policy Scenario 70
Conclusions 84

6 Industrial-Policy Impacts on the U.S. Steel Industry: A Simulation Study 85
F. Gerard Adams, Trevor Alleyne, Christopher Bell, Richard Koss, Brian Pinto, and *Mikko Puhakka*

Issues and Experience in the U.S. Steel Industry 86
The International Issues 90
An Econometric Model of the U.S. Steel Industry 91
Validation of the Econometric Model 113
Policy Analysis 119
Conclusions 130

7 Industrial Policy and the Electrical Machinery Industry: The Case of Transformers 133
Vladimir Kontorovich

The Transformer Industry 134
The Structure of the Model 135
Model Validation: Baseline Simulations and Multiplier Analysis 141
Policy Analysis 144
Conclusion 151
Appendix 7A: Mnemonics and Definitions of Variables 153

8 Quantity and Quality of Capital Impacts on Productivity in the Chemical Industry: An Empirical Study 161
Menahem Prywes

Data and the Production Function 162
The Effect of New Regulation on the Quantity of Capital and Productivity 163
Energy and the Quality of Capital 165
R&D and Productivity 168
Conclusion 172
Appendix 8A: The Three-Level Nested CES Production Function 175
Appendix 8B: Estimation of the Regulatory Capital Stock 177

9 Industrial Policy and Optimization in the Coal Industry 181
Robert F. Wescott

An Overview of the International Trade Flow Model for Coal 182
The Baseline Forecast 189

Analyzing the Impact of Potential U.S. Coal Policies   195
Conclusions   207

10 Empirical Evaluation of Industrial Policy: An Appraisal   211
F. Gerard Adams

Experience with Empirical Studies of Industrial Policy   214
The Gaps   221

Bibliography   229

Index   233

About the Contributors   241

About the Editor   243

Preface and Acknowledgments

T his book is based on a research project on industrial policy carried out at the Economics Research Unit, Department of Economics, University of Pennsylvania during 1980–1983 under sponsorship of the U.S. Departments of Labor and Commerce. This is the second book drawn from this research.

The chapters presented in this book are econometric studies of industrial policy and are concerned with policy impacts on the international economy, the United States, its various regions, and various individual industries. Although the literature on industrial policy is long, there have been few econometric studies of industrial policy impacts, so that these econometric investigations are unique in focus.

The authors wish to thank Arnold Packer, who helped initiate this research effort, and Nancy Barrett, Roland Droitsch, Samuel Woods, Warren Farb, and Allen Olsen, who were involved with the original Department of Labor and Department of Commerce project, for helpful suggestions and support. We also wish to thank the numerous other people who have worked with us and have influenced these studies of industrial policy.

The information presented in this book is entirely the responsibility of the authors and in no way represents the views of past or present staff of the Departments of Labor and Commerce.

Lynnmarie Costello deserves thanks for an excellent job of typing.

1
Empirical Analysis of Industrial Policies: The Challenges

F. Gerard Adams

lmost all countries have some kind of industrial policies (IPs). Although industrial policies tend to be associated with the targeted industry-specific efforts typical of Japan and France, many more traditionally free-enterprise countries such as West Germany also have industrial policies. The United States has had no formal industrial policy for many years, although general incentives to savings and investment have been enacted under both Democratic and Republican administrations. Implicit industrial policies favoring agriculture, defense industries, and transportation have long been a part of the economic scene, and industry-specific policies intended to protect or aid the restructuring of particular industries or firms are becoming more frequent. As the challenges in the world economy have grown, proposals have been made that the United States also turn toward an explicit industrial policy, a broad and coherent policy effort to rejuvenate U.S. industry. There is, however, no consensus; indeed, there are considerable differences of opinion on whether an industrial policy would be useful and, if so, what forms it should take. Such policy proposals hang not only on economic issues but also on broad philosophic and political considerations, which the economist alone cannot weigh. Even many of the purely economic questions about the effectiveness of industrial policy, however, are subject to considerable disagreement.

Most strong opinions about industrial policy rest on theoretical and philosophical thinking, sometimes on little more than repeated vigorous assertion. Little systematic work has been done to evaluate the effectiveness of the industrial-policy experience or to measure the impact of potential policy alternatives. Our survey of worldwide thinking and experience with industrial policy (Adams and Klein 1983) suggests that the record of success or failure ranges widely. Although there have been failures, even spectacular ones such as the Anglo-French Concorde, other efforts, such as the Japanese strategies, are seen by many experts as largely successful.[1] Most such evaluations are judgmental, however, and provide scant basis for making decisions about specific policy alternatives.

One complication is the fact that the impacts of industrial policies are likely to be specific not only to the particular policy but also to the environment in which it is applied. Thus, for example, the fact that a particular policy has been successful in Japan does not mean that the policy will work in the setting of U.S. industry. Conversely, one need not automatically reject a policy as unsuitable for the U.S. environment just because it has been used by the Japanese.

The central point is that industrial policies must be evaluated quantitatively as well as qualitatively, specifically as well as generally. Ideally, one would consider IPs from the same cost-benefit perspective as other public-policy proposals. This may not always be possible because it may be difficult to obtain a complete quantified measure of all the benefits. An IP that is intended to open broad new technological options may be hard to evaluate empirically, for example; or a protectionist policy may impose costs that are not easily measured. Many aspects of industrial policy, however, can be measured quantitatively from the perspective of both their costs and their benefits. For this purpose the tools of econometric modeling can be particularly useful. The key issue is to measure the impact of alternative policies. Econometric models of an economy or of an industry provide a comprehensive framework in which alternative policy scenarios can be considered quantitatively: the model of the industry in order to measure the impact on the particular industry and on related activities, the model of the nation (and of the international system) to measure the impacts of industrial policy on national (and international) economic development. Even if the nature of some IP initiatives resists direct quantitative appraisal, modeling studies can contribute in many cases to evaluating how the economy would be affected in many crucial dimensions.

This volume looks at industrial-policy questions from an empirical perspective. What are the potentials and barriers to empirical evaluation of IPs? How can industrial-policy alternatives be integrated into econometric models and their impact evaluated? What does such analysis show about the effect of industrial-policy strategies at the level of the international economy, the level of the nation, and the level of particular regions and industries?

The Concept of Industrial Policy

Proposals aimed at increasing the nation's productivity and competitiveness have gone under a variety of names: reindustrialization, revitalization, structural-adjustment policies, bailouts, even supply-side policies. Some economists have taken the position that the best industrial policy is no policy at all, that the unfettered operation of the market will result in optimal resource allocation and the best industrial structure.

The debate on a potential U.S. IP continues despite the fact (or perhaps because of the fact) that there is little agreement on the meaning of the term *industrial policy*.[2] What is industrial policy? What kinds of measures does an industrial policy include? What are its ultimate objectives?

At the heart of the industrial policy debate is the question of whether policies for growth and competitiveness should be targeted on particular industries or whether they can be broadly general without specific industrial focus. In this connection, a terminological distinction is sometimes drawn between *micro* industrial policies that are industry-specific and *macro* industrial policies, which are not.

The choice between a narrowly focused industrial policy and a broader system of incentives was at the center of the policy dispute on reindustrialization during the last phase of the Carter administration in 1980. Some economists took the position that the United States should adopt an industrial policy like that of France. The idea was to identify the so-called winner industries and then to adopt industry-specific or even project-specific measures in order to advance these fields. Presumably they would be high-technology, synthetic-energy and other highly capital-intensive industries. Opponents of this idea argued that it would be difficult to pick the winners, that there would be only a slim chance that government bureaucrats or committees representing labor, management, and the public sector could effectively choose potential winner industries.

The outcome of the dispute was a decision to go for a non-industry-specific policy, a series of proposals for tax incentives to industrial investment and modification of the depreciation guidelines, not altogether different from the business tax legislation ultimately enacted by the Reagan administration.[3]

One may, of course, view the distinction between industry-specific and general policies as a semantic issue, giving policies outside the scope of the narrow definition of industrial policy a different name. But there is merit to viewing industrial policies broadly to include nontargeted policies, since a variety of policy tools that are not narrowly focused on particular industries or projects may play an important, even dominant, role in achieving the objectives of economic restructuring. This is particularly important in the United States, where past experience with public decision making about business matters or with public enterprise has not always been favorable.

We have found it useful in our work to take a broad view of industrial policy, including both industry-specific and general measures. Thus IPs may include measures intended to improve industrial structure or to aid in its adjustment, to provide incentives for investment in new industrial capacity, to stimulate research and development, to build new industries, and to ease transition from old sectors. In short, we see industrial policies as supply-side instruments. We include all policies intended to improve industrial productivity and competitiveness and to adapt the productive potential of the U.S.

economy to the needs of the 1980s. Some of these policies focus narrowly on specific fields, but others have broad impacts on many sectors. Some are directly concerned with industries; others are oriented more widely toward industrial infrastructure, human capital, and basic research.

IPs can be looked at from the perspective of their *purpose,* their *specificity,* and their *mechanisms.*

Purpose

The purposes of industrial policy are often summarized in three categories: policies intended to advance the winners, policies to help the losers, and policies to aid industrial transitions. A fourth category—policies to improve the economic setting for industry—must be added.

Advancing the Winners. The objective of advancing potential winner industries has undeniable attraction. Many countries, among them Japan and France, have directed their policies toward this goal to find the industries in the forefront of technology and to help them establish a leading position in the world economy. Such policies can be more or less specific and more or less interventionist. At one extreme they represent simply the effort to identify the types of sectors that offer long-run comparative advantage—for example, high technology, agriculture, advanced services—and to give them maximum incentives. At the other extreme are specific picking-the-winner policies, which call for selection and development of particular technologies or projects.

Aiding the Losers. Bailouts for industries in financial difficulty have not been uncommon in the United States, the United Kingdom, and elsewhere. It is inescapable that major industries will seek public-sector assistance when they run into trouble. Industrial retrenchment and failures have social and political consequences. The regional concentration of certain industries, with resulting high incidence of unemployment in certain areas, increases pressures to support declining industries. There may also be economic justifications for aiding troubled industries, however—for example, if the difficulty is temporary, or if the industry represents an essential link to a larger industrial structure. It is important in this connection to make realistic calculations of the long-run prospect for the sector and the firm. Can it be salvaged into an efficient competitive enterprise? Do the ultimate gains from maintaining or supporting such a sunset industry justify the costs incurred?

Smoothing Transitions. The foregoing leads naturally to the next category of policy—that intended to smooth transitions. Even if ultimately the elimination of certain industries and their replacement by other activities is justified, the social and economic costs of the transition are often very high. This means there is often justification for policies intended to ease transitions—to retrain or move unemployed workers, to find alternative uses for plant facilities, to make effective use of the managerial staff that is being displaced.

Improving the Setting for Industry. Much can be accomplished by improving the setting in which industries operate. This could involve improved infrastructure and public services, a better-trained labor force, or a legislative setting that reduces arbitrary interventions and facilitates adaptation to new technologies—for example, in communications. The United States has allowed public capital to deteriorate, and much needs to be done to redress these losses. Requirements for improved human capital through investment in education and training are also important in a world that is moving increasingly from muscle power to brain power.

Specificity

Industrial policies may be specific to particular industries or even to particular firms or projects. On the other hand, our broad definition includes industrial policies that are non-industry-specific—directed to all industries or to eligible industries in a particular sector.

General industrial policies (GIPs) intended to encourage investment may be an important part of an industrial policy that seeks to advance capital-intensive industries or sectors that need to renew their stock of machinery and equipment. Even policies that are general in coverage offer advantages to specific industries, a fact that is not lost on their supporters.

Industrial policies need not focus specifically on narrowly defined industries or enterprises, but targeting—*industry-specific policies* (ISPs)—has been an important feature of many industrial-policy efforts.

Mechanisms

The range of policy mechanisms is wide. In one dimension one may evaluate these policies for their *comprehensiveness*. At the narrowest level, we can conceive of a specific measure or a specific regulation. A program of industrial policy embraces a set of measures that are seen as a coordinated whole by the policymaker. Finally, an industrial strategy can be seen as a broad economywide program intended to reorient the entire economy.

From another perspective, one may ask to what extent industrial policies are indicative, provide incentives, or are compulsory. At one extreme are indicative programs whose sole purpose is to establish targets and to provide a background against which private decision making can be evaluated. Indicative planning—the so-called visions of the Japanese Ministry of International

Trade and Industry (MITI)—are typically supplemented with more concrete measures. These may range from general incentives for investment and research, taking the form of tax credits, preferential credit terms, accelerated depreciation, subsidies, and grants—all measures that are not compulsory in character but are intended to supplement the incentives provided by the market mechanism. Finally, one can turn to direct public intervention in the economy through regulatory measures, public enterprises, direct investments, contracts, or guaranteed markets for the private sector. Note the range—from one extreme, where the measures are indicative, to the other, where they represent direct government intervention. In the United States the advantages of the private-sector-oriented approach, in terms of entrepreneurial innovation and in terms of the so-called test of the market, appear to be considerable compared to the perceived problems associated with public enterprise. Most countries, however, have at one time or another used the entire range of policy options.

Evaluating the Success of Industrial Policy

Criteria are necessary to evaluate the success or failure of industrial policies. Since the intent of industrial policies typically extends beyond the aims of the industrial business enterprise, the criteria on which industrial policy must be judged also are considerably broader than those applying to the success of business investments. Thus, for example, it is not sufficient to ask, as some analysts do, whether an industry that has been promoted by industrial policies is earning a competitive return on its invested capital. Indeed, had there been a reasonably certain expectation of such a return, private business might well have developed such industry without aid from the public sector. The Japanese steel industry is such a case. During the earlier stages of Japanese industrialization, the steel industry could not be evaluated only in terms of its profitability as a separate industry. By the standard of its low rate of return, the Japanese steel industry is not a success. It can be seen, however, as an essential link in the broader industrial objective of an integrated modern industry, which the Japanese have sought to achieve.[4] This is not to say that return on capital should be disregarded, but it does mean that the success of an incentive favoring one sector over others must be evaluated on the basis of other criteria as well as profitability—impact on employment, trade balance, production costs, technological development, industrial structure, and so on. The success of these measures must be considered with respect to their effect on all industries and on the economy as a whole.

The objectives of industrial policy have ranged widely. Starting from the narrowest industry-specific policy (ISP) to the broadest general industrial policy (GIP), we can develop the following list of relevant considerations:

For a particular industry: Return on capital, international competitiveness, employment, low cost of production and price of product, modernization of equipment, development of new technology.

For a region: Growth of regional product and other regional development measures; improved infrastructure—roads, communication, transportation costs—development of integrated regional, commercial, and industrial structure; employment; public-sector revenues; improvement of health and education.

For the nation as a whole: Growth of national product and other measures of improved national economic performance; improved utilization of industrial capacity; competitiveness in world markets; reduced inflationary pressures; development of advanced industries and improvement in productivity; phasing out of old, declining industries; reduction of unemployment, particularly structural unemployment; improved national infrastructure; building of technical research and development base; improved national security; improvements in the national stock of capital and improved utilization of national resource base; improved social conditions; improved education and human-capital stock.

Not all these considerations are readily measureable. Even if the measurement is possible, it is not always clear how these diverse factors can be compared to one another. What, for example, is the relative weighting to be given to improved productivity versus reduced employment as a result of an IP measure? What is the trade-off between industrial, regional, and national benefit? What is an optimal industrial structure from the perspective of the region and from that of the nation? These multiple considerations intervene almost inevitably in the process of industrial policymaking. Admittedly they pose some significant problems to policy management. There is evidence around the world (Adams and Klein 1983) of cases where industrial-policy decisions have been dominated by social and political considerations, or have assumed economic justifications without adequate quantification. Under those circumstances, who is to say whether the policies have succeeded or failed. (In some cases, of course, the evidence of failure or of success is so apparent in the results that it is difficult to argue to the contrary.)

As this discussion makes clear, multidimensional quantitative analysis of the costs and benefits of industrial-policy proposals is a sine qua non of efficient decision making. This quantitative analysis need not be precise, however. Even an approximate estimate, the best one can do under admittedly difficult circumstances, is better than no estimate at all. Fortunately, economic aspects of the results of industrial policy are somewhat more amenable to quantification than are the social-political considerations.

What does this mean for empirical economic studies of IP? First, quantitative studies are appropriate wherever possible. As already noted, such studies may be more readily carried out for some aspects of industrial policy than for others. Measuring the direct impacts of investment incentives on investment is relatively straightforward; it is much harder to evaluate the effects of policies favoring research or education. Second, it is important to recognize the impacts of policy not only on the level of a particular industry, which may benefit, but also on other industries, on the region, and on the nation as a whole. Indirect effects may contribute to or may offset the direct impacts on a particular industry. Third, the appraisal must be multidimensional. Profitability is not the only criterion. Indeed, if the usual assumptions about competitive markets apply (and in the absence of market failure), profitability should be a sufficient guide for private decision making, and there may be no need for industrial policy. Industrial policy often supplements the private market, however, presumably because the private market will not accomplish the desired tasks, or will accomplish them too slowly or at too high an economic or social cost. Consequently, the results of industrial policy usually must be appraised from a broader perspective, which takes into account measures of effectiveness such as those noted earlier.

The Methodology of Policy Simulation

Econometric or simulation modeling offers the opportunity to measure the impact of industrial policy on many, but not all, of the dimensions of concern.

The typical methodology of policy simulation applies.[5] This methodology can be summarized in the following steps:

1. *Development of the econometric model describing the industry:* The model of the policy impact points is at the heart of industrial-policy modeling. For this purpose, an industrial model of the econometric type or of the simulation model variety (Naylor 1979) is the appropriate vehicle. Short of building a complete industry model, the relevant behavioral functions may be introduced into a macro model. As we will note later, it is possible, for example, to introduce industrial-policy incentives into the investment functions of a macro model or to develop special shift parameters to recognize industrial policies in a broad national model framework by shifting the coefficients of the input-output system.

2. *Integration of the industry model into a national (or international) model:* Since the impacts of industrial policy are likely to be broader than the effects on a particular industry (indeed, in most cases they are supposed to be), the relation between the industry model and the national model system is critical.

3. *Derivation of the base (control) solution without industrial policy:* Standard practice in policy simulation is the development of a base solution. This solution may apply to a historical period or, for maximum relevance to the proposed policy options, it could be a forward projection or a base forecast. In either case, the objective is to have a base in the absence of industrial policy against which the policy alternatives can be compared.

4. *Introduction of industrial-policy alternatives into the model system:* The appropriate way to introduce policy alternatives into the model system depends greatly on the particular proposed policy. As we will note later, some policy possibilities—tax incentives, for example—are relatively easy to integrate into a conventionally structured econometric model. Others, however, pose significant difficulties. Obviously, the strategy for introducing the policies into the model simulations must be thought through at the time the specification of the industry model is worked out, since the model design must be adapted as much as possible to its proposed use.

5. *Simulation of alternative industrial-policy scenarios:* Alternative industrial policy scenarios are simulated in the model. The impact of industrial policies is measured by comparing policy simulations with the base simulation. It is possible to measure the impact of single specific policy measures as well as broad policy programs that combine numerous measures.

6. *Evaluation of alternative policies:* Empirical results of alternative policy simulations must be evaluated along with broader political, regional, or social considerations that the econometric model does not consider. A cost-benefit framework is the optimal evaluation strategy.

Although the methodology of econometric modeling and simulation is fairly mature, it is less clear how best to accommodate industrial policies into the econometric models of national economies, as well as into industrial models.

Certain types of policy initiatives can be handled readily along traditional lines since econometric models incorporate so-called policy handles that allow certain policies to be introduced. Investment-incentive policies such as investment tax credits or accelerated depreciation and preferential financing fit directly into the investment equations of the macro models, which traditionally relate business fixed investment to output, prices, and the user cost of capital (where the term *capital* incorporates the interest rate, tax rate, investment tax credits, and depreciation (Jorgenson 1963). In turn, the stimulus to investment should feed through the model by way of the supply side as increases in capital stock, which will favor productivity and potential output, and through demand side effects as a result of increased investment demand as well. Industry-specific measures call for a macro model system with industrial disaggregation and extensive detail at the industry level. Protective tariff measures also can be introduced by adjusting the relationship between import prices and domestic prices, although here a highly disaggregated structure of import functions may be necessary to show the impact of specific protectionist measures.

Other policy measures are more difficult to accommodate since most econometric macro models do not include the necessary linkage relationships. For example, suppose IP takes the form of aid to research and development. Few existing macro models show research and development (R&D) expenditures explicitly, and even fewer are able to handle the tenuous but important relationship between expenditures on R&D and technical progress. This is a problem not simply at the macro level but also at the level of particular industries, where the association between investment in research and gains in productivity is imprecise and involves long lag periods. Moreover, if the research results in new industrial processes, it ultimately may shift the industry's production function or the nature of its product. Such changes, which are frequently the object of an industrial policy, are difficult to recognize in most models. One common approach is to install a shift parameter in the production function or to make technologically determined adjustments in the input-output coefficients, but it is often difficult to establish what the magnitude and/or the timing of such shifts is likely to be. Similar problems arise when policy is directed toward education and training or toward infrastructure development.

Industry-specific assistance—credits or contracts—is also difficult to factor into the model system unless highly disaggregated industrial structure is available, as in an industry model. Even in that case it may be necessary to make approximate adjustments in the model to account for the changes that will ultimately take place. Visualize, for example, the problem involved in handling econometrically the Japanese efforts with respect to the 64K RAM chip and related microelectronics, or the French effort to stimulate the production of computer peripheral equipment. Equally difficult to take into account are the changes in industrial organization that are sometimes carried out under the guise of industrial policy—for example, the French efforts to rationalize major lagging basic industries, or the Japanese recession cartels. Explicit adjustment on the basis of the expected impact of these policies would need to be made to the model system. This is not a counsel of despair, however, since a well-structured and detailed model offers many opportunities to make adjustments and to check to see that their effect is reasonable in terms of expected behavioral changes. Moreover, once the changes have been introduced, the remainder of the model system serves to evaluate their impacts elsewhere in the economy and to catch indirect as well as direct effects.

Comprehensive industrial-policy strategies have often been justified on the basis that a coherent integrated industrial structure will create economies and gains that exceed the sum of its parts. Such a policy of restructuring the economy or altering its industrial composition is intended to reorient the entire economy and, presumably, to produce broad advantages. It is not clear whether most econometric models draw a sufficiently subtle picture of the economy to capture the macro interaction effects of such broad structural economic changes.

On the other hand, econometric modeling has great advantages. Traditionally, econometric simulation has been a way to quantify the dimensions of proposed policy changes. Such quantification is particularly important in the case of industrial policy, since more than a simple change in some aspects of the economic system is desired. Industrial policies intended to restructure the economy are likely to have impacts throughout the system. The indirect effects may be as important, whether in a positive or in a negative direction, as the direct impacts of the policies. For this purpose, insertion of the proposed policies in a complete simultaneous system of the economy offers the possibility to take the interaction effects into account and to evaluate the total impact of these policies—of course, as we have indicated, within the limits of the econometric model's capabilities.

Outline of This Book

This book presents a series of empirical studies of industrial policy. These studies are intended to illustrate the application of econometrics to the study of industrial policy, to show the potentials for research in this direction, and to provide empirical information on various important questions of policy effectiveness on the national and industrial level.

The first study, chapter 2, is concerned with the international impact of industrial policies. The policy mechanisms considered here are traditional and general ones—investment tax incentives and interest rates. The basic idea is not simply to examine the effectiveness of these policies within one country but to see what the impact of industrial policy is on trade-partner countries as well—that is, on the world economy—and to ask whether coordinated policy carried on by several countries is more effective than a separate policy strategy by one country. Using the models of Project LINK, a linked system of country models covering the world economy, the study investigates the impact of investment-stimulus policy carried on separately in the United States as compared to a joint investment-stimulus effort by the major industrial countries. The results indicate that investment-incentive policies can have significant impact on economic expansion in the country carrying on the stimulus policy and also, though to a lesser extent, in its trade partners. A joint stimulus policy in which many countries participate appears to be more effective as a stimulus to world trade than a policy led by the United States alone.

Chapter 3 is concerned with the impacts of general as opposed to industry-specific industrial policies. Using a large-scale macroeconometric model with an embedded input-output system, the Wharton Annual and Industry Model as specially adapted for this project, the model simulations contrast general industrial policies with policy incentives that have broad industrial targeting. Not surprisingly, the study shows that a general policy still has greatly differentiated impacts on different industries. The simulations indicate that targeted policies, in this case quite broadly targeted ones on high-technology and metals-using industries, make more efficient use of the available financial resources than do general policies available equally to all industries or than do policies targeted on basic industries. The study also contrasts the efficacy of alternative investment incentives and concludes that the investment tax credit is a more efficient stimulus measure than alternatives such as general reductions in corporate-profits taxes.

Chapter 4 is concerned with the regional impacts of industrial policy. Drawing on the simulations discussed in chapter 3, a regional econometric model of the United States has been used to appraise regional impacts. It is not surprising that general as well as industrially targeted industrial policies have differential impacts on different parts of the country. Some regions appear to benefit from industrial policies more than other regions, however, regardless of the nature or industrial focus of the IP measures.

Chapter 5 attempts to weigh the effect on the United States economy of industry-specific imports from abroad. In simulations of the Wharton Annual and Industry Model, it has been assumed that foreign IPs or export supports account for large increases in imports of machinery and transportation equipment into the United States. The impact on the import-competing industries, on other industries linked to them by input-output relationships, and on the economy in general is readily apparent. However, allowing the international adjustment process to operate through a change in the exchange rate significantly modifies the result. The resulting stimulus to exports and reduction in imports brings the economy back to its original growth path after a few years—a strong argument for free trade and exchange-rate adjustment.

Chapters 6 through 9 are concerned with industrial econometric modeling. Industrial econometrics is a field that is much less developed than the application of models to macroeconomies. Consequently, these modeling efforts are not simply applications of existing models to questions of industrial policy, but rather newly developed models at different levels of detail and sophistication intended to evaluate different aspects of industrial policy. Chapter 6 considers the development and application of a model of the U.S. steel industry. This detailed structural representation of the steel industry considers demand for and imports of various classes of steel products, inputs of materials and labor, production costs, price determination, and investment. It is the basis for extensive simulations of alternative industrial-policy scenarios.

Chapter 7 is a small model of the U.S. power-transformer industry. It is a good example of what can be accomplished with a relatively small model system.

Chapter 8 deals with some econometric production-function estimates for the U.S. chemicals industry. This project, which focuses on specification of a limited part of the industry model, considers the impact of government policy on the quality and quantity of capital inputs.

Chapter 9 deals with an elaborate model of the coal industry in the United States and in the world, using programming methodology to obtain optimal results. The coal model shows that U.S. potentials in the world coal market will be influenced only moderately by policies in the United States, although market intervention in other countries could have substantial impact.

Summary conclusions are drawn in Chapter 10.

Notes

1. For a contrary opinion, see Trezise (1983).
2. For a taxonomic discussion, see Adams and Klein (1983), Chapter 2.
3. The latter, of course, extended the idea through the concept of the Kemp-Roth supply-side personal income-tax cuts. Their ultimate objective was also improvement in productivity, but through the indirect mechanism of increased private saving and work incentives through lower personal income-tax rates.
4. For a discussion, see Adams and Ichimura (1983) and Shinohara (1982).
5. For a discussion of policy simulation, see Klein and Young (1980).

2

International Interactions of Industrial Policy: Simulations of the World Economy, 1982–1990

Lawrence R. Klein,
Andrea Bollino, and
Shah Fardoust

The world economy suffered two of its most severe postwar recessions in the decade of the 1970s. This disappointing economic performance has plunged the growth rate of real output for the industrial countries to rates below those of the 1960s and 1970s.

As is well known, the main apparent cause for the two economic recessions of 1974–1975 and 1979–1980 was the abrupt increase in oil prices. Most economists also agree that unlike the Great Depression of the 1930s, which was brought about mainly by an inadequacy in aggregate demand leading in turn to a gradual fall in prices, the recessions of the 1970s were produced mainly by disruptions in aggregate supply and were accompanied by acceleration in the rate of inflation.

For the industrial countries the average growth rate of real output in the period 1973–1981 was only a little more than half the growth rate for 1962–1972. The inflation rate for the 1970s, however, was more than twice that of the 1960s (table 2–1).

In most industrial countries the fall in aggregate demand, resulting from the decrease in real income, has been exacerbated by restrictive monetary policy and, occasionally, restrained fiscal policy in order to slow down the rate of inflation.[1] Especially in the period 1977–1980, this policy prescription "reflected a general view on the part of national authorities that the reduction of inflation and inflationary expectations was a necessary condition for the restoration of better investment performance and sustained economic growth."[2]

High nominal interest rates, resulting partly from competitive increases across countries and partly from domestic monetary conditions, have led to

We would like to thank Victor Filatov for his help in implementing the simulation exercises.

Table 2–1
World Output, Prices, and Trade Performance, 1962–1981
(*All figures are growth rates except as indicated*)

Economic Grouping	Average, 1962–1972	Average, 1973–1981	Change from Preceding Year			
			1973	1975	1980	1981
Industrial countries						
Real output	4.8	2.8	6.3	−0.6	1.2	1.5
GNP deflator	4.1	8.6	7.3	11.2	9.0	8.9
Unemployment rate[a] (rate of unemployment)	3.0	5.2	3.3	5.6	5.7	6.6
Volume of exports	9.0	5.5	13.5	−4.0	4.5	1.5
Volume of imports	9.6	4.0	12.0	−8.0	−1.0	0.0
Current account balance[b] (in billion U.S.$)	(8.1)	(−18.8)	(−19.3)	(17.1)	(−44.0)	(−30.0)
Trade balance[b] (in billion U.S.$)	(9.4)	(−20.3)	(8.3)	(5.5)	(−65.0)	(−50.0)
Developing Countries						
Nonoil developing countries						
Real output	5.8	5.1	6.3	4.0	4.4	5.0
Consumer prices	9.1	28.4	22.1	27.0	37.7	33.7
Volume of exports	7.0	7.1	10.0	0.5	8.0	7.0
Volume of imports	6.0	6.2	14.0	−4.0	6.0	5.0
Current account balance[b] (in billion U.S.$)	(−8.1)	(−47.4)	(−11.5)	(−46.8)	(−80.4)	(−96.7)
Trade balance[b] (in billion U.S.$)	(−7.3)	(−32.6)	(−10.5)	(−40.4)	(−65.2)	(−75.2)
Oil-exporting developing countries						
Real output	9.0	4.1	10.7	−0.3	−3.0	0.1
Consumer prices	8.0	14.0	11.3	18.8	13.4	12.0
Volume of exports	9.0	−1.1	13.0	−11.5	−13.0	−8.0
Volume of imports	9.0	16.8	20.5	41.5	15.5	16.5
Current account balance[b] (in billion U.S.$)	(0.6)	(51.1)	(−6.6)	(35.0)	(112.2)	(96.0)
Trade balance[b] (in billion U.S.$)	(8.5)	(83.0)	(18.8)	(53.4)	(163.00)	(151.23)

Source: Calculated from *World Economic Outlook*, IMF, 1980 and 1981 issues.
[a]Includes only Canada, the United States, Japan, France, West Germany, Italy, and the United Kingdom.
[b]The figures for current account and trade balance for the 1962–1972 column are for 1970–1972.

substantial declines in the rate of investment by the private sector in many industrialized countries. In addition, for the non-oil-developing countries high interest rates are posing a serious threat to long-term economic viability by substantially increasing the cost of borrowing funds for their development projects. Even if interest rates begin to decline, a set of policies specifically designed to encourage capital formation must be developed in order to counter the supply-side setbacks of the 1970s.

The real challenge to the industrial countries in the 1980s is to find a policy mix that could slow down the rate of inflation and simultaneously provide incentives to the private sector for higher rates of investment. The policy mix should be directed at the source of problem—the obsolescence of the energy-inefficient stock of capital and the consequent fall in labor productivity. It has been increasingly recognized by economists from a variety of perspectives that there is an urgent need for some form of industrial policy, general or industry-specific, aimed at stimulating the supply side of the economy in order to cope simultaneously with high unemployment and high inflation.[3]

The aim of this study is to measure the impact of a medium-term industrial-policy strategy involving the major industrial countries on world output, prices, and trade, using the LINK system.[4]

Specifically, we try to answer the following questions:

1. In the face of a neutral monetary policy and initially depressed economic conditions, would a fiscal policy directed at stimulating both the supply side and the demand side of an industrial economy result in a higher growth rate of real output and a lower or unchanged rate of inflation?
2. Is there a gain for the world economy as a whole if the industrial countries follow an industrial policy in concert with one another (a *convoy* policy) in comparison to a situation where only one major industrial country (for example, the United States) follows an industrial policy (a *locomotive* policy)?
3. What are the comparative effects of the convoy and locomotive types of industrial policies on the dynamic path of real output, prices, and trade for the non-oil-exporting developing countries?

Theoretical Framework

The task of modeling industrial policy (IP) within the LINK system is not a trivial one. An IP program aimed at stimulating capital formation in the economy could embrace specific measures, such as investment tax credits, accelerated depreciation, and corporate tax rate changes. The complex dimensionality of the IP policy alternatives does not conform easily to existing macroeconometric models.

Although it would be interesting to consider different selective policies in order to investigate important policy alternatives such as a picking-the-winner approach, this study will not make such an ambitious attempt. Instead, it will focus on policies specifically designed to spur capital formation generally in the manufacturing sector.[5]

In the LINK system each country model possesses unique characteristics reflecting the basic economic structure of the country being modeled. A detailed discussion of econometric specification of capital formation in each country model is beyond the scope of this chapter. Most of the LINK system's national models used in the present simulations use one form or another of the neoclassical investment-equation specifications.[6]

The fiscal measures that may spur capital formation in this model are: lower corporate-profits tax rate, higher investment tax-credit rate, and higher (faster) depreciation rate.

The monetary channel, influencing investment through interest rates, is more complicated since interest-rate changes would directly affect exchange rates.

Scenario Assumptions

We now turn to the assumptions that have been made for the time path of the industrial-policy efforts during the period 1982–1990. These scenarios attempt to capture various views expressed by policymakers in the major developed economies, reinterpreted to conform to the LINK framework. We have refrained from formulating any miraculous scenarios; it is unlikely that we could quickly return the world economy to the fast growth track of the 1960s. Instead, we have tried to respect the feasibility and plausibility constraints imposed by the current debate on government intervention. The policies assumed in the alternative scenarios are summarized in table 2–2.

The Baseline Scenario

The baseline scenario established trends in exogenous inputs for the LINK system up to 1990.[7]

In countries belonging to the Organization for Economic Cooperation and Development (OECD), policy actions adopted in the recent past were used as a guideline for determining future policymaker activity. Fiscal and monetary policy is assumed to be somewhat restrictive in the early part of the decade. As inflation subsides and payment deficits become smaller, this policy stance is relaxed in a number of countries.

With respect to developing countries, extrapolation of policy variables was provided by the United Nations Conference on Trade and Development

(UNCTAD). The ratio of net capital inflow to gross domestic product (GDP) is held at the historical level for the decade—a fairly optimistic assumption given the difficulties in obtaining external financing faced by non-oil-exporting developing countries.

Oil prices are assumed to increase in real terms along a smooth path at an average of 3.6 percent per annum, corresponding to an average annual nominal increase of 11.3 percent.

As a result, this scenario envisages for the 1980s:

1. A real growth rate of world output slightly lower than in the previous decade.
2. Oil-exporting countries' surplus and OECD countries' deficit, progressively fading over time.
3. A slower growth of world trade (in volume) and a pattern of terms of trade turning against non-oil-exporting developing countries.
4. A lower growth rate of centrally planned economies with respect to their historical trend.

A Locomotive Scenario

The second scenario assumes that only the United States engages in an industrial-development strategy. Policymakers are assumed to increase the investment tax-credit rate (approximately double) to achieve total additional investment (nominal nonresidential) of $215 billion in the period 1982–1990.

This scenario represents the starting point of our analysis of IP.

A Convoy Scenario

Abandonment of a simple bilateral view—the United States versus the rest of the world—constitutes the thrust of the third scenario, which assumes that a group of other OECD countries responds to the U.S. IP.

As each country model reflects the different characteristics of various economies in the LINK system, we have assumed that policymakers in each country use an appropriate combination of instruments, in line with both traditional experience and prevailing philosophical attitudes toward IP (table 2–2). For a group of nine countries (Australia, Austria, Belgium, Canada, Italy, the Netherlands, Finland, Sweden, and the United Kingdom), we have assumed a policy commitment comparable to that of the United States.

To quantify this notion, we have assumed that for each country the total additional (nominal) investment in the decade relative to U.S. total additional investment equals that country's gross national product (GNP) relative to U.S. GNP (evaluated at 1981 exchange rates in current U.S. dollars). For Germany, France, and Japan, we have assumed a relatively more aggressive

Table 2–2
Alternative Policy Assumptions, Prelinkage
(*Cumulative additional nominal investment for the period 1982–1990 over the base solution*)

	Target Variable	Target Variable[a] as % of Total Investment	Locomotive		Convoy		Nature of Stimulus
			Amount in Local Currency	Target %Δ of GDP	Amount in Local Currency	Target %Δ of GDP	
Australia	Private investment in equipment	58.1	—	—	5,816	0.3	+ Increased capital tax allowance − Decreased corporate tax rate
Austria	Private investment in equipment	47.4	—	—	13.50	0.2	− Decreased corporate tax rate
Belgium	Private investment	73.9	—	—	279.87	0.7	+ Increased call money interest rate − Increased autonomous investment
Canada	GPCF in machinery	39.2	—	—	25.31	0.8	− Lower user cost of capital
Finland	Total investment	100	—	—	20,709	1.0	− Lower implicit corporate tax rate + Increased autonomous investment
France	Total investment	100	—	—	344.60	1.3	− Lower fiscal pressure on investment price − Lower corporate tax rate + Increased autonomous investment

Country	Variable						Effects
Germany	Private fixed investment	100	—	498.66	3.1	—	− Lower implicit corporate tax rate + Increased autonomous investment
Italy	Private investment	100	—	24,510	0.8	—	+ Increased government transfer to firms
Japan	Private investment	100	—	63,749	2.4	—	+ Increased implicit depreciation rate + Increased autonomous investment
Netherlands	Investment in equipment	91.6	—	23.44	0.7	—	+ Increased total depreciation + Increased autonomous investment in equipment
Sweden	Investment in equipment (manufacturing)	36.4	—	18.12	0.4	—	− Lower local government corporate tax rate − Lower center government corporate tax rate + Increased autonomous investment in equipment
U.K.	Private investment	100	—	45.62	2.1	—	− Lower marginal corporate tax rate + Increased autonomous investment in equipment
U.S.	Nonresidential investment	75.1	214.42	214.42	0.77	0.77	+ Increased investment tax credit

a Average 1982–1990.

response to the U.S. IP. The sum total of additional investment in the private sector as a result of the assumed national industrial policies for the 1982–1990 period amounts to approximately $430 billion.

Empirical Results

Tables 2–3 through 2–8 summarize the outcome of these two scenarios in comparison to the baseline solution for real output, inflation, productivity, and trade variables. All the results reported are for flexible-exchange-rate regimes, a relative version of the purchasing-power-parity rule that has been implemented in the LINK system.[8]

The following general conclusions apply:

1. The growth rate of output for the world economy is on average higher by 0.1 percent per year for the locomotive policy and by 0.2 percent per year for the convoy policy in comparison to the control solution.

2. The rate of inflation for the world economy falls by 0.1 percent per year, on average, for the locomotive policy, but remains unchanged for the convoy case in comparison to the control case. Even in the latter case, however, there is a fall in the rate of inflation comparable to that for the locomotive case in the initial years of simulation.

3. The distribution of gains in real output and lower inflation varies widely across industrial countries under both scenarios. As one would expect, however, besides the United States, Canada and Japan are the main beneficiaries of the locomotive policy. *The United States gains more than any other country, in terms of lowering its rate of inflation and increasing its real output growth, when it pursues industrial policy alone.* Under both scenarios, the country that gains in terms of productivity increases is Japan. The exceptional case among the countries selected for tabulation is Germany, where nominal wage increases seem to outstrip gains in productivity, resulting in a higher inflation rate than for other countries. However, the results indicate that all countries benefit in terms of higher real output growth, with gains on inflation being irregular. Italy's gain in terms of real output growth is less than that of any other "major country" under both scenarios.

4. World trade benefits from both scenarios, although gains from the convoy case are larger by a factor of 3 than those from the locomotive case. This indicates that in the convoy scenario for the world as a whole, gains in trade outstrip gains in output, resulting in a higher trade/output ratio, in real terms, by the end of the 1980s. In both scenarios Japan and Canada benefit more than any other countries, including the United States in

Table 2-3
Real GDP Growth Rate, Control Scenario
(All figures are differences in percentages)

	1982		1985		1990		1980–1990	
	A	*B*	*A*	*B*	*A*	*B*	*A*	*B*
Canada	+0.0	0.7	+0.0	0.2	+0.0	0.1	0.15	0.32
France	+0.0	0.4	0.1	0.5	+0.0	0.7	0.02	0.41
Germany	0.0	0.6	+0.0	0.4	-0.1	0.3	0.01	0.30
Italy	-0.0	0.3	+0.0	0.1	-0.0	0.0	0.01	0.09
U.K.	+0.0	0.4	0.0	0.2	0.0	0.1	0.02	0.21
U.S.	0.3	0.4	0.1	0.1	0.4	0.3	0.45	0.42
Japan	+0.0	0.6	+0.0	0.1	0.1	0.9	0.10	0.48
OECD[a]	0.20	0.50	0.10	0.20	0.20	0.40	0.20	0.40
Developing countries (nonoil)	+0.0	1.0	0.10	0.10	0.0	0.10	0.05	0.10
World	0.10	0.30	0.10	0.20	0.15	0.20	0.10	0.20

Note: A = locomotive, B = convoy.
[a] 13 major OECD countries.

Table 2–4
Rate of Change of Consumption Deflator, Control Scenario
(All figures are differences in percentages)

	1982		1985		1990		1980–1990	
	A	B	A	B	A	B	A	B
Canada	-0.1	-0.2	0.1	0.8	0.0	-0.1	-0.02	0.30
France	-0.1	-0.2	-0.8	-1.0	0.1	0.2	-0.0	-0.01
Germany	0.0	0.1	0.1	0.5	0.1	1.4	0.04	0.62
Italy	0.0	0.1	0.0	0.1	0.0	-0.2	0.0	-0.02
U.K.	-0.0	-0.0	0.1	0.1	0.0	-0.2	-0.01	-0.05
U.S.	-0.4	-0.4	-0.4	-0.6	-0.2	-0.2	-0.32	-0.30
Japan	0.0	0.3	0.0	0.0	0.0	-0.3	0.0	0.19
OECD[a]	-0.2	-0.2	-0.3	-0.3	0.0	0.10	-0.1	-0.0
Developing countries (nonoil)	-0.1	-0.1	-0.1	-0.1	0.0	0.0	-0.0	-0.0
World	-0.1	-0.1	-0.2	-0.2	-0.1	0.1	-0.0	0.0

Note: A = locomotive, B = convoy.
[a] 13 major OECD countries.

Table 2–5
Labor Productivity, Control Scenario
(Percentage change in output per man-hours)

Selected Countries	1982		1985		1990		1980–1990	
	A	B	A	B	A	B	A	B
Canada	0.03	0.46	0.06	0.14	-0.12	0.13	0.05	0.25
France	+0.0	0.26	0.0	0.0	-0.01	0.37	0.0	0.27
Germany	+0.0	0.19	0.0	0.13	+0.0	0.61	0.0	0.20
Italy	0.0	0.29	0.0	0.34	0.0	0.0	0.23	0.48
U.K.	0.0	0.25	0.0	0.11	0.0	0.10	0.0	0.25
U.S.	0.3	0.3	0.1	0.1	0.0	0.0	0.15	0.20
Japan	0.41	0.85	0.0	0.1	0.0	0.72	0.38	0.56

Note: A = locomotive, B = convoy.

Table 2-6
Real Growth of Merchandise Exports, Control Scenario
(All figures are in percentages)

	1982		1985		1990		1980–1990	
	A	B	A	B	A	B	A	B
Canada	0.1	0.4	−0.1	0.2	+0.0	+0.0	0.37	0.41
France	0.1	0.8	0.1	0.5	−0.2	0.1	0.1	0.36
Germany	+0.0	1.0	+0.0	0.4	−0.2	−0.2	0.1	0.32
Italy	0.0	0.7	+0.0	0.4	−0.1	−0.1	+0.0	0.26
U.K.	+0.0	0.4	+0.0	0.2	+0.0	−0.1	+0.0	0.16
U.S.	0.3	0.8	0.6	−0.2	+0.0	−0.0	0.23	0.39
Japan	+0.0	0.7	+0.0	0.3	+0.2	0.4	0.4	0.60
OECD[a]	+0.0	0.7	+0.0	0.3	−0.1	0.0	0.2	0.4
Developing countries								
Oil exporters	+0.0	0.7	+0.0	0.4	0.1	0.5	0.0	0.4
Oil importers	0.1	0.5	0.1	0.2	+0.0	0.1	0.2	0.3
Centrally planned[b]	−0.1	0.5	0.1	0.3	+0.0	0.2	0.0	0.2
World	0.1	0.7	+0.0	0.3	0.0	+0.1	0.1	0.3

Note: A = locomotive, B = convoy.
[a]13 major OECD countries.
[b]Eastern Europe and USSR.

Table 2-7
Real Growth of Merchandise Imports, Control Scenario
(All figures are in percentages)

	1982		1985		1990		1980–1990	
	A	B	A	B	A	B	A	B
Canada	0.1	0.7	0.1	1.0	0.3	0.4	0.2	0.72
France	+0.0	1.2	0.2	0.2	−0.1	−2.1	+0.0	−0.32
Germany	+0.0	1.3	−0.1	0.9	−0.1	0.7	+0.0	0.73
Italy	+0.0	0.6	+0.0	0.1	−0.1	0.0	+0.0	0.25
U.K.	+0.0	0.7	−0.0	−0.0	+0.0	0.1	+0.0	0.15
U.S.	0.1	0.1	−0.1	1.1	0.1	0.2	0.40	0.43
Japan	+0.0	1.1	+0.0	+0.0	+0.0	0.8	0.10	0.56
OECD[a]	+0.0	0.9	+0.0	0.5	+0.0	0.1	0.20	0.40
Developing countries								
Oil exporters	+0.0	0.4	−0.1	−0.1	+0.0	0.0	0.0	0.0
Oil importers	+0.1	0.6	+0.0	0.2	−0.1	−0.1	0.3	0.4
Centrally planned[b]	0.0	0.2	0.0	0.2	+0.0	0.1	0.0	0.2
World	0.1	0.7	+0.0	0.3	+0.0	0.1	0.1	0.3

Note: A = locomotive, B = convoy.
[a]13 major OECD countries.
[b]Eastern Europe and USSR.

Table 2-8
Trade Balance (Levels)
(*All figures in billions of current U.S. $*)

	1982			1985			1990			1980–1990[c]		
	C	A	B	C	A	B	C	A	B	C	A	B
Canada	0.2	0.3	0.0	-2.2	-1.8	-5.3	3.3	8.9	0.4	—	—	—
France	1.4	1.3	-0.7	-0.4	-0.4	-0.3	3.6	4.5	28.6	—	—	—
Germany	18.1	18.2	15.6	7.1	7.8	-2.0	56.4	61.0	16.2	—	—	—
Italy	-3.1	-3.0	-2.8	4.0	4.2	3.4	6.1	7.2	6.7	—	—	—
U.K.	-3.4	-3.3	-3.5	-12.4	-12.2	-11.8	-12.4	-10.6	-10.3	—	—	—
U.S.	-15.0	-15.3	-13.0	-20.4	-22.2	-17.4	29.7	4.6	19.0	—	—	—
Japan	7.5	7.6	6.8	32.4	34.1	32.5	58.0	68.2	52.7	—	—	—
OECD[a]	3.9	3.8	1.2	3.1	3.9	-7.5	110.8	112.3	69.3	27.4	28.6	11.3
Developing countries												
Oil exporters	140.6	140.7	143.5	146.4	146.7	158.8	169.6	176.3	218.8	151.3	153.0	170.4
Oil importers	-94.4	-94.5	-95.4	-145.5	-146.6	-149.1	-280.0	-288.0	-292.9	-165.0	-168.0	-170.6
Centrally planned[b]	-8.5	-8.4	-7.6	-0.9	-0.7	1.4	3.6	5.1	9.6	-2.4	1.8	0.6

Note: A = locomotive, B = convoy, C = control.
[a]13 major OECD countries.
[b]Eastern Europe and USSR.
[c]Arithmetic averages.

terms of real export growth. In terms of balance of trade, Canada, Japan, and Germany gain in the locomotive case at the expense of the United States. However, the convoy case leads to more convergence as most of large surpluses are washed away especially in comparison with the control solution. The exception is France where export growth by far outstrips import growth.[9]

5. The non-oil-exporting developing countries also benefit from both scenarios in terms of real output and trade. However, this gain from the convoy policy seems to be smaller relative to that of the industrial countries. The trade balance for these countries worsens in the convoy case in comparison with the locomotive case. This is essentially due to a higher response in import growth relative to export growth, as the industrial countries stimulate their economies.

6. Oil-exporting countries obviously gain as higher growth rates in world output lead to higher rates of growth of fuel demand. These countries especially increase their trade surplus in the convoy case.

Notes

1. During the 1974–1975 recession some governments chose to have a lax fiscal policy by deliberately running large deficits, perhaps to moderate the fall in aggregate demand.

2. International Monetary Fund (IMF), *World Economic Outlook*, 1981, p. 30.

3. For a comprehensive discussion of measuring and experience with industrial policy in developed economies, see Adams and Klein (1983), chapter 2, "The Meaning of Industrial Policy." The notion of *supply side* referred to in this study is in the spirit of L. R. Klein, "The Supply Side," presidential address to the AEA, *AER* (March 1978).

4. For a detailed discussion of the LINK system, see Klein (1976) and Ball (1973).

5. The precise implementation of this policy obviously depends on the degree of disaggregation within each of the national models in the LINK system. In a few smaller models, where the manufacturing sector is not modeled explicitly, the policy was directed at stimulating capital formation by the private sector as a whole.

To take into account the continual changes in the international and national economic structure, the LINK system itself is in continuous evolution as equations within existing models are reestimated and new country models are added to the system. The specific version of the system used in the present simulations is the 1979–1980 version of the long-term system composed of thirteen industrial country models (Australia, Austria, Belgium, Canada, Finland, France, West Germany, Italy, Japan, the Netherlands, Sweden, the United Kingdom, and the United States); seven models of Eastern European socialist countries and the USSR; and a developing-countries model composed of regions of Asia, Africa, Latin America, and the Middle East.

6. Jorgenson (1963).

7. This scenario is discussed in detail in L.R. Klein, V. Filatov, and S. Fardoust (in press).

8. For implementation of purchasing-power-parity doctrine in the LINK system, see Klein, Fardoust, and Filatov (1981).

9. In the case of France, imports have been restrained in simulations of industrial policy to allow for the government's response to chronic external imbalances.

3
General versus Industry-Specific Industrial Policies: Quantifying the National and Sectoral Impacts

F. Gerard Adams and
Vijaya G. Duggal

O ne issue at the heart of the debate on industrial policy (IP) has been whether stimulative policies should be general or whether measures with specific industry focus are required. In the United States economic policies traditionally have operated at the macro level seeking to stimulate demand or occasionally pushing supply, largely through economy-wide fiscal and monetary measures. In principle, specific industrial development and restructuring has been left to market forces, although in practice, even in the United States there have been some important market interventions.

In contrast to the U.S. approach, some leading industrial nations and advanced developing countries have directed their industrial policies toward development of specific sectors (Adams and Klein 1983). Such policies have sought to promote import substitution or export promotion. In many cases they have been targeted on high-technology industries. Frequently they provided financial aid to declining industries, seeking to rebuild the troubled sector or to ease the transition to other types of activities. The mechanics of these policies have varied greatly, ranging from tax incentives to direct grants and public enterprises. The essential point is not that general policies have only general impacts and industry-specific policies only industry-specific impacts. On the contrary, general policies may affect some industries more than others, and industry-specific policies may also have important economywide impacts. Industry-specific approaches force policymakers to make explicit choices among target industries. Making such choices may or may not improve the effectiveness and efficiency of policy.

The aim of this chapter is to use macroeconometric model simulations to establish quantitatively the dimensions of the effects on particular industries and on the U.S. economy as a whole of tax incentives for investment. The questions to be posed are the following:

> What are the impacts of tax-incentive policies to stimulate industrial investment and productivity (1) at the level of specific industrial sectors? (2) on the performance of the macroeconomy?

> How do these impacts differ when the policies are general (not industry-specific) rather than focused on particular sectors?

> What is the payoff—in terms of benefits to industries and to the national economy and costs to the U.S. Treasury—of general versus industry-specific incentives?

A dynamic macro model framework is necessary in order to measure the net effects of alternative industrial-development strategies in a general equilibrium context. For this purpose we have simulated the Wharton Annual and Industry Model, a system that is particularly well suited for such analysis. This large-scale macroeconomic model of the U.S. economy consists of more than 2,400 equations. It has embedded in it a 56 × 56 input-output matrix, an integral part of the model whose elements change in response to relative prices and technological trends. The breakdown of manufacturing industries is at the two-digit SIC (standard industrial classification) level, making it possible to implement some industry-specific policies, though only for fairly broad groups of industries. The model has a variety of policy handles, such as corporate tax rates, investment tax-credit rate and depreciation tax lives by industrial sectors, and interest rates. Unfortunately, it would be difficult to introduce into the model other types of policies, such as aid to research and development, which might have been interesting to study.

One limitation of studying industry-specific policies within a macro model framework is that it confines us to studying the effect of policies directed at fairly broad groups of industries in order to have a visible impact on the economy as a whole with a reasonable policy incentive. Despite the fact that the model has twenty separate industries within manufacturing, we cannot narrow the policy option to the level of the individual industries because providing a reasonable incentive to only one such industry will not, in the model, have a discernible effect on the total economy. For example, although incentives provided to the steel industry will have a significant impact on the employment, capital, production, price level, and competitivness of the steel industry, it would be difficult to distinguish their effects on the aggregate economy. Our concern here is precisely to see macro effects as well as impacts at the industry level.

Industry Policy Simulations

The approach used in this study is to compare the results of alternative simulations of the Wharton Annual and Industry Model—simulations without an explicit industrial policy as compared to simulations with general and industry-specific policy assumptions. The differences between the simulations, in various dimensions of industry and macroeconomic performance, indicate the impact such policies might be expected to have in the real world.

As a starting point for the simulations, we use the Wharton base forecast of June 1981. This base forecast represents an evaluation in 1981 of the most probable developments of the U.S. economy over the long term. It is not a constant policy solution since it includes approximations of the recently enacted program changes and contains adjustments in fiscal and monetary policy during the forecast period designed to put the economy on a long-run growth path. This path projects growth for the U.S. economy of some 3 percent per year. The impacts of the alternative industrial-policy scenarios are then measured in terms of the difference from the base solution.

To provide a measure for purposes of comparison, the industrial-policy scenarios have been standardized around a direct U.S. Treasury revenue cost of $26 billion over a six-year period, 1982–1987. The timing of the revenue loss varies depending on the proposed policy program; and, of course, so does its allocation by policy tools and by industry. Yet overall the objective was to design a sustained policy change in each case that ex ante costs the Treasury $26 billion. This does not mean, however, that the ultimate direct and indirect cost to the Treasury is at all close to $26 billion. On the contrary, the stimulative effect of the programs varies; the ultimate revenue cost after all endogenous reactions of the economy to demand- and supply-side developments and the impacts on tax receipts will also vary, depending on the program. For this reason, program impacts should be measured not only in terms of *dollar effect per dollar of direct tax revenue reduction,* but also in terms of *dollar effect per dollar of direct and indirect revenue impact.*

We have considered various tools: investment tax credit, shortening depreciation tax lives, corporate tax rate, and interest rate. These were implemented first as general—that is, non-industry-specific—policies, and then on the following three sets of industries:

Basic industries: Agriculture, mining, lumber, stone, clay, glass, primary metals, textiles, paper, chemicals.

Metal-using industries: Fabricated metal products, nonelectrical machinery, electrical machinery, motor vehicles, nonauto transportation equipment and miscellaneous manufacturing, instruments.

High-technology industries: Chemicals, electrical machinery, nonelectrical machinery, nonauto transportation equipment, miscellaneous manufacturing and instruments.[1]

The changes in the fiscal instruments (as percentage changes from the base solution levels) that bear the ex ante cost to the Treasury of $26 billion over the period 1982–1987 are as follows:

	Investment Tax Credit (%)	Corporate Tax Rate (%)	Tax Lives (%)
All industries, nonspecific (ALL)	+ 17	– 13	– 6
Basic industries (BASIC)	+ 70	– 17	– 26
Metal-using industries (METALS)	+ 100	– 25	– 35
High-technology industries (HI-TECH)	+ 100	– 25	– 12

Comparison of Policy Instruments

The alternative policy instruments considered have very different impacts both on the level of the economy in general and on the level of specific industries. We consider these differences here before considering the contrast between industry-specific and general policy scenarios.

The push given in the investment-tax-credit scenario results in a much greater change in the user cost of capital than that which results from a comparable push given in the corporate-tax-cut or the tax-lives scenario. The tax credit directly reduces the cost of an investment good; a firm can take advantage of an investment tax credit only if the firm is going to invest. The corporate tax cut, on the other hand, allows the firm to keep a larger share of any profits that may be earned, regardless of whether or not it invests. The firm may indeed invest more because of the expectation of a larger profit per unit of output, but the investment effect is only an indirect consequence of the tax saving. Thus the investment incentive to the firm from a dollar lost by the Treasury is greater when the incentive takes the form of the investment tax credit than when it takes the form of a cut in taxes on corporate profits. This is reflected in the bigger impact on the user cost of capital in the ITC scenario.

The results of the simulations with respect to the impact on real GNP (as compared to the base solution) are shown in table 3–1. In all cases GNP increases, and the impact of policy is to increase GNP relative to the base solution until 1987, after which the impact declines. The investment-tax-credit policy is clearly the most powerful instrument.

The marked contrast in the impact on GNP of the investment-tax-credit incentive and of the corporate tax cut suggested the possibility of a mixed

Table 3–1
Alternative Industrial-Policy Scenarios: Effect on Real GNP (Compared to Base Forecast)
(billions of 1972$)

	1982	1983	1984	1985	1986	1987
Investment tax credit, all industries	.5	2.3	4.5	6.7	8.7	9.6
Corporate tax cut, all industries	.3	.9	1.9	2.7	3.4	3.7
Capital consumption allowance, all industries	.2	1.0	2.1	3.1	4.0	4.5
Mixed policy	.2	2.1	4.3	6.7	9.3	11.0

policy scenario in which GNP is raised by increasing the tax credit and the corporate tax rate simultaneously. The ex ante cost of this scenario to the Treasury is set at zero; yet the GNP effect turns out to be higher than in the separate case of a corporate tax cut or of a reduction in tax lives.

Industrial Impacts of Incentive Policies

The industrial impacts of alternative investment tax credit scenarios are shown in table 3–2 for a general ITC policy and in tables 3–3 and 3–4 for the metals-using industry-specific scenario.

The impact of an across-the-board investment incentive varies significantly between industries. As can be seen in table 3–2, by 1986 investment is higher as a result of the tax credit by 2.3 percent in chemicals, 4.2 percent in primary metals, 7.9 percent in motor vehicles, and 11.8 percent in nonelectrical machinery.

On the other hand, industry-specific policies may have economywide effects even though only specific industries are affected directly. When the direct effects work themselves into the overall economy, all industries are affected.

To illustrate, we trace the effect on the automobile industry of increasing the investment tax credit in the metal-using manufactures scenario (table 3–3). The tax incentive directly reduces the user cost of capital. Labor is more expensive relative to capital, and additional investment is made to achieve the new desired labor/capital ratio. The change in the desired labor/capital ratio depends on the elasticity of substitution between labor and capital, which varies from industry to industry. In the short run, capital changes slowly, and the labor/capital ratio remains above the desired level for a few years. In table 3–3 the initial additional investment of 2.7 percent gradually increases by 34.2 percent in 1986. Productivity increases by 11.2 percent in 1986; wage rates are higher by 5.2 percent. The increase in the wage rates in conjunction with a decrease in the user cost makes capital more attractive. By 1986 relative capital and labor cost changes by 20.6 percent, leading to a change in the labor/capital ratio of 14.8 percent. There is 11 percent more capital and 6 percent less labor.

In turn, let us examine the indirect effects on an industry that was not directly a target industry in this simulation—primary metals (table 3–4). Output in primary metals is up as a general response to increased activity in the economy. The induced response in this industry is probably greater than average since it supplies the industries targeted for incentives. Again focusing on 1986, user cost is lower by 1.6 percent and wage rates are up by 1.8 percent because of increase in productivity. Relative prices of factors of production change by 3.3 percent in 1986, bringing the labor/capital ratio down and pushing investment up 6.4 percent. The indirect effects alone in this case increase productivity in primary metals by 1.1 percent by 1986. Similar examples of general and specific effects can be shown for all industries.

Diverse industry effects are found not only in the industry-specific scenarios but also as a result of nonspecific scenarios. The stimulus of a 17 percent increase in investment-tax-credit rates results in a decrease in the user cost of capital that varies between 1.3 and 2.6 percent in 1982. At the peak of the effect (1986 or 1987), the impact varies between 2.3 and 3.2 percent before declining.

Macroeconomic Impacts of Incentive Policies

To evaluate the effects of general and industry-specific incentives, we consider only the investment-tax-credit policy. Table 3–5 and figure 3–1 depict the effect on real GNP traced by the simulations of alternative ITC scenario's—general (ALL) and industry-specific.

In all cases, GNP increases and the difference between the base solution and the scenario reaches a peak in 1987, after which it rapidly declines. Initially, the increase in investment due to incentives increases demand at the same time as it increases the economy's productive potential. There are increases in productivity and aggregate real output. The real income generated should be sufficient to create enough demand to take advantage of the higher potential output. But unemployment in all scenarios is increased in comparison with the base solution when simulations are extended further into the future. As Keynes theorized, supply does not seem to create its own demand (at least not in the Wharton model). Investment incentives have

Table 3–2
General Investment Tax Credit: Impact on Major Industries
(Percentage deviations from base solution)

	1982	1983	1984	1985	1986	1987	1988
Chemicals							
User cost of capital	-2.4	-2.6	-2.8	-3.0	-3.1	-3.1	-3.0
Investment	0.2	0.7	1.3	2.0	2.3	2.1	1.5
Output per man-hour	0.5	1.3	2.1	2.8	3.3	3.6	3.8
Primary Metals							
User cost of capital	-2.1	-2.2	-2.4	-2.6	-2.7	-2.7	-2.5
Investment	0.2	0.9	2.0	3.3	4.2	4.2	3.3
Output per man-hour	0.1	0.4	0.8	1.5	2.1	2.6	2.8
Motor vehicles							
User cost of capital	-2.6	-2.7	-2.9	-3.1	-3.2	-3.2	-3.1
Investment	0.5	2.1	4.9	7.3	7.9	6.0	3.1
Output per man-hour	0.6	1.3	1.9	2.0	1.9	1.6	1.6
Nonelectrical machinery							
User cost of capital	-1.7	-1.8	-2.0	-2.2	-2.3	-2.3	-2.2
Investment	0.5	1.9	1.7	8.4	11.8	13.2	11.3
Output per man-hour	0.1	0.3	0.4	0.5	0.6	0.8	0.7

Table 3–3
Investment Tax Credit for Metals-Using Industries: Impact on Motor Vehicle Industry
(Percentage deviations from base solution)

	1982	1983	1984	1985	1986	1987	1988
User cost of capital	−15.0	−15.4	−15.9	−16.4	−16.4	−16.2	−16.0
Wage rate	1.1	3.0	4.5	5.3	5.2	4.7	4.7
Value added output	0.1	1.0	2.4	3.8	4.8	5.0	3.3
User cost/wage rate	−15.9	−17.8	−19.6	−20.6	−20.6	−20.0	−19.7
Labor/capital ratio	−3.7	−8.3	−12.2	−14.3	−14.8	−14.2	−14.6
Man-hours	−3.4	−6.7	−8.3	−7.7	−5.7	−3.9	−4.7
Capacity-utilization rate	2.4	5.5	7.5	7.6	6.0	3.9	2.5
Investment	2.7	10.4	23.6	33.7	34.2	22.9	7.3
Capital stock	0.4	1.7	4.3	7.7	10.7	12.1	11.5
Output per man-hour	3.6	8.3	11.7	12.4	11.2	9.2	8.4

Table 3–4
Investment Tax Credit for Metals-Using Industries: Impact on Primary Metals Industry
(Percentage deviations from base solution)

	1982	1983	1984	1985	1986	1987	1988
User cost of capital	-0.2	-0.7	-1.3	-1.7	-1.6	-1.2	-0.9
Wage rate	0.1	0.3	0.6	1.2	1.8	2.4	2.7
Value added output	0.1	0.6	1.2	1.7	2.0	1.9	1.0
User cost/wage rate	-0.3	-0.9	-1.9	-2.8	-3.3	-3.5	-3.5
Labor/capital ratio	0.1	0.3	0.4	0.1	-0.6	-1.8	-3.2
Man-hours	0.1	0.4	0.8	1.0	0.9	0.2	-1.0
Capacity-utilization rate	0.1	0.5	0.8	0.9	0.8	0.5	-0.3
Investment	0.2	1.2	3.0	5.1	6.4	6.1	3.6
Capital stock	0.0	0.1	0.5	0.1	1.5	2.0	2.2
Output per man-hour	0.0	0.2	0.3	0.6	1.1	1.6	2.0

raised the economy's aggregate supply schedule. That in itself does not guarantee that aggregate supply and demand will intersect at full employment. It may be necessary to use fiscal or monetary tools to obtain a corresponding shift in aggregate demand.

The contrast between the industry-specific and the general policy is striking. Among the sets of industries tested, policies focused on high-technology industries and metals-using manufacturing show the highest impact on GNP (figure 3–1 and table 3–5). Across-the-board incentives lead to the least growth, with incentives to basic industries only a little more effective than the across-the-board policy. This pattern is due to the fact that incentives given to HI-TECH and METALS increase manufacturing productivity by amounts much greater (0.52 and 0.49, respectively, in 1986) than a similar dollar amount incentive to BASIC (0.25) and to ALL (0.18) (table 3–6).

The higher the impact on productivity, the greater the downward impact on the price level (table 3–7). The HI-TECH policy reduces the deflator the most among the industry-specific policies. The ALL policy has the least impact on inflation. It is noteworthy, however, that the effect on the deflator begins to fade away after a few years.

Similar patterns, though with less impact, can be observed for the other policy instruments tested. These results are summarized in tables 3–5, 3–6, and 3–7.

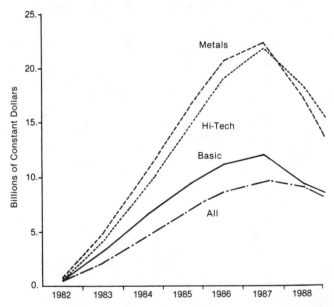

Figure 3–1. General versus Industry-Specific Investment-Tax-Credit Incentives: Effect on GNP

Table 3-5
Alternative Investment Tax Credit Scenarios: Effect on Real GNP (Deviation from Base Solution)
(In billions of 1972 dollars)

	1982	1983	1984	1985	1986	1987	1988
Industry-Specific							
Basic	0.7	3.4	6.4	8.9	11.2	12.0	9.4
Metals	0.8	4.9	10.2	15.6	20.6	22.4	17.2
Hi-tech	0.6	4.2	8.8	13.9	19.0	21.9	18.3
General							
All	0.5	2.3	4.5	6.7	8.7	9.6	9.1

Table 3–6
Alternative Investment-Tax-Credit Scenarios: Effect on Manufacturing Productivity (Deviation from Base Solution)
(In thousands of 1972 dollars per person)

	1982	1983	1984	1985	1986	1987	1988
Basic	0.04	0.09	0.15	0.20	0.25	0.29	0.31
Metals	0.07	0.18	0.30	0.41	0.49	0.54	0.56
Hi-tech	0.07	0.18	0.31	0.42	0.52	0.58	0.61
All	0.02	0.06	0.10	0.14	0.18	0.21	0.22

Table 3–7
Alternative Investment Tax-Credit Scenarios: Effect on GNP Deflator (Deviation from Base Solution)

Investment-Tax-Credit Policy	1982	1983	1984	1985	1986	1987	1988
Basic	−0.15	−0.47	−0.85	−1.07	−1.13	−1.05	−0.74
Metals	−0.16	−0.62	−1.14	−1.37	−1.30	−1.05	−0.64
Hi-tech	−0.17	−0.65	−1.25	−1.64	−1.69	−1.43	−0.83
All	−0.07	−0.25	−0.48	−0.66	−0.78	−0.82	−0.74

Note: 1972 = 100.

Evaluating the Costs and Benefits

It is appropriate to compare the gain in GNP with the cost to the Treasury in foregone taxes. Such a computation can be made on the basis of the ex ante cost estimates, which amounted to $26 billion (except in the mixed policy scenario). In fact, however, the feedback of the stimulus to economic activity increases tax revenue and reduces the cost to less than the initial ex ante cost estimate. We call the resulting change in Treasury receipts the ex post cost, and we note that in some cases ex post revenue losses turn out to be negative. We do not consider the value of other gains to the economy, such as productivity gains, or improvements in the price level. Nor do we take into account the difficulty resulting from the fact that some of the policy scenarios cause higher unemployment unless offset by demand management policies.

Since the ex ante loss to the Treasury is the same across all scenarios, except for the mixed scenario, the bigger the impact on GNP and incomes in general, the lower the final cost to the Treasury (table 3–8). The nominal net cost in the METALS and HI-TECH scenarios is negative in the mid period of the simulation, implying that the gain in receipts due to induced increases in incomes more than offsets the reduction in receipts due to the reduced effective tax rate. However, this does not happen in the first few periods of the simulations and in most cases, the increase in receipts is less than the cost accumulated over the period of the simulation.

Table 3–9 presents the impact on GNP per dollar of real net cost to the government. It is calculated by summing the impact on real GNP over the period 1982–1987 and dividing it by the sum of real net cost to the government over the same period. In contrast to the impact per dollar of cost measured ex post, the table also shows the impact on GNP per dollar of the ex ante stimulus. The table shows that among the policy tools available, maximum impact per dollar of ex ante or ex post cost is achieved in the investment tax credit scenarios. Within the investment tax credit scenarios, the ALL industry scenario is least effective, generating six additional dollars of GNP per dollar of ex post cost over the period. The High Technology scenario generates an increase in real GNP of $17.5 per dollar of cost while BASIC generates an increase of $8.5. The MIXED policy which ex ante has zero cost associated with it generated a lower deficit than in the absence of the policy.

We find that there are significant differences in the cost effectiveness of various policy instruments to stimulate investment and economic activity. An interesting finding is the tendency of supply side measures to result in rising unemployment unless supplemented with demand stimulus. We also find that there are significant differences between general, i.e., non-specific-industry measures, and industry-specific incentive programs. Among the latter the measures directed toward a broad class of high-technology and metals-using industries have the greatest impact.

Table 3-8
Alternative Investment-Tax-Credit Scenarios: Nominal Net Cost to Government
(*In billions of current dollars*)

	1982	1983	1984	1985	1986	1987	1988
Basic	2.5	3.8	3.0	1.7	0.1	0.8	0.6
Metals	3.0	4.3	2.3	-1.9	-6.1	-5.8	-2.1
Hi-tech	3.2	5.0	4.2	1.2	-2.7	-3.4	-1.8
All industries	2.0	3.6	3.2	2.1	1.2	1.3	3.9

Table 3–9
Gain Real GNP per Dollar of Real Cost

	Average Impact on Real GNP	Average Real Stimulus	Average Real Net Cost	Gain in Real GNP/Real Stimulus	Gain in Real GNP/Real Net Cost
Investment tax credit					
Basic	7.1	1.7	.83	4.3	8.5
Metal users	12.4	1.6	−.07	7.7	—[a]
Hi-tech	11.4	1.7	.65	6.8	17.5
All industries	5.4	1.7	.92	3.2	5.9
Corporate tax cut					
All industries	2.2	1.7	1.47	1.2	1.5
Capital consumption allowance					
All industries	2.5	1.6	1.26	1.5	2.0
Mixed policy					
All industries	5.6	0.0	−.3	—[b]	—[a]

Note: The gain is calculated on an ex ante and ex post basis by averaging the impact on real GNP over the period 1982–1987 and dividing it respectively by the sum of real stimulus and real net cost to the government over the same period.

[a]The average real cost to the Treasury was negative. The Treasury increased its total revenues.
[b]The denominator is zero by definition.

Note

1. Unfortunately, since the model does not permit a narrower focus on specific industries, it was not possible to study specific high-technology industries such as bio-engineering. In any case this would raise issues relating to technical change that are not yet well handled econometrically.

4

Regionalized Analysis of Industrial Policy

John A. Del Roccili and
Priscilla Luce

N ational policies have regionally diverse impacts. This is particularly true of industrial policies, whose regional effects are closely linked to the location of the industries that benefit, directly or indirectly, from the industrial-policy initiatives. The preceding chapter evaluated the effects of alternative investment incentive policies in the framework of the Wharton Annual and Industry Model. The objective in this chapter is to provide a quantitative assessment of the regional impact of the same changes in policy instruments designed to enhance corporate investment.

The principal analytical tool utilized to assess the regional ramifications of changes in industrial-policy instruments was the Wharton Census Region Model, an econometric model designed to act as a satellite to the Wharton Annual and Industry Model in order to provide a regional disaggregation of the national economy. The model is geographically disaggregated according to nine census regions as defined by the U.S. Bureau of the Census. Simply speaking, the model is designed to take certain variables, such as sector gross output, from the projections of the Wharton Annual and Industry Model as inputs,* and then to disaggregate these totals to their respective regional levels on the basis of intraregional feedbacks and interregional competitiveness. This is accomplished through the use of a set of econometric equations designed to share down the national aggregates and to recognize intraregional feedbacks. The equations make use of such factors as regional wage rates, region-specific energy price indices, and user costs of capital to arrive at the regional estimates. This is commonly referred to as a *top-down* approach. A brief description of the regional model is provided in the next section.

The model was used to prepare seven regionally disaggregated simulations, a baseline forecast, and six alternative scenarios. The baseline forecast incorporates the same assumptions as the baseline used in chapter 3 and includes national programs prevailing or expected to prevail at the time the forecast was made (June 1981). All the alternatives involve assumptions

---

*The Wharton forecasts for the U.S. economy used in this study are documented in chapter 3.

about policies designed to stimulate national economic growth through use of industrial-policy instruments: The first three represent *general* industrial incentives, tax reductions available to all industries, whereas the next three are industry-specific policies targeted specifically on basic industries, high-technology industries, and the metals using industries. As discussed in the previous chapter, the effects of alternative investment incentive policies differ not only in the aggregate but also in terms of their impact on specific industries. This is true not only for industrial policies targeted at particular industries, but also for general incentives available to all industries on the same terms.

The effect of the regional disaggregation is summarized in table 4–1, which shows the impact of the principal alternative policies on gross real regional output for 1987. In each case the table shows the percentage difference between the industrial-policy solution and the baseline forecast. The relative effects of each policy within each region have been indicated in brackets. In general, the differences between the regions appear to be noteworthy, though not as important as the differences between the policies.

Table 4–1 shows that industrial policies have very different impacts on the various regions. The West South Central region gains in almost all cases, followed by the East North Central and West North Central Regions. The gains for the New England and Middle Atlantic regions are typically less than in the other regions.

As noted in chapter 3, the industry-specific high-technology and metals-using industries policies showed greater effects than did the basic industries or the general nontargeted policy. But the different policies showed important diverse regional effects; some types of policies are more beneficial to some regions than others. For example, in the Middle Atlantic region the metals-using policy has far more impact than the basic industries policy, even though the effect of all policies is generally lower in this region than elsewhere. The basic industries policy appears to have the most pronounced impact in the West South Central region, which is relatively favored by industrial policy in general, as noted earlier.

The Structure of the Regional Model

The Wharton Census Region Model is an extension of the Wharton Annual and Industry Model providing a regional disaggregation of the national economic model and projections. The regional disaggregation is to nine census regions: (1) East North Central, (2) East South Central, (3) Middle Atlantic, (4) Mountain, (5) New England, (6) Pacific, (7) South Atlantic, (8) West North Central, and (9) West South Central.

A flow chart of the model structure is displayed in figure 4–1. The major

Table 4-1
Effects of Alternative Targeted Policies on Regional Gross Real Output in 1987
(*Percentage deviation from baseline forecast*)

	General	Targeted		
	All Industries	*High-Tech*	*Metal-Using*	*Basic*
New England	0.47	1.00 (2.1)[a]	1.04 (2.2)	0.54 (1.1)
Middle Atlantic	0.39	0.90 (2.3)	1.23 (3.2)	0.19 (0.5)
East North Central	0.80	1.68 (2.1)	1.77 (2.2)	0.87 (1.1)
West North Central	0.75	1.59 (2.1)	1.59 (2.1)	1.00 (1.3)
East South Central	0.57	1.33 (2.3)	1.61 (2.8)	0.53 (0.9)
West South Central	0.88	2.16 (2.5)	1.96 (2.2)	1.35 (1.5)
South Atlantic	0.49	1.35 (2.8)	1.45 (3.0)	0.58 (1.2)
Mountain	0.70	1.35 (1.9)	1.28 (1.8)	0.90 (1.3)
Pacific	0.65	1.25 (1.9)	0.99 (1.5)	1.22 (1.9)
U.S.	0.64	1.4 (2.2)	1.47 (2.3)	0.8 (1.2)

[a]Relative to general industrial policy within each region.

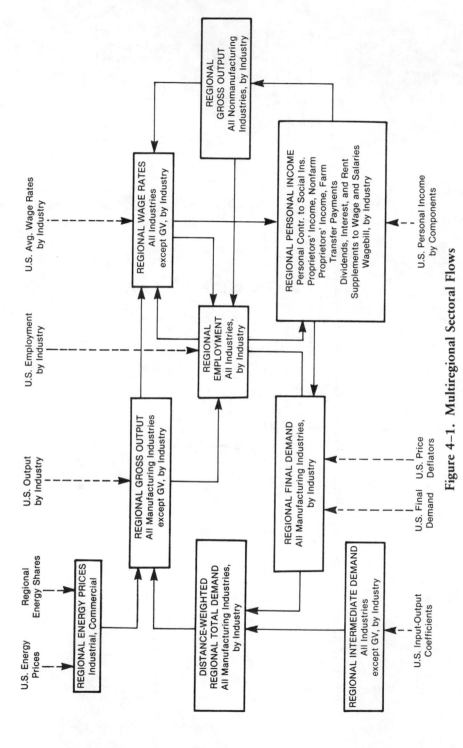

Figure 4–1. Multiregional Sectoral Flows

link from the national model to the multiregional system occurs in the output and personal-income blocks. That is, it has been hypothesized that the demand for manufactured goods is essentially *national* demand.

The disaggregation for manufacturing output is accomplished through the use of a logit procedure from which the regional output shares by industry are derived. The shares are specified as functions of regional total demand and regional input prices such as wage rates, energy prices, and user cost of capital. Consistency between the regional and national projections is enforced by constraining the sum of the regional output shares by industry to equal one. The regional gross outputs are then computed via identity and used as inputs into the manufacturing-employment equations, along with the local wage rates relative to the U.S. average wage rate for the particular industry.

The industry- and area-specific wage rates are determined as a function of the national wage rate and usually a regional measure of productivity. Indicators for the nonmanufacturing sector are computed in an analogous fashion, with the exception of real gross output, which is estimated directly. Intermediate demand is determined by assuming that the values of the regional input-output coefficients are identical to that of the nation, and these are used in conjunction with regional gross outputs by sector to generate intermediate demand. Final demand is determined as a function of regional employment, regional personal income, or per capita income. The sum of intermediate and final demand is then computed to define total demand. Wagebills are computed via identity, and the other components of regional personal income, with the exception of the residence adjustment, are linked to the national totals. These are then summed to derive personal income. Through an iterative procedure, the sum of regional variables is made to coincide with the national values forecast by the Wharton Annual Model at each level of the model.

For each region, equations are estimated for output, employment, wage rates, total demand, final demand, intermediate demand, and wagebills by industrial sector disaggregated for the major two-digit Standard Industrial Classification industries, along with their regional totals, personal income and its components, and price indices for commercial and industrial energy use. In all there are 2,804 endogenous variables, 161 exogenous variables, and 310 variables taken from the Wharton Annual and Industry Model. The model contains five nonmanufacturing sectors (contract construction; regulated industries; finance, insurance, and real estate; services; and wholesale and retail trade) and nine manufacturing sectors (food and kindred products; textiles and apparel; chemical and allied products; primary metals; fabricated metals; nonelectrical machinery; transportation; and other manufacturing). Agriculture, mining, and government are exogenous to the model.

In addition to the strong interregional linkages built into the model structure, an important feature of this model is the strong intraregional links, as figure 4–1 indicates. The feedback effect of wage rates and energy prices in the manufacturing sector is a significant part of the determination of industrial location and, therefore, of regional development. In addition, these manufacturing wage rates are employed in the determination of wage rates in some of the nonmanufacturing sectors. A further source of simultaneity is sectoral employment, where both output and wage rates play a role in the endogenous determination of labor requirements. Also, after the total wagebill and other components of personal income are estimated, total personal income leads to the determination of output in the nonmanufacturing sectors.

Alternative Simulations of Regional Growth

This section will examine the implications of the baseline forecast and of the alternative industrial-policy scenarios on regional economic development.

The Baseline Forecast

The baseline forecast corresponds to the Wharton Annual Model Post-Meeting Forecast of June 1981. This forecast was formulated before all the details of congressional response to the Reagan economic proposals were known, but it incorporates broadly most of the programs that were later enacted. The result was an economy with real GNP growth averaging 2.8 percent annually between 1981 and 1990. It shows real personal income increasing 2.4 percent annually, and employment growing 1.3 percent per year, over the same period.

The composition of the output produced by the economy as a whole is projected to change over the next decade, in part as a continuation of long-term trends and in part in response to the federal government's increased emphasis on defense spending. The service-based industries are projected to continue to grow at a rate above the average, further increasing their share of total output. Using the Census Region Model's industry delineation, this means growth in parts of the wholesale and retail trade and other manufacturing sectors, as well as in services. Manufacturing industries that produce finished goods, such as transportation equipment (SIC37), electrical (SIC36) and nonelectrical (SIC35) machinery, and fabricated metal products (SIC34), are also expected to be high growth sectors, as they benefit from increased defense spending and recover from a low recession-year base in 1981. Basic-materials industries are expected to grow as a result of defense demand and of their increased use as intermediate inputs in other sectors. These industries include primary metals (SIC33), textiles (part of SIC22 + 23), and chemicals (SIC28). Below-average growth is forecast for the energy and government sectors.

The predicted trends in output, employment, and personal income anticipate a pattern of regional development that is somewhat different from that experienced historically.

1. The differences between regional rates of growth are not anticipated to be as dramatic over the forecast horizon as they were over history. We expect a more balanced pattern of growth in regional economic activity, resulting from the higher projected rates of growth in both energy prices and wage rates in the Sunbelt relative to the Frostbelt, which should mitigate the industrial migration experienced historically.
2. The Pacific region is expected to grow at a rate slightly less than the U.S. average, whereas historically it grew at a rate slightly above the average.
3. Employment is expected to grow at a significantly slower rate than that experienced over history, both for the nation as a whole and for the nine census divisions.
4. Although the New England, Middle Atlantic, and East North Central states are still expected to grow at rates below the national average, the growth rates in income and output are improved both relatively and absolutely compared with those experienced over history.

Three commonly used indicators of regional economic activity—the annual average rates of growth of real gross output, real personal income, and employment—are presented in table 4–2 for the forecast period 1981 1990. They suggest the Mountain Region will display the fastest rate of growth, followed by the West South Central and the South Atlantic Regions. All these areas are expected to experience rates of growth above the national average, regardless of the yardstick employed. The New England, Middle Atlantic, and Pacific states are anticipated to be the slowest growing, experiencing below-average growth in real gross output, real personal income, and employment. In the East North Central states gross output and personal income are envisioned to increase at an above-average rate, whereas employment is expected to grow at a rate below the norm. Similar patterns can be discerned in both the West North Central and East South Central divisions.

The forecast and historical annual average rates of growth in manufacturing output and commercial output are displayed in table 4–3. They suggest that the distribution of output between the manufacturing sector and the commercial sector may be changing in some of the regions.

In the New England and Middle Atlantic states both manufacturing output and commercial output are anticipated to grow at rates above their his-

Table 4–2
Forecast Annual Average Percentage Growth Rates, 1981–1990

	Real Personal Income	Real Output	Employment
New England	2.25	2.21	.62
Middle Atlantic	2.15	2.31	.92
East North Central	2.72	2.92	1.15
West North Central	2.46	2.40	1.12
East South Central	2.80	2.94	1.20
West South Central	3.28	3.54	2.02
South Atlantic	3.15	3.17	1.61
Mountain	4.51	4.33	2.88
Pacific	2.33	2.02	.72
U.S.	2.38	2.79	1.28

Table 4–3
Historical and Forecast Annual Average Percentage Growth Rates

	History		Forecast	
	Manufacturing Output	Commercial Output	Manufacturing Output	Commercial Output
New England	1.08	2.23	2.37	2.12
Middle Atlantic	0.85	1.84	2.11	2.44
East North Central	1.81	2.53	3.08	2.84
West North Central	2.73	3.46	2.31	2.53
East South Central	3.65	4.05	3.33	2.77
West South Central	5.84	5.10	3.64	3.75
South Atlantic	3.32	4.39	3.19	3.30
Mountain	5.12	5.98	4.08	4.79
Pacific	3.61	3.46	1.75	2.21
U.S.	2.55	3.13	2.81	2.88

torical levels. In New England, however, as well as in the East North Central and East South Central states, we expect the distribution of gross output to change somewhat over the forecast period. In those areas we envision the manufacturing sector to grow at a slightly faster rate than the commercial sector. Historically, the opposite occurred in all the census regions with the exception of the Pacific states, where manufacturing output grew at a slightly higher rate than commercial output. In the Pacific region, however, the rate of growth in the commercial sector is expected to surpass that of manufacturing, although both rates are lower absolutely than historical experience. In the West North Central, West South Central, South Atlantic, and Mountain regions, the commercial sector is expected to expand at a faster rate than the manufacturing sector, thus maintaining the historical pattern of output distribution.

Alternative Forecasts of General Industrial Policy

Three of the alternative simulations involve assumptions of general industrial-policy incentives, available on the same basis to all industries. As shown in chapter 3, even general policies have industry-specific impacts. The question here is primarily one of their regional implications—whether and to what quantitative extent general policies have region-specific effects.

The general industrial policies examined are:

Investment tax credit: Assuming an increase in the investment tax credit of 1.17 percent.

Corporate tax cut: Assuming a 0.97 percentage point cut in the corporate income-tax rate.

Capital-consumption allowance: Assuming an increase in capital-consumption allowances through a reduction of 0.94 percent in average tax lives of equipment and structures.

The results of these simulations are summarized on a regional basis in figure 4–2 and in tables 4–1 and 4–4.

Investment Tax Credit
The investment-tax-credit alternative, with its increase in the tax-credit rate of 1.17 percent, produces moderate shifts in both total U.S. activity and regional indicators in the 1980s. Total output for the nation moves slightly above the baseline forecast beginning in 1982, with the difference between the two forecasts growing to 0.64 percent in 1987 before tapering off. The additional output is distributed fairly evenly: The largest difference in 1987 is 0.88 percent of the baseline output in the West South Central region; the smallest change is 0.39 percent in the Middle Atlantic states.

In both output and employment certain regions tend to have slightly higher growth or slightly smaller declines from base simulation, although the changes in employment are a bit more evenly distributed between regions. In general, the West South Central, West North Central, and Mountain regions have the least to lose and the most to gain from an increased investment tax credit, whereas the New England and Middle Atlantic regions have the worst prospects. In addition, regional shifts are more pronounced in the capital-intensive durable-goods industries and less pronounced in nonmanufacturing.

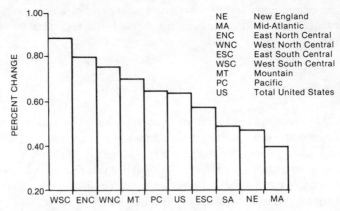

Figure 4–2a. Percentage Change from Control in Real Output in 1987 Investment Tax Credit

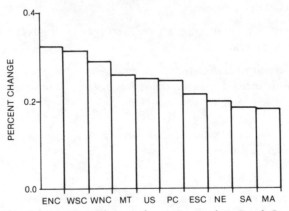

Figure 4–2b. Percentage Change from Control in Real Output in 1987 Corporate Tax Cut

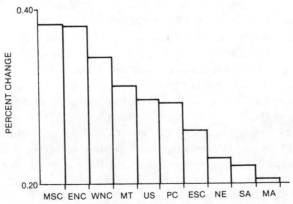

Figure 4–2c. Percentage Change from Control in Real Output in 1987 Capital-Consumption Allowance

Table 4–4

Effects of Alternative Policies on Regional Gross Real Output in 1987

	Investment Tax Credit	Corporate Tax Cut	Capital-Consumption Allowance
New England	0.47	0.20	0.23
Middle Atlantic	0.39	0.18	0.20
East North Central	0.80	0.32	0.38
West North Central	0.75	0.29	0.34
East South Central	0.57	0.21	0.26
West South Central	0.88	0.31	0.38
South Atlantic	0.49	0.18	0.22
Mountain	0.70	0.26	0.31
Pacific	0.65	0.24	0.29
U.S.	0.64	0.25	0.29

Corporate Tax Cut

This alternative, which incorporates a cut in corporate tax rates of 0.97 percent, exhibits effects on the Census Region Model that are quite similar in direction, smaller in size, to those produced by the increased investment-tax-credit rate. Not only are the overall effects smaller, but the differences between regions are less pronounced. Thus, whereas the investment tax credit caused total national output to grow by a maximum of 0.64 percent in 1987, the corporate tax cut causes a maximum change of 0.25 percent in the same year. In addition, whereas the spread of effects between regions ranged from 0.88 percent in the West South Central region to 0.39 percent in the Middle Atlantic region with the investment tax credit, the corresponding range with the corporate tax cut is only 0.32 to 0.18 percent.

The personal-income effects of this business tax cut are also mild, with the largest national change from the baseline forecast at 0.17 percent in 1990. This increase is distributed fairly evenly between regions, with the West South Central region gaining the most, at 0.26 percent, and the East South Central region gaining the least, at 0.13 percent of the baseline level.

Capital-Consumption Allowance

Another general tax cut that has been examined for its regional and interindustry effects is an increase in capital-consumption allowances, which results in tax lives 0.94 percent below those in the baseline forecast. The changes produced by this form of tax cut are virtually identical to those produced by a corporate tax cut of 0.97 percent. Whereas the corporate tax cut causes a maximum change in total national output of 0.25 percent in 1987, the capital-consumption-allowance increase causes a maximum change of 0.29 percent in the same year. The interindustry and interregional distributions of this change are also similar. The total employment effect is the same as that of the corporate tax cut, reaching 0.07 percent in 1987, again with the same industry and regional shifts. Wage rates, productivity, and income are also affected in the same way.

Alternative Forecasts of Industry-Specific Industrial Policy

It is not surprising that targeted industrial policies, specifically available to some industries but not to others, would have differential industrial impacts. The issue here is to quantify their diverse regional effects. For purposes of comparison, three scenarios involving an increased investment tax-credit rate were applied to different industrial sectors, as follows

1. A 1.7 percent increase in the investment tax-credit rates applied to the basic industries.
2. A 2.0 percent increase in the investment tax-credit rates applied to the high-technology industries.
3. A 2.0 percent increase in the investment tax-credit rates applied to the metals-using industries.

The results of these simulations can be contrasted with the comparable—in terms of direct cost to the U.S. Treasury—general investment-tax-credit scenario presented earlier.

The results of these simulations are summarized in figure 4–3 and tables 4–1 and 4–5.

The Investment-Tax-Credit/High Technology Alternative

This scenario incorporates the assumption of a 2.0 percent increase in the investment tax-credit rates applicable to the following industries: chemicals (SIC28), electrical machinery (SIC36), transportation equipment (SIC37), and instruments (SIC38). The use of this industrial-policy instrument is expected to result in a rise in both total U.S. and regional economic activity over the forecast period. Total output for the nation moves slightly above the baseline forecast in 1982, with the difference between the two forecasts growing to 1.4 percent in 1987. The additional output is envisioned to be distributed somewhat unevenly among the regions, with the principal beneficiaries being the West South Central, East North Central, and West North Central areas (table 4–1, figure 4–2). Strikingly, the New England and Pacific regions, where high-technology industries are particularly strong, show relatively modest gains. As one would expect, the fastest-growing sectors are those that benefit—particularly from the investment tax credit—and output increases in these sectors also spur modest growth in the commercial sectors.

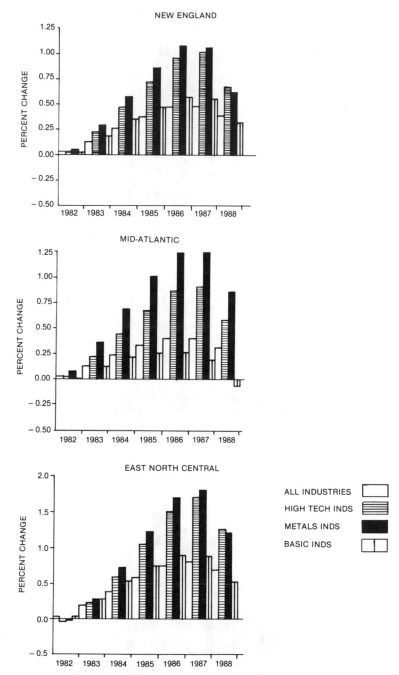

Figure 4–3. Investment Tax Credit Alternatives Percentage Change from Control in Real Output

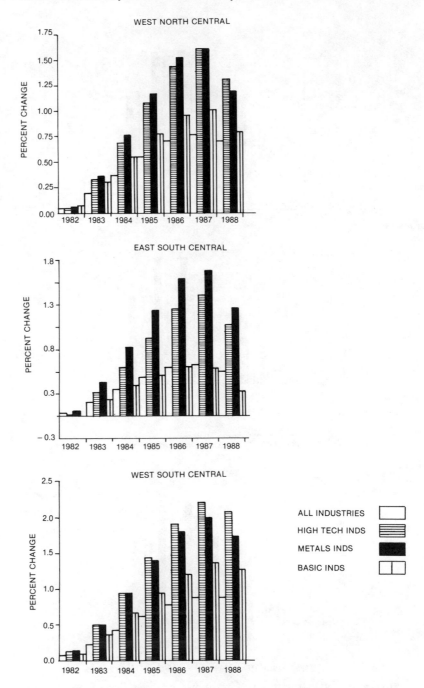

Figure 4–3 (continued)

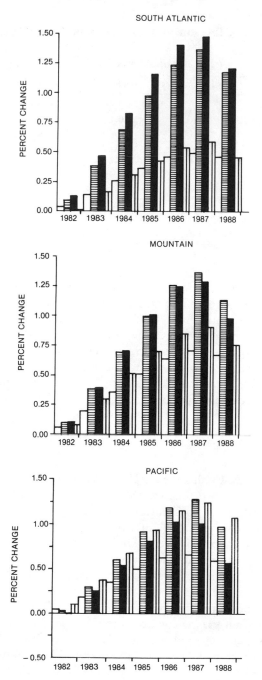

Figure 4–3 (continued)

Table 4–5
Effects of Alternative Investment Tax Credits on Regional Employment in 1987
(Percentage deviation from baseline forecast)

	All Industries	High-Tech	Metals-Using	Basic
New England	−0.11	−0.49	−0.02	0.54
Middle Atlantic	−0.07	−0.25	0.34	0.19
East North Central	0.08	−0.27	0.47	0.87
West North Central	0.23	0.24	0.61	1.00
East South Central	−0.09	−0.15	0.72	0.53
West South Central	0.39	0.88	1.14	1.35
South Atlantic	−0.02	0.25	0.76	0.58
Mountain	0.34	0.28	0.44	0.99
Pacific	0.13	0.01	0.04	1.22
U.S.	0.08	0.04	0.52	0.79

Total employment remains close to the baseline simulation for the United States as a whole; but regional employment decreases slightly in the New England, Middle Atlantic, East North Central, and East South Central areas and is relatively stable in the remaining regions (table 4–5). This is due to the increase in the investment tax-credit rates, which reduces user cost of capital in the industries affected, which in turn stimulates the substitution of capital for labor, causing a reduction in employment in the high-technology industries. The increased output, however, also stimulates employment in the commercial sectors, although the reduction in the high-technology sector tends to offset this increase.

The Investment-Tax-Credit/Metals-Using Alternative
This scenario incorporates the assumption of a 2.0 percent increase in the investment tax-credit rates applied to the following sectors: fabricated metals products (SIC34), nonelectrical machinery (SIC35), electrical machinery (SIC36), transportation equipment (SIC37), and instruments (SIC38). With this change, total output for the nation moves above the baseline forecast beginning in 1982, with the difference between the two forecasts growing to 1.47 percent in 1987 before tapering off.

Table 4–1 shows the differential effect on real output by region. This policy has somewhat greater impact in the Middle Atlantic and East South Central regions that does a policy targeted on high technology, but in turn the impact is somewhat smaller in the Pacific region. The employment effects are generally somewhat more favorable, particularly in the East and West South Central regions.

The Investment-Tax-Credit/Basic-Industries Alternative

This alternative analyzes the impact on regional economic activity of a 1.7 percent increase in the investment tax-credit rate applied to basic industry. The industries included in this grouping are agriculture, mining, lumber (SIC24); printing and publishing (SIC26); chemicals (SIC28); stone, clay, and glass (SIC32); and primary metals (SIC33).

The effect on real gross output is modest, with a percentage difference of 0.8 percent as compared to the baseline forecast in 1987 (table 4–1). The West South Central, West North Central, and—curiously—Pacific regions are the principal beneficiaries of this policy.

With respect to employment, the basic-industries tax credit is somewhat more favorable than the other policies, yielding the greatest improvement in the West North Central, West South Central, and Pacific regions, where the effect on output is also the strongest.

Conclusions

Industrial policy clearly has regional as well as sectoral implications, a factor of great importance in a political system that puts great emphasis on the regional dimension. This chapter has explored the regional impacts of industrial policy using a model with *intra*regional as well as *inter*regional linkages. The results point strongly toward regional diversity:

1. Some regions appear to be more favorably and others less favorably influenced by industrial policies. Strikingly, the greatest impact on output almost always is in the West South Central region, with the smallest effects in the New England and Middle Atlantic regions.
2. Targeted industrial policies have more focused impact than general policies also in a regional dimension, with the West South Central, East South Central, and South Atlantic regions benefiting particularly from the high-technology and metals-using investment tax-credit policies.

The regional impacts of industrial policies will surely be taken into account when policy decisions are made.

5

The Effects of Foreign Export-Promotion Policies on the United States: Macro Model Simulations

F. Gerard Adams,
Lawrence R. Klein, and
Vijaya G. Duggal

T he industrial-policy issue is taking on a new dimension as major U.S. industries are being challenged by imports. Protectionism is becoming the battleground of industrial policy. Industrial policies in our trade-partner countries are being blamed for the problems of many industries; specifically, the industrial targeting contained in many such policies is being termed an unfair trade practice. Since industrial policies covering a wide range of industries are an important ingredient in the economic policies of all our international competitors, this could open a Pandora's box of retaliatory trade restrictions. Such a view, if it should prevail, represents a serious threat to the international free-trading system.

This chapter poses two related questions: (1) What is the impact in the United States of imports resulting from foreign export promotion or industrial policy? (2) What is the effect of the adjustment process following an industrial-policy-induced increase in imports?

International Aspects of Industrial Policy

One important consideration is whether an industrial policy represents interventions in international trade. Some countries' policies have been explicitly mercantilist, protecting domestic industries and providing incentives for exports. Others have had broader economic-development objectives. We

The empirical work in this chapter is based on Adams, Klein, and Duggal (1984).

must recognize, however, that industrial policy, even when it aims primarily at domestic development, almost always has implications for international trade.

Broad industrial-development strategies with significant protectionist features, along lines proposed almost two hundred years ago by Alexander Hamilton (1791), have been widely used and are accepted for developing countries even within the framework of international tariff agreements. Unfortunately, it is difficult to determine where an industrial-development strategy stops and protectionism begins, particularly in a technologically dynamic world. Broad industrial strategies frequently encompass narrow, specific industry-targeted mechanisms. Indeed, industrial targeting is often the central feature of an industrial-development strategy—the building of a steel industry, for example. Protectionism for infant industries and/or export promotion are also typical of industrial-development policy. The success stories of economic development in East Asia are evidence of the powerful effect of an export-oriented economic-development strategy.

The Japanese case, only the first of several in recent history, is a good illustration. During the early 1950s, after completing the immediate tasks of reconstruction, the Japanese faced a major industrial-policy decision about what kind of an economy to develop: a labor-intensive economy consistent with the large available supplies of labor, or capital-intensive industry capable of taking advantage of modern technology and competing in the world market. The Japanese Ministry of International Trade and Industry (MITI) pushed hard and successfully for the latter view, urging in particular that products should have high value added, should have a high demand elasticity with respect to income, and should be competitive in world markets. There is still debate on how much (or how little) of Japanese economic development can be attributed to industrial policy, and to what extent it influenced the development of particular industries. (Trezise 1983). There is no question, however, that Japan built an integrated industrial structure at the technological frontier, one that is highly effective in world competition. This development was influenced by a great variety of industrial-policy measures (Adams and Ichimura 1983; Shinohara 1982). These policies make up an industrial-development strategy. They have included measures that are general but also many that are industry-specific. They have also included protection to allow new industries to reach viable scale and technology, but export competitiveness has been a persistent guiding objective.

More recently, Japanese industrial policy has turned toward a new target—building the so-called knowledge-intensive industries. This represents even more of a challenge than previous industrial-policy aims, since it means stretching the technological frontier into new domains. As a result, it has also been more product- or industry-specific, seeking by funding research and production to direct Japanese technology into promising new fields—for example, the successful development of the 64K chip and the massive effort to build a fifth-generation computer. The current policy is often seen as a direct threat to advanced industries in the United States, where many products of Japanese high technology will be directed. It is hardly likely, however, that pressure from the United States will persuade the Japanese to limit their efforts, or that our trading partners will be willing to recognize such policies as unfair trade practices.

The Impact of Foreign Industrial Policies

Paradoxically, many of the people who maintain that industrial policy does not work nevertheless complain bitterly about the impact of foreign industrial policies on U.S. industry.[1]

There has been little theoretical or empirical work specifically on the impact of foreign industrial policies. In this respect, the distinction between narrow, beggar-thy-neighbor export promotion and broad industrial-development strategies is crucial. If one is dealing with policies designed to gain advantage for particular industries in foreign competition through subsidies or low-cost export credits, the well-known materials on intervention in international markets apply. Public agencies—the U.S. International Trade Commission (ITC), for example—are accustomed to evaluating the impact of export subsidies and similar measures. It may be more difficult, however, to measure the impact of other industrial-policy trade-intervention measures: contracts for research and development, preferential capital allocations, or public-sector support of new high-technology enterprises, for example. In principle, however, the traditional methodologies to measure impact and the traditional policy responses to trade intervention appear to be called for.

The issue is altogether different if industrial policies are broader. To begin with, it is not clear that an industrial-development strategy in one country must have adverse impact on other countries. Industrial-development policy is not a zero-sum game. We are undoubtedly all better off as a consequence of Japan's economic development.[2] U.S. consumers have gained greatly from low-cost, high-quality imports from Japan. As Japan has become a powerful competitor, it also has become a much larger purchaser of U.S. exports. The Japanese contribution to the development of modern technology will have positive externalities worldwide. On the other hand, of course, the development of the Japanese economy has also had significant negative impact on certain U.S. industries—for example, automobiles and electronic equipment. There are fears, perhaps justifiable ones, that Japanese industries will take over additional markets.

The quantitative impact of foreign industrial-development strategies on the U.S. economy and on other world economies is more difficult to determine than in the case of narrow trade-intervention policies. It involves economywide effects, albeit with specific industry impact. It may affect the aggregate trade balance temporarily, although the international adjustment process is likely to modify that result. Finally, it may involve long-run shifts in technology and growth that are hard to capture quantitatively.

This chapter considers a quantitative evaluation of industrial policies.

U.S. Foreign Industrial-Policy Scenario

This econometric-modeling scenario is intended to examine the effect of a foreign industrial policy on the U.S. economy. The issue is one of the changes in industrial structure as well as of the macroeconomic effects that would occur as a result of increased imports of particular classes of industrial products.

We make use of the Wharton Annual and Industry Model. The industrial disaggregation of this model is important, since the impact of industrial policies falls on particular sectors. Imports of particular product categories affect the output of the corresponding domestic industries.

Three model solutions are compared:

1. *Base solution:* Without new foreign industrial policy (Wharton long-term solution of November 1983).
2. *Foreign-industrial-policy solution:* Assuming increased imports of industrial products as a result of foreign industrial policies.
3. *Foreign-industrial-policy solutions with readjustment:* Assuming adjustment of the exchange rate.

The base solution (solution 1) is simply a standard recent Wharton model forecast (November 1983). It takes into account various forces operating in the U.S. and world economies, including existing foreign industrial policies. It shows (table 5–1) a cyclical recovery in 1983 and 1984 and a growth-recession cycle thereafter. It obtains a merchandise trade deficit ranging from $61.8 billion in 1983 to $86.5 billion in 1988 and a current account of −$11.5 billion in 1983 and $10.4 billion in 1988.

In solution 2 it has been assumed that, beginning in 1984, new foreign industrial policies enable foreign producers to increase their shipments into the U.S. market by $10 billion (1972$) per year.[3] These increased U.S.

Table 5–1
Comparison of Alternative Simulations: Macro Variables

		1983	1984	1985	1986	1987	1988
GNP: Percent change per year (1972$)	1[a]	3.5	5.8	3.6	.5	4.5	2.8
	2[b]	3.5	4.7	3.6	.4	4.6	3.0
	3[c]	3.5	4.9	4.1	1.0	4.9	3.2
GNP (billions of 1972$)	1	1,536.8	1,626.6	1,685.4	1,694.4	1,769.8	1,819.7
	2	1,536.8	1,608.7	1,666.2	1,672.5	1,749.0	1,801.1
	3	1,536.8	1,612.1	1,678.9	1,695.5	1,778.7	1,834.5
GNP deflator (1972 = 100)	1	215.7	226.2	239.2	249.8	262.6	275.7
	2	215.7	226.32	239.35	249.79	262.17	275.39
	3	215.7	226.7	240.1	250.6	263.3	277.0
Employment (millions)	1	100.79	104.26	106.78	106.80	109.91	111.80
	2	100.79	103.84	106.04	105.83	108.83	110.74
	3	100.79	103.96	106.38	106.55	109.56	112.23
Unemployment (percent)	1	9.74	8.6	7.8	8.8	7.6	7.2
	2	9.74	9.00	8.42	9.60	8.40	7.99
	3	9.74	8.94	8.13	8.98	7.48	6.82
Productivity: all industries (thousands of 1972$ per worker)	1	15.248	15.601	15.783	15.864	16.103	16.276
	2	15.248	15.492	15.713	15.803	16.070	16.264
	3	15.248	15.516	15.786	15.917	16.126	16.349
Merchandise trade balance (billions of 1972$)	1	−11.2	−14.7	−12.3	−5.7	−1.8	.1
	2	−11.2	−24.1	−21.4	−14.8	−14.1	−10.8
	3	−11.2	−20.9	−12.6	−1.7	1.6	5.4
Merchandise trade balance (billions of current $)	1	−61.8	−85.1	−88.9	−76.9	−89.2	−86.5
	2	−61.8	−106.7	−110.9	−100.8	−115.6	−114.8
	3	−61.8	−111.7	−115.3	−92.2	−100.2	−97.0

Table 5–1 (continued)

		1983	1984	1985	1986	1987	1988
Current account balance (billions of 1972$)	1	12.5	11.8	17.5	28.2	31.4	37.3
	2	12.5	2.5	8.6	19.3	22.6	28.7
	3	12.5	6.6	19.1	34.2	40.0	46.6
Current account balance (billions of current $)	1	−11.5	−26.0	−18.1	5.6	−.4	10.4
	2	−11.5	−47.3	−39.7	−17.9	−26.6	−17.6
	3	−11.5	−49.0	−36.6	−.4	−1.6	10.5

[a]1 = base solution.
[b]2 = foreign industrial-policy solution.
[c]3 = foreign industrial policy with readjustment.

imports occur specifically in five industrial categories—electrical machinery, nonelectrical machinery, automobiles, aircraft, and other transport equipment—and reduce the output of the corresponding domestic industries. We have not attempted to identify the particular industrial policies used by foreign countries to achieve this result. However, one could readily visualize programs of special export credits (the case of U.S. imports of subway cars, for example) or export subsidies, or other targeted industrial policies that would have this effect.

In solution 3 we recognize that the resulting disequilibrium in the trade balance could not persist for long without some adjustment. The aim here was to simulate the operation of the adjustment process with floating exchange rates. In this case an adjustment in the dollar exchange rate amounting to − 6.9 percent in 1984 and − 12.5 percent thereafter has been assumed. This is approximately enough to return the U.S. current-account balance in nominal terms to its base solution value in 1986. In this simulation, import and export responses to the exchange rate have been allowed to operate as they normally would in the model, without any attempt to modify their sectoral composition.

A comment on the impact of changes in the dollar exchange rate in the model and, presumably, in the U.S. economy is appropriate here. Import and export elasticities with respect to price are relatively low, and the lags are fairly long. The immediate impact of changes in the exchange rate shows up as expected on real trade movements: A decline in the value of the dollar reduces imports and increases exports. The immediate effect on the nominal trade balance is unfavorable, however. In terms of dollars, imports become more costly, and the value of exports is not quickly increased. The balance of trade deteriorates. As anticipated, there is eventually a readjustment of trade, even in nominal terms, but that takes two or more years.

Another important element is the relationship between factor income and the exchange rates. Under conventional valuation procedures, foreign earnings are translated at the current exchange rate. Since factor-income flows in constant dollars are exogenous in the model, we have adjusted the factor-income deflator to reflect the change in the exchange rate. This variable is an important consideration in the current-account balance in nominal terms. The results of these simulations are summarized in tables 5–1 through 5–4.

At the level of the macroeconomy (table 5–1) the increased imports assumed in simulation 2 cause a 1.1 percent reduction in the rate of growth of GNP in 1984. The merchandise trade balance in real terms is affected by a little less than the $10 billion (1972$) shock imposed because lower economic activity calls for some offsetting reduction in imports and expansion of exports in 1984. The current account in nominal terms goes from − $26.0 billion in the base simulation to − $47.3 billion as a result of the increased imports assumed, and remains significantly in the negative through 1988.

Table 5-2
Comparison of Alternative Simulations: Real Gross Output by Sector
(1972$)

		1983	1984	1985	1986	1987	1988
Manufacturing	1[a]	926.7	1,016.9	1,066.9	1,051.3	1,121.0	1,155.4
	2[b]	926.7	984.4	1,033.5	1,015.0	1,086.5	1,123.9
	3[c]	926.7	988.4	1,049.5	1,044.1	1,123.9	1,165.2
Durable manufacturing	1	498.4	561.5	595.1	581.0	631.5	565.1
	2	498.4	535.7	568.8	552.6	604.4	631.0
	3	498.4	538.2	579.4	572.1	625.6	659.0
Nondurable manufacturing	1	428.3	455.5	471.8	470.3	489.5	499.2
	2	428.3	448.6	464.7	467.5	482.2	492.9
	3	428.3	450.2	470.1	472.0	494.3	506.2
Commercial and other	1	1,197.0	1,259.0	1,299.4	1,309.8	1,360.4	1,395.5
	2	1,197.0	1,254.6	1,294.2	1,302.8	1,353.8	1,390.1
	3	1,197.0	1,255.9	1,299.2	1,312.4	1,367.2	1,406.2
Nonelectrical machinery	1	97.4	108.6	117.5	117.5	127.1	134.0
	2	97.4	104.5	113.0	112.6	112.3	129.6
	3	97.4	105.2	115.3	116.7	127.6	135.5

Electrical machinery	1	93.2	102.3	108.7	109.0	115.9	119.8
	2	93.2	98.7	104.9	104.9	111.9	116.0
	3	93.2	99.1	106.2	107.3	114.9	119.5
Motor vehicles	1	75.2	87.7	91.0	84.5	95.3	100.5
	2	75.2	82.8	86.5	79.4	90.5	95.5
	3	75.2	82.6	87.6	82.7	95.1	101.1
Aircraft	1	18.9	32.1	25.7	24.6	27.5	28.4
	2	18.9	21.5	24.0	22.9	25.9	27.0
	3	18.9	21.6	24.5	23.8	26.9	28.1
Other transportation equipment	1	22.2	24.6	26.1	25.7	27.9	28.8
	2	22.2	23.2	24.6	24.2	26.4	27.4
	3	22.2	23.2	24.8	24.7	27.0	28.1
Iron and steel	1	17.7	21.9	23.6	22.0	25.2	26.2
	2	17.7	19.0	20.7	19.0	22.4	23.6
	3	17.7	19.4	22.0	21.1	25.0	26.3

[a]1 = base solution.
[b]2 = foreign industrial-policy solution.
[c]3 = foreign industrial policy with readjustment.

Table 5–3a
Comparison of Alternative Simulations: Composition of Output
(constant $; percentage of total)

		1983	1984	1985	1986	1987	1988
Agriculture, forestry and fisheries	1[a]	3.0	3.0	3.0	2.9	2.9	2.9
	2[b]	3.0	3.0	3.0	3.0	3.0	2.9
	3[c]	3.0	3.0	3.0	3.0	3.0	3.0
Durable manufacturing	1	13.8	14.7	15.0	14.7	15.2	15.4
	2	13.8	14.2	14.6	14.1	14.8	15.0
	3	13.5	14.2	14.7	14.4	15.1	15.3
Nondurable manufacturing	1	9.5	9.6	9.6	9.6	9.6	9.5
	2	9.5	9.6	9.6	9.5	9.9	9.5
	3	9.5	9.6	9.6	9.6	9.6	9.6
Commercial and other	1	51.3	50.9	50.8	51.0	50.7	50.6
	2	51.3	51.3	51.1	51.4	51.0	50.9
	3	51.3	51.3	51.0	51.1	50.7	50.6

[a]1 = base solution.
[b]2 = foreign industrial-policy solution.
[c]3 = foreign industrial policy with readjustment.

Table 5–3b
Real Gross Output
(growth rates, percentage per year)

		1983	1984	1985	1986	1987	1988
Durable manufacturing	1[a]	8.2	12.7	6.0	-2.4	8.7	3.9
	2[b]	8.2	7.5	6.2	-2.8	9.4	4.4
	3[c]	8.2	8.4	8.2	-1.6	9.6	4.5

Nondurable manufacturing	1	5.6	6.3	3.6	-.3	4.1	2.0
	2	5.6	4.8	3.6	-.5	4.3	2.3
	3	5.6	5.1	4.4	.4	4.7	2.4
Nonelectrical machinery	1	3.7	11.6	8.1	.1	8.2	5.4
	2	3.7	7.4	8.1	-.4	8.4	5.9
	3	3.7	8.0	9.6	1.1	9.4	6.1
Electrical machinery	1	7.9	19.8	6.2	.3	6.3	3.4
	2	7.9	5.9	6.3	.0	6.6	3.7
	3	7.9	6.3	7.2	1.0	7.1	4.0
Motor vehicles	1	20.2	16.6	3.8	-7.2	12.8	5.4
	2	20.2	10.1	4.4	-8.2	14.0	5.9
	3	20.2	9.7	6.2	-5.5	14.9	6.3
Aircraft	1	.1	21.9	11.2	-4.0	11.4	3.3
	2	.1	13.3	11.8	-4.4	12.8	4.2
	3	.1	14.0	13.4	-2.5	13.2	4.2
Other transportation equipment	1	23.1	11.0	5.9	-1.3	8.4	3.2
	2	23.1	4.4	6.2	-1.6	9.2	3.7
	3	23.1	4.6	7.0	-.7	9.5	3.9
Iron and steel	1	5.0	23.5	8.0	-6.8	14.6	3.8
	2	5.0	7.1	9.1	-8.3	17.9	5.4
	3	5.0	9.4	13.7	-4.2	18.3	5.5
Agriculture, forestry and fisheries	1	4.3	5.9	3.0	-1.1	4.5	1.8
	2	4.3	5.3	3.0	-1.1	4.7	2.1
	3	4.3	5.8	4.1	-.1	5.2	2.2
Mining	1	-1.5	4.9	2.1	-1.5	4.2	2.0
	2	-1.5	1.8	2.0	-1.7	4.5	2.4
	3	-1.5	2.6	3.5	-.4	5.2	2.6

[a]1 = base solution.
[b]2 = foreign industrial-policy solution.
[c]3 = foreign industrial policy with readjustment.

Table 5–4
Comparison of Alternative Simulations: Imports
(billions of 1972$)

		1983	1984	1985	1986	1987	1988
Goods and services	1[a]	126.1	134.6	141.5	137.3	143.0	146.3
	2[b]	126.1	144.3	151.1	146.7	152.3	155.7
	3[c]	126.1	142.1	146.2	141.3	146.8	150.4
Merchandise	1	87.8	93.5	92.5	94.2	98.8	101.2
	2	87.8	102.9	106.9	103.4	108.0	116.4
	3	87.8	101.2	103.1	98.9	103.3	105.7
Food and beverages	1	7.7	8.0	8.1	8.2	8.2	8.2
	2	7.7	7.9	8.1	8.1	8.1	8.2
	3	7.7	7.8	7.9	7.8	7.8	7.8
Consumer goods	1	20.0	21.5	22.3	22.4	22.9	23.2
	2	20.0	21.4	22.1	22.1	22.6	22.8
	3	20.0	20.5	20.0	19.4	19.7	20.0
Industrial supplies excluding petroleum	1	18.8	19.6	20.5	19.4	20.4	20.7
	2	18.8	19.3	20.2	19.1	20.1	20.4
	3	18.8	18.7	18.8	17.6	18.6	19.0
Capital goods	1	19.8	20.4	21.2	21.6	22.9	24.0
	2	19.8	28.4	28.7	29.1	30.4	31.5
	3	19.8	28.4	28.7	29.1	30.4	31.5

Autos and parts							
	1	13.5	14.1	15.6	12.9	14.2	14.6
	2	13.5	16.6	18.1	15.4	16.7	12.1
	3	13.5	16.6	18.1	15.4	16.7	17.1
Petroleum							
	1	5.2	6.4	6.7	6.7	7.2	7.4
	2	5.2	6.3	6.6	6.6	7.2	7.3
	3	5.2	6.3	6.7	6.8	7.3	7.5
Factor income							
	1	17.3	20.6	24.0	23.8	24.6	25.4
	2	17.3	20.6	24.0	23.8	24.6	25.4
	3	17.3	20.6	24.0	23.8	24.6	25.4
(billions of current $)							
Goods and services							
	1	346.0	399.1	451.3	470.9	537.2	591.0
	2	346.0	422.1	475.2	496.8	564.9	621.2
	3	346.0	437.6	507.4	530.4	604.1	666.1
Merchandise							
	1	259.9	301.8	342.0	356.4	407.4	446.8
	2	259.9	324.2	365.8	381.7	434.6	476.4
	3	259.9	335.2	385.2	404.2	460.8	506.5

[a] 1 = base solution.
[b] 2 = foreign industrial-policy solution.
[c] 3 = foreign industrial policy with readjustment.

At the industry level (table 5–2), simulation 2 shows large impacts specifically on the sectors affected by the additional assumed imports and those closely linked to them by the input-output scheme. Specifically, in 1984 durable manufacturing gross output is $25.8 billion (1972$) lower than in the base solution, with big impacts in machinery, automobiles, and so on. It is noteworthy that output in iron and steel, which was not directly affected, is down $2.9 billion (more than 13 percent) and nondurable manufacturing is reduced almost $7 billion. These impacts continue through 1988 (in simulation 2). Although these changes show only small shifts the composition of aggregate industrial structure (table 5–3a), they show pronounced effects on the growth rates of particular industries (table 5–3b) in 1984, when the new imports begin. Note particularly a growth rate of 7.5 percent as compared to 12.7 percent in durable manufacturing and 7.1 percent as compared to 23.5 percent in iron and steel. Import and export performance are shown in tables 5–4 and 5–5. As noted, the injection of $10 billion (1972$) of imports is partially offset by small reductions elsewhere as a result of slower economic activity, and there is a minimal improvement in exports. Since there is no change in the exchange rate, however, the readjustment is minimal, and the deterioration in the trade balance and in the current account continues. This result is unacceptable since natural forces for readjustment must reassert themselves, in the case of floating exchange rates by a deterioration of the exchange rate for the dollar.

The readjustment has been introduced in simulation 3, which will be considered next. On the basis of some experimentation, we found that a 12.5 percent change in the exchange rate would bring the balance on current account to its base solution values in 1986–1998. In simulation 3, after a year of reduced growth in 1984, the readjustment of exchange rates brings aggregate economic activity back to its base-year values by 1986 (table 5–1). Employment and unemployment also show only a temporary divergence from the base-year path. The important point is that the readjustment of the exchange rate has great effect. The effect on income and employment of an increase in imports is only temporary, and the readjustment process brings the economy back to its original aggregate level.

The inflation rate is very slightly accelerated in 1984, somewhat less than we would have anticipated (by less than 0.5 percent). This may reflect the failure of the model to elaborate fully the links between exchange rates and domestic prices. It is probable that a 12.5 percent decline in the dollar would have a somewhat greater impact on inflation than is obtained here.

With regard to the balance on merchandise trade, the difference between nominal and constant dollar values should be noted. The J curve does work; consequently, the immediate impact of devaluation of the dollar is a deterioration of the merchandise trade and current-account balances even with respect to simulation 2. In constant-dollar terms, however, there is significant improvement, even with respect to simulation 1, as real trade flows readjust.

Turning now to the sectoral effects (tables 5–2, 5–3a, 5–3b), real gross output is somewhat better as a result of devaluation (and the resulting improved trade performance) in simulation 3 than in simulation 2; but there are still significant effects on growth (table 5–3b) in 1984. Note, however, that the impact of the change in the exchange rate causes most industries to show faster real growth in 1985. The responsiveness of activity to trade is responsible. The remarkable result is that by 1988 output in all the industrial sectors is back to the base solution level. If we were to examine individual plants or very narrow sectors, we would undoubtedly find permanent effects; but at the level of aggregation shown here there appears to be no significant long-run structural impact. Composition of output after readjustment is not much different from what it was before the inflow of imports. This does not, however, deny the fact of considerable temporary impact on particular industries, nor does it account for the cost of the dislocations that may take place as a result of the readjustment and during the readjustment period.

The explanation is in the trade figures shown in tables 5–4 and 5–5. In real terms, imports are reduced in most sectors, and exports show shifting positive growth, particularly after a lag of two to three years. Real merchandise imports by 1986 are $4.5 billion less in simulation 3 than in simulation 2, though still $4.7 billion higher than in simulation 1 (note that the policy-related import inflow assumed was $10 billion). By 1986 real merchandise exports, which showed only minimal changes between simulation 1 and simulation 2, are $9.8 billion higher in simulation 3 than in the base solution. With respect to terms of trade, more exports are paying for imports.[4] As we have noted, the effects in current dollars are quite different. Merchandise imports are affected unfavorably by devaluation, and, as one would expect, current-dollar exports of merchandise show only the effect of real changes. The adjustment of factor-income receipts on the basis of the exchange rate does, however, make a significant difference in the nominal current-account balance.

To summarize, the impact of exchange-rate readjustment tends after a few years to offset the impact of the increased imports. If the exchange rate is allowed to respond to bring the current account back to its original position, the adjustment process works. The impact on sectoral structure is perceptible, particularly in the industries that competed against the new imports and those that are closely linked to them by the input-output system. Ultimately, however, the growth of real exports causes readjustments that bring the industries back to the base solution levels even where substantial imports continue. From the perspective of readjustment under free trade with floating exchange rates, this is a sanguine result.

Table 5-5
Comparison of Alternative Simulations: Exports
(billions of 1972$)

		1983	1984	1985	1986	1987	1988
Goods and services	1[a]	138.6	146.4	159.1	165.6	124.4	183.6
	2[b]	138.6	146.8	159.7	166.1	174.9	184.3
	3[c]	138.6	148.7	165.4	175.4	186.8	197.0
Merchandise	1	76.6	78.8	85.3	88.5	93.8	99.3
	2	76.6	78.8	85.5	88.6	93.9	99.6
	3	76.6	80.3	90.5	97.2	104.9	111.3
Food	1	13.8	13.7	14.5	15.0	15.8	16.5
	2	13.8	13.7	14.5	15.0	15.8	16.5
	3	13.8	14.0	15.3	16.2	17.2	18.0
Consumer goods	1	7.0	7.4	8.1	8.5	9.0	9.5
	2	7.0	7.4	8.1	8.5	9.0	9.4
	3	7.0	7.6	8.6	9.2	9.8	9.9
Industrial supplies excluding petroleum	1	20.7	22.0	24.0	25.0	26.9	28.6
	2	20.7	22.0	23.9	24.8	26.8	28.5
	3	20.7	22.6	26.6	28.3	31.3	33.3
Consumer goods	1	25.6	25.5	27.9	28.7	30.4	32.7
	2	25.6	25.5	27.8	28.6	30.3	32.6
	3	25.6	25.6	28.5	31.2	34.0	36.7
Autos and parts	1	5.7	6.0	6.4	6.8	7.0	7.3
	2	5.7	6.0	6.4	6.8	7.0	7.3
	3	5.7	6.3	7.1	7.5	7.8	8.0

Other merchandise	1	3.8	4.1	4.3	4.4	4.6	4.8
	2	3.8	4.3	4.8	5.0	5.1	5.3
	3	3.8	4.2	4.7	4.7	4.8	5.1
Factor income	1	38.5	43.5	48.1	50.3	52.6	55.0
	2	38.5	43.5	48.1	50.3	52.6	55.0
	3	38.5	43.5	48.1	50.3	52.6	55.0
Other services	1	23.5	24.1	25.7	26.7	28.1	29.4
	2	23.5	24.5	26.1	27.1	28.4	29.8
	3	23.5	24.8	26.7	27.5	29.4	30.8
(billions of current $)							
Goods and services	1	334.6	373.2	433.1	476.5	536.7	601.4
	2	334.6	374.6	436.1	478.9	538.3	603.6
	3	334.6	398.6	472.9	530.0	602.6	676.6
Merchandise	1	198.1	216.7	253.1	279.5	318.2	360.3
	2	198.1	217.4	254.9	280.9	319.0	361.5
	3	198.1	223.5	273.8	312.0	360.6	409.5
Factor income	1	82.7	97.9	113.3	123.8	136.1	149.3
	2	82.7	97.9	113.5	123.9	135.8	149.1
	3	82.7	104.0	127.5	139.3	153.1	168.0

[a] 1 = base solution.
[b] 2 = foreign industrial-policy solution.
[c] 3 = foreign industrial policy with readjustment.

Conclusions

What, then, can be said about the impact of foreign industrial policies? Industrial policies are likely to affect the international competitiveness of foreign and U.S. industries and are likely, for some time at least, to impose burdens on the industries directly affected and on others as well. Our simulations have demonstrated the potential for readjustment based on movement of the exchange rate. Imports impose costs of dislocation on domestic industries, and policymakers should not ignore the problems of industries that have become noncompetitive and need help to modernize or to make a transition into other activities. The empirical study suggests, however, that the exchange-rate adjustment process will ultimately cause the economy to regain its earlier growth path. This is a powerful argument for free trade.

Notes

1. Of course, even if foreign policies do not work, they might damage U.S. industry. In most cases, however, proponents of this position see U.S. industry as damaged because of the superior competitiveness of foreign industries as a result of targeted industrial policies, or export subsidies.

2. This statement can be made even if there is no agreement on whether industrial policy influenced Japanese growth.

3. This is a large, sudden change, amounting to approximately $26 billion in nominal terms. It is probably unrealistic to visualize such a sudden change; it would certainly evoke a hefty policy response. For our purpose here, however, a change of this magnitude is useful to show clearly the impact on the macroeconomy. Smaller shocks would evoke roughly proportional results.

4. Note that in 1986 merchandise exports are up $9.8 billion and imports are up $4.7 billion in simulation 3 as compared to the base solution.

6
Industrial-Policy Impacts on the Steel Industry: A Simulation Study

F. Gerard Adams,
Trevor Alleyne,
Christopher Bell,
Richard Koss,
Brian Pinto, and
Mikko Puhakka

The United States steel industry has been exhibiting the classic symptoms of a crisis: layoffs, closures of inefficient plants, excess capacity, and rising import shares in domestic markets. At the same time, steel occupies a central place in the industrial nexus, serving as a crucial input component in most other U.S. industries. Thus the fortunes of the steel industry are a matter of concern to the well-being of the entire U.S. economy.

The objective of this simulation study was to provide a basis for choosing appropriate industrial-policy instruments to combat the long-term problems faced by the steel industry. The empirical approach involves the estimation and simulation of an econometric model of the steel industry. The impact of industrial policies is evaluated by comparing simulations embodying alternative assumed industrial-policy measures with a base model solution.

The first section considers the crucial steel-industry issues. The next section is devoted to a description of the econometric model. This section describes the causal sequence linking the blocks of the model and also elaborates on the underlying logic of the various individual equations and the explanatory variables they contain.

This second section summarizes validation of the model through dynamic sample-period simulation and multiplier tests. The model adequately explains the critical variables of the steel industry—production, domestic demand, import shares, employment, capacity utilization, price, and cash flow.

The third section analyze five broad classes of policy. Some, such as monetary policy affecting interest rates, belong to the category of general policy, not specific to a particular industry. Others, such as investment tax credits, trade intervention, and incomes policies, are specific to the steel industry.

We find that the steel industry does respond to measures designed to stimulate investment and production. The effect on unemployment is not always beneficial, however, because stimulus to investment increases labor productivity and lowers employment unless demand grows strongly.

Issues and Experience in the U.S. Steel Industry

The crucial issue for the U.S. steel industry is its ability to sustain itself in an environment of severe international competition. Most controversy and suggested remedial measures in the recent past have been aimed at this question. The trends, as conveyed by the figures in table 6–1, are unmistakable: Imports as a share of apparent domestic consumption have been steadily on the rise,[1] and U.S. relative cost-effectiveness has been on the decline. Three major facts are relevant in this context:

Table 6–1
Statistics on Import Share, Relative Cost and Capacity Utilization

Year	Imports/U.S. Apparent Consumption %	Unit Cost $/MT in U.S. / Unit Cost $/MT in Japan	% Cap. Util. U.S. / % Cap. Util. Japan & EEC
1956	1.7	0.925	0.9244
1957	1.5	0.826	0.8886
1958	2.9	1.239	0.7199
1959	6.1	1.266	0.7245
1960	4.7	1.413	0.7108
1961	4.7	1.337	0.7078
1962	5.6	1.456	0.7658
1963	6.9	1.468	0.8700
1964	7.3	1.529	0.9228
1965	10.3	1.479	1.0250
1966	10.9	1.575	1.0844
1967	12.2	1.693	0.9740
1968	16.7	1.762	0.9872
1969	13.7	1.791	1.0070
1970	13.8	1.758	0.9625
1971	17.9	1.796	0.9847
1972	16.6	1.856	1.0564
1973	12.4	1.597	1.0982
1974	13.4	1.463	1.0908
1975	13.5	1.697	1.1237
1976	14.1	1.820	1.1762

Source: Developed from FTC Report (1977).

Note: U.S. Apparent Consumption = Factory Shipments plus imports minus exports, it ignores inventory build-ups/reduction by users.

1. The industry has been marked by low rates of capacity utilization and new investment. As a result, facilities in the United States are generally older than those abroad and have not taken advantage of the latest technological developments.
2. Return on equity from primary iron and steel was occasionally more than 25 percent smaller than the average for manufacturing from 1958–1978.[2] Thus in 1978 the return on equity for the former was 8.9 percent, whereas that for all manufacturing was 15 percent.
3. Imports as a percentage of apparent domestic consumption rose from 1.2 percent in 1955 to a peak of 17.9 percent in 1971, and touched 14.1 percent in 1976, despite sporadic episodes of protection.

Background on the Steel Industry and the Domestic Issues

Most studies of the domestic steel industry have focused on that industry segment constituted by the twelve or more companies in the category of integrated carbon-steel producers, which account for 85 percent of domestic output.[3] There are basically three types of steel—carbon, alloy, and stainless steel—of which the first accounts for the bulk of production. There are four types of furnaces—basic oxygen (BOF), open-hearth and electric, and continuous-casting—which vary widely with regard to production efficiency, type of raw material used, and implications for pollution control. Thus electric furnaces, which use virtually 100 percent scrap, are consequently energy efficient, are the cheapest when it comes to pollution control, and can operate at small scale. BOFs are far more efficient than the older open-hearth furnaces. There has been a marked decline in the share of open-hearth furnaces in production over time. On the other hand, continuous casting, though increasingly used in Japan, is only at its beginnings in the United States.

An important consideration in a heavy investment industry such as steel is the ability to operate at a level where economies of scale can be reaped. The two places in an integrated steel plant where this can be done most profitably are the blast furnace and the hot strip mill. The minimum efficient scale for a blast furnace is 2 to 3 million tons per year. The second source of large-scale economies is the hot strip mill. With regard to production itself, integrated steel production includes the whole complement of iron ore yards, coal yards, coke ovens, and blast furnaces. Coke is produced from metallurgical coal and feeds into the blast furnace with iron ore. Limestone is added to the blast furnace, the combination being converted into pig iron and slag. The equipment required up to this stage accounts for a significant share of total investment in a steel plant. It also has serious implications for pollution control. Blast furnaces and coke ovens are a source of pollution, and the mandatory control of this pollution has diverted investment funds from alternative productive uses.

Consequently, investment in pollution control equipment is an important policy issue. Electric-furnace production, on the other hand, relies almost entirely on steel scrap and does not require investment in facilities for producing pig iron. The next stage is the production of raw steel in a basic oxygen, open-hearth, or electric furnace. Raw steel either may be formed into ingots and then rolled into semifinished products, or may be continuously cast into these semifinished forms.

Traditionally, the two big customers for steel have been the construction and automotive industries. Table 6–2 shows the distribution of U.S. domestic steel shipments by customer class for two years, 1973 and 1979. In the 1950s the auto industry accounted for 16 percent of the industry's shipments. This figure climbed to 19 percent in the early 1970s and was 24 percent in 1976–1977. With the energy crisis and the subsequent downsizing of cars, accompanied by a search for substitute lightweight materials, the automotive market may decline as a steel-user segment in the future. In the construction industry, there has been a more or less persistent decline in the use of steel in the 1960s and 1970s.

With the twin prongs of sluggish growth in domestic demand and competition from abroad, the industry has been plagued with considerable excess capacity over the past twenty-five years (see table 6–3). The rate of expansion slowed from 2.5 percent per year in the late 1950s to about 1 percent per year in the 1960s, and in the 1970s only 5 million tons of new capacity were added, with obvious consequences for the age of steel-making facilities. This

Table 6–2
Net Shipments of Steel Products by Market Classifications
(Thousands of net tons)

Market Classification	1979		1973	
	Shipments	%	Shipments	%
Construction and contractors' products	13,723	13.7	17,190	15.4
Automotive	18,621	18.5	23,217	20.8
Rail transportation	4,111	4.1	3,228	2.9
Shipbuilding, aircraft, oil and gas, mining, etc.	5,292	5.3	5,027	4.6
Steel service centers and distributors	18,246	18.2	20,383	18.3
Machinery, industrial equipment and tools	5,996	6.0	6,531	5.7
Others	34,273	34.2	36,034	32.3
Total shipments	100,262	100.0	111,430	100.0

Source: AISI *Annual Statistical Reports* (various issues).

Table 6–3
Average Capacity Utilization in the Steel Industry, 1956–1978

Years	Average Utilization Rate (%)
1956–1960	74.5
1961–1965	77.2
1966–1970	87.7
1971–1975	85.2
1976–1978	82.0

Source: Crandall (1981).

was accompanied by a sharp decline in the profit rates. The following figures give an impression of this trend.[4]

Period	Earnings/Sales (%)	Imports/Total Market (%)
1950s	6.5	2.3
1960	5.3	9.3
1970	3.3	15.3
1977–1979	1.7	17.0

Changes in technology, coupled with stagnant demand for U.S.-produced steel, have led to falling labor use over time in the steel industry. Although steel production averaged more than 133 million tons from 1965 to 1969, it rose only marginally to 137 million tons in 1978, a relatively good year. At the same time, total industry employment fell from about 650,000 employees to 550,000 employees. Productivity grew by 1.4 percent per year between 1966 and 1978, but total output grew by a mere 0.2 percent per year.

The ratio of wage payments to value added has been extremely high in steel even when compared with the electronics or apparel industries. From 1972 to 1976 this ratio averaged 51 percent for manufacturing but was 64 percent for steel. This ratio, an indicator of labor-intensiveness or at least of labor cost, suggests that the steel industry is more disadvantageously placed with respect to labor use than is generally true in manufacturing. This has an important bearing on the notion of comparative advantage (more appropriately *dis*advantage) in the U.S. steel industry relatively to foreign steel producers.

Clearly, high wage rates have not been offset by reduced use of labor. The logical questions that then arise are: how much labor-capital substitution is possible? and why did the US steel producers not shift to modern, new plants where the dependence on costly labor might be reduced? The possibilities for substitution are limited. Hence, it is clear that the cost of labor is crucial in determining comparative advantage.

Environmental Regulation

The costs associated with adequate pollution control and the strict monitoring of regulations have been a bone of contention in the past few years, with the industry claiming this results in a cost disadvantage relative to foreign producers.

There are two aspects to regulation: worker safety and pollution control. According to the industry's estimates, the first accounts for about one-sixth of environmental costs. As with every controversial issue, however, the evidence is conflicting and does not point to clear conclusions. Thus the OTA study (OTA 1980) concluded:

> Regulatory requirements have been and will continue to be a major cost burden on the domestic steel industry. As additional pollution control equipment is installed during the next few years, the industry's capital, operating, and maintenance costs will increase accordingly. . . . Economic considerations have recently been receiving greater weight in the identification of qualifying control technologies, and the industry hopes that the feasibility of future regulatory technologies will also be fully considered.

The EPA-commissioned study of the cost impact of full compliance with environmental regulations projected that the 1983 cost would be $20 per ton in 1975 prices. The industry was, however, far from full compliance in 1977, a situation that has not altered much in more recent years.

Estimating the cost impact of EPA and OSHA regulations is not easy. It also is not clear whether the conclusions of the past studies are still valid in light of the recent changes introduced, notably the so-called bubble concept and the key changes in regulations and their implementation by the Reagan administration.

The International Issues

In virtually all studies that look into the historical origins of the steel problem, there is agreement that the following international trends played a major role:

1. An increase in the world supply of raw materials, which gradually eliminated the U.S. steel industry's advantage in this sphere.
2. A decline in shipping costs, which further lowered the cost of materials.
3. A rapid diffusion of steel-making technology abroad.
4. The rapid, and apparently excessive, rise of wages in the United States.

Two important details illustrate graphically the competitive position of the U.S. steel industry relative to foreign producers of steel: (1) Continuous casting, which is seen as a major breakthrough with major implications for savings in energy and operating costs and higher quality, accounted for 50 percent of Japanese output and 29 percent of European Economic Community (EEC) output, but only 15 percent of U.S. output in the late 1970s; and (2) economies of scale are crucial in the steel-making industry. By 1976 the average annual capacity of the ten largest plants in Japan was 12.7 million tons, for the EEC 7.1 million tons, and for the United States 6.5 million tons.

Crandall argues that the problem of imports is one of comparative advantage.[5] With raw materials no longer a constraint in terms of supply or price, and easy access to modern technology, Japan's low wage rate combined with high productivity has made a substantial difference in its competitive position. In addition, from 1961–1971 Japan was able to expand its capacity by 80 million tons far more cheaply than either Europe or the United States.

The most significant instance of protection was the institution of the trigger-price mechanism (TPM). More recently on the trade front, important policy issues are the continuation of protection via quotas and negotiation of voluntary restraint agreements (VRAs). In addition, the effects of export incentives to foreign competitors are also extremely important and need exploring.

An Econometric Model of the U.S. Steel Industry

This section contains a detailed description of an econometric model of the steel industry. The model serves as a basis for examining various industry policy scenarios, as well as for forecasting steel-industry activity.

The Model as a System

Before considering the causal sequence of the steel model, it is helpful to highlight the variables of primary interest.[6] The main exogenous inputs are:

1. Indicators of economic activity in steel-using industries, such as construction, autos, and the like.
2. Prices of substitutes for steel products, elaborated in the description of functional forms for the demand block.

3. Government and institutional policy with respect to pollution control, tax rates, protection, and so on.
4. Factor costs: wages and prices of material and energy inputs.
5. Foreign variables, principally unit cost of production in Japan and capacity utilization in Japan and the EEC.

The main endogenous variables are:

1. Domestic demand.
2. Foreign trade in steel.
3. Production of steel.
4. Price of steel.
5. Cash flow.
6. Revenues and profits.

Figure 6–1 describes the relationships between the exogenous and endogenous variables. Domestic demand (in the top left-hand corner) is derived from activity levels in steel-using industries and prices. In conjunction with imports and exports of steel, this determines domestic production of raw steel. Steel prices are affected both by the level of demand (which prices affect in turn) and by costs, the latter being determined by the requirements of factor inputs as dictated by the level of production. Employment, or the labor requirement, is obtained from an inverted production function (to be explained later in this section) and depends on level of both output and investment. Material-input requirements (including energy) are determined on a fixed-coefficient basis that specifies the amount of input per unit of output. In addition to determining these inputs, production feeds into capacity utilization rates and required investment levels, whereas price, together with production, indicates the revenues forthcoming. Revenues and costs feed into cash flow, determined as a residual. Investment in turn is a function of the user cost of capital (or, alternatively, can be related to cash flow).

Demand Block

Steel is an intermediate good, and the demand for steel is almost totally derived from the level of production and demand in the steel-using industries. The demand for steel in this study has been estimated by major product category on the basis of equations that depend largely on the activity level in the steel-using industries. Table 6–4 presents the major steel product categories, and table 6–5 shows the principal steel-using industries.

The explanatory variables used include a steel-user production index, a

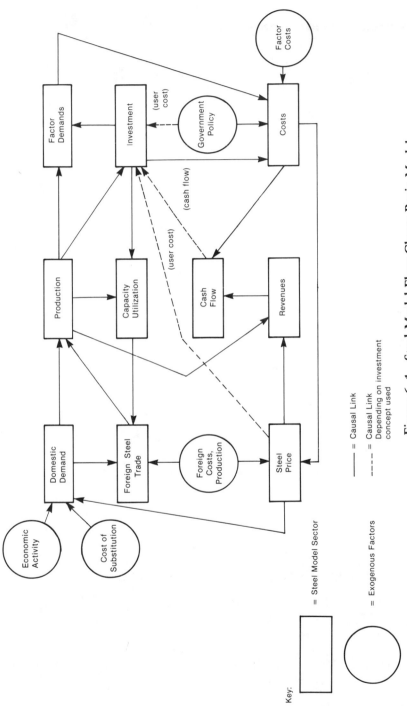

Figure 6–1. Steel Model Flow Chart: Basic Model

Table 6–4
The Major Steel Product Categories

Code	Product	1979 Production (thousands of net tons)
SEMI	Semifinished (ingots, blooms, billets, slabs, sheet bars, tube, rounds, skelp, wire rods)	5,495.7
SHAPE	Structural shapes (heavy) and steel piling	5,596.1
PLATE	Plates	9,035.2
RAIL	Rails and accessories	2,025.9
BAR	Bars and tool steel	17,601.4
PIPE	Pipe and tubing	8,242.4
WIRE	Wire	2,448.7
TIN	Tin mill products	6,310.0
SHEET	Sheets and strip	43,506.8
	Total	100,262.1

Source: AISI *Annual Statistical Report* 1979.

Table 6–5
The Principal Steel-Using Industries

Data Bank Code	Industry
IBFX	Construction
IPMF0371	Motor vehicles and parts
IPMF035	Nonelectrical machinery
IPMF	Total manufacturing
IPMF0374	Railroad equipment
IPMG13	Oil and gas extraction
IPMF036	Electrical machinery
IPMF0341	Metal cans

Source: Wharton Econometric Forecasting Associates.

distributed lag index of relative prices, and in several instances an adjustment variable. The general specification of the functional form is:

$$DDOM_i = F(DD_i, DDRD_i, PREL_i) \ i = 1, 2, \ldots, 9$$

(9 steel product categories)

where

$DDOM_i$ = domestic production plus imports less exports for the ith steel product category.

DD_i = steel-user production index for the ith steel product category.

$DDRD_i$ = adjustment variable for the ith steel product category defined as $DD_i / DD_{i(-1)}$.

$PREL_i$ = relative price index for the ith steel product category.

The steel-user production index (DD_i) is a constructed variable obtained by weighting the activity index of the user industry by the pertinent input coefficient. Specifically,

$$DD_i = \sum_{j=1}^{n} a_{ij}^0 A_j$$

where

A_j = activity index for the jth steel-using industry.

a_{ij}^0 = proportion of demand for the ith product category from the jth steel-using industry in 1967.

The A_js are indexes of value added by the user industries with a 1967 base. The a_{ij}s have been calculated for 1967 using data on domestic shipments of steel products by market classification compiled by the American Iron and Steel Institute (AISI). It has been assumed that the shipment patterns for imported steel are identical to those for domestically produced steel.

The relative price index, $PREL_i$, is constructed as follows:

$$PREL_i = \sum_{k=1}^{n} b_{ik} P_{ik} / \sum_{l=1}^{n} c_{il} P_{il}$$

where

P_{ik} = producer price index for the kth subcategory of the ith steel product.

P_{i1} = producer price index for the lth rival product of the ith steel product—that is, price of substitute product.

b_{ik} = proportion of the kth subcategory of the ith steel product, relevant to P_{ik}.

c_{il} = proportion of rival product for markets catered to by the ith steel product, relevant to P_{il}.

The PREL variable enters the equation with a distributed lag. Table 6–6 presents the producer price indexes used in this study. The b_{ik}s are estimated

Table 6–6
The Producer Price Indexes Used in This Study

	Steel Products
Data Bank Code	*Index*
WPU101301	Semifinished steel
WPU10130248	Structural shapes
WPU10130245	Plate
WPU10130241	Rail
WPU10130255	Bars, reinforcing
WPU10130252	Bars, hot rolled
WPU10130256	Bars, cold finished
WPU10130269	Pipe, black
WPU10130272	Pipe, oil well casing
WPU10130273	Pipe, mechanical
WPU10130282	Tin plate
WPU10130261	Sheet, hot rolled
WPU10130262	Sheet, cold rolled
WPU10130263	Sheet, galvanized
WPU10130286	Wire, drawn

	Competitive Materials
Data Bank Code	*Index*
WPU133	Concrete
WPU033	Plywood
WPU134	Structural clay
WPU102501	Aluminum
WPU066	Plastic
WPU1025	Wire and cable
WPUDUR-0110	Durable goods

Source: Wharton Econometric Forecasting Associates.

using the data on domestic shipments of steel products by market classification compiled by AISI for 1967.

It was hypothesized that the impact of strikes in the steel industry should be taken into account in the equations determining steel demand. The bust-boom pattern of demand that characterizes a strike tends to be absorbed in annual data, however, so none of these terms proved significant. Nonsignificant results were also obtained for the adjustment variable, $DDRD_i$, in many cases. In these instances it too was dropped.

A variable capturing changes in product design that have an impact on steel consumption by the user industries could perhaps be included in the demand equations. Such a variable is difficult to specify. In the absence of such a variable, adjustments in the demand equations may be necessary if known changes in final product specifications are in prospect—for example, the reduced weight of automobiles.

Table 6–7 summarizes the estimated activity and price elasticities for the various steel categories. Of the nine steel categories, three had activity elasticities significantly greater than one (that is, if economic activity in the industries using the type of steel in question increases by 1 percent, the demand for that type of steel increases by more than 1 percent). These categories were semifinished steel, steel structural shapes, and steel plate. Two other categories, steel pipe and tin mill steel, exhibited elasticities significantly less than one. This difference may be accounted for by the technological questions raised in the previous paragraph: For instance, automobiles in 1967 are not perfect substitutes for automobiles in 1979. Price elasticities vary from 0.6 for steel wire to 2.08 for steel plates, depending on the ease with which each type of steel may be substituted for its competitors.

Imports

Imports of steel in the United States have reached the point where the United States has become the world's largest importer of steel.

Steel imports are explained as a function of domestic demand and a distributed lag of relative unit steel-making costs and capacity utilization in the United States and abroad. Import restrictions have been introduced in these equations where appropriate. The basic equations are for the share of imports in domestic demand for the nine steel categories presented in table 6–4. Equations take the following general form:

$$\frac{M_i}{DDOM_i} = f(\,U,\,CU,\,MR\,)$$

where

M_i = imports for category i.

$DDOM_i$ = domestic demand for category i (factory shipments plus imports minus exports)

U = unit-cost ratio in the United States to that of Japan for steel-making with a distributed lag.

CU = capacity-utilization ratio in the United States to that of Japan and the EEC with a distributed lag.

MR = import restriction dummy variables.

Table 6–7
Summary of Elasticities for Estimated Demand Equations

Category	Elasticity with respect to	
	Steel User Production Index DD_i [a]	Relative Price Index PREL[a]
SEMI	1.51	1.22
SHAPE	1.57	.48
PLATE	1.58	2.08
RAIL	.90	1.27
BAR	1.00	.83
PIPE	.76	.77
WIRE	1.18	.06
TIN	.73	1.26
SHEET	1.05	.27

[a]For detailed definitions of these variables, see text.

The rationale for the various explanatory variables is as follows:

1. *Domestic demand for steel* ($DDOM_i$): This is an obvious choice, because the demand for steel is *derived* from the demand for automobiles, construction activity, etc. It is reasonable to expect that a rise in domestic demand will increase imports;
2. *Unit cost per metric ton* (U): If users of steel are profit-maximizing, then, subject to a quality threshold, they will opt for the cheaper source of supply. Hence one would expect a positive coefficient for the cost ratio; that is, as relative costs in the United States rise, one would expect imports to rise as well. The cost variable used in the ratio of the unit cost per MT in the United States to that in Japan.
3. *Capacity utilization* (CU): The variable used is capacity utilization in the United States relative to that in Japan and the European Community. The importance of relative capacity utilization stems both from the ability to meet delivery schedules, as well as its impact on unit cost via the scale of operations.[3]
4. *Import restriction variables* (MR): These are dummy variables that assume a value of 1 in periods of significant deviation from a normal trend owing to a specific occurrence, and 0 in the other periods. It was decided to experiment with dummy variables for the voluntary restraint agreements (VRA) introduced during 1969–74, and for the trigger price mechanism (TPM) applicable during 1978 and 1979. The results with the dummy variables for the VRA's were statistically nonsignificant. Those for the TPM were, however, significant and of the right sign (negative, except in the case of rail imports), indicating that the TPM had

a significant effect on restricting the volume of imports and/or, that foreign producers of steel were extraordinarily restrained in exporting to the United States. Whatever the reason, in the absence of the dummy variables for the TPM, imports "predicted" by the dynamic solution of the whole model tended to be far in excess of actual imports for 1978 and 1979. In addition, separate dummy variables were used for the TPM in 1978 (year of introduction) and 1979, because it was felt that there would be a difference between its operation in the two years owing to inevitable lags and "learning" in administration and implementation.

A summary of the import elasticities is given in table 6–8. The sensitivity of import shares to relative cost efficiency is of a high order, confirming the hypothesis that relative costs in the United States and abroad play a significant role in determining the volume of imports. Thus a 1 percent rise in unit production costs in the United States relative to Japan will, in the long run, raise the share of semifinished steel imports in domestic demand by 2.06 percent, for wire products by 0.79 percent, for sheet and strip steel by as much as 5.05 percent, and so on. Capacity utilization in the United States relative to that in Japan and the EEC also has a significant impact on import shares for most of the categories, presumably via its effect on delivery schedules, cost efficiency, and price markup. The effect is particularly pronounced in the cases of plate and rail products, where a rise of 1 percent in U.S. capacity utilization relative to that in Japan and the EEC will raise the import shares for these products by 3.83 percent and 3.36 percent, respectively.

Table 6–8
Summary of Elasticities for Estimated Import Share Equations

	Elasticity with Respect to	
Category	*Relative Unit Cost UCUSJ*[a]	*Relative Capacity Utilization CUUSJEC*[a]
SEMI	2.06	—
SHAPE	2.35	.34
PLATE	3.45	3.83
RAIL	1.69	3.36
BAR	.99	—
PIPE	2.28	1.10
WIRE	.79	.42
TIN	2.64	3.31
SHEET	5.05	3.03

[a]For detailed definitions of these variables, see text.

Production and Factor Demands

Once domestic demand and imports have been determined, the total requirement for domestically produced steel can be expressed:

$$X\,RAWS = DDOM + X - M$$

where,

DDOM = total domestic demand for steel.

X = total exports of steel.

M = total imports of steel.

Exports are given exogenously. Market-clearing requires that steel production in the United States be the sum of total demand and the change in inventories. Since this is an annual model, however, the inventory-accumulation decision takes place with a frequency that is short relative to the annual frequency of the model; hence inventories are excluded. The variable $X\,RAWS$ is used as a proxy for total U.S. steel production.

Given a particular level of steel production, a steel-making firm faces several decisions to determine how best to meet this requirement. These decisions may be classified as long-run or short-run. The primary long-run decision, that of capital investment, is discussed in the next section. Given a particular configuration of installed capital stock, three shorter-term production decisions remain to be determined:

1. Which of the available processes will be utilized in the production of steel?
2. What energy and materials inputs does the chosen capital require?
3. How many workers will be employed by the industry?

Production Shares

Figure 6–2 gives a rough idea of the steel-making process and of the inputs involved.

Technology in steel-making is embodied in the three major raw steel production processes: open hearth, electric, and basic oxygen. Since at any point in time the capital stock is fixed, the industry will choose the means of production that is feasible and that minimizes costs. Table 6–9 gives the historical distribution of the share of the three different processes used in total raw steel production. The dominant process in the early 1960s was the

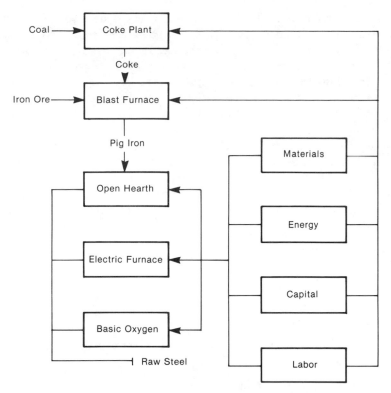

Figure 6–2. Flow Chart of Raw Steel Production

Table 6–9
Relative Shares of Various Raw Steel-Making Processes in Total Raw Steel Production

	Basic Oxygen	Electric	Open Hearth
1960	.03	.08	.86
1965	.17	.11	.71
1970	.48	.15	.37
1975	.62	.19	.19
1979	.61	.25	.14

Note: May not sum to 1.00 in earlier years because negligible share of Bessemer process has been excluded.

open-hearth process, which was responsible for 86 percent of total production. By 1979 this had dropped off to 14 percent. This pattern may be contrasted with the basic-oxygen process, which went from a 3 percent share in

1960 to 61 percent in 1979. The electric-process share also grew over the same period, but at a much slower rate, from 8 percent in 1960 to 25 percent in 1979. It is clear from the data that the electric and basic-oxygen processes must be efficient relative to the open-hearth process. The speed with which the industry shifts from inefficient to efficient processes depends on the rate at which efficient processes grow less costly than inefficient ones. The industry does not shift over immediately because of the costs of closing down old plants and opening new ones. The relative-cost variable measures the incentive industries feel to absorb these costs. This shift is constrained by the amount of capital accumulation in the industry as a whole. Hence, assuming that capacity utilization is less than 100 percent (the highest historical level is 96 percent in 1975), the share of production in the most productive process, basic oxygen, depends on the rate of decline of costs in this process compared to that for the industry as a whole, and on the value of capital investment:

$$X_1 = F (\text{INET}, Y_1)$$

where

X_1 = share of raw steel production by the basic-oxygen process.

INET = total investment (net of pollution-control expenditures) in the steel industry.

Y_1 = cost of production in the basic-oxygen process relative to all processes.

Estimation of the parameters of this expression yields the result that, over the long run, a 1 percent decrease in the cost of production by the basic-oxygen process relative to the other processes results in a 1.5 percent increase in the share of production attributed to basic oxygen.

The electric process is also efficient compared to the open-hearth process, and relative costs represent the strength of the pressure to move to more efficient production. Since basic oxygen has become the most preferred process, however, the electric process is used most intensely when production requirements are near capacity. The specification then becomes:

$$X_2 = F (\text{CAPUR}, Y_2)$$

where

X_2 = share of raw steel production by the electric process.

CAPUR = capacity-utilization rate in steel production.

Y_2 = cost of production in the electric process relative to all processes.

In the long run a 1 percent increase in the capacity-utilization rate increases the share of steel production by the electric process by 0.53 percent, and a 1 percent decrease in the relative cost of the electric process relative to other processes increases the production share by 2.8 percent.

Finally, steel production by the open-hearth process is now largely residual. This method is used primarily when capacity utilization is high. This notion is expressed:

$$X_3 = F\,(\text{CAPUR, TIME})$$

where

X_3 = share of raw steel production by the open-hearth process.

CAPUR = capacity-utilization rate in steel production.

The production share of the open-hearth process decreases by about 11 percent of its share each year, and a 1 percent increase in the capacity-utilization rate increases by the share by 7 percent in the long run. Since no explicit constraint requiring that these shares sum to one has been imposed in estimation, in the model, once X_1, X_2, and X_3 are calculated, they are renormalized to sum to one.

The relative-cost variables used in the estimation of the production share equations are based on the relative uses of four key inputs: pig iron, scrap, fuel oil, and electricity. The weights used to compute the variables are based on engineering data from 1972 and are assumed to be constant (given the particular technology in question) over the estimation period. Table 6–10 provides the relative uses by process of each of these inputs, as well as for fluxes. Once the weights are calculated, total costs are computed using producer-price-index data for each of the inputs. Data by process for other factor inputs, notably labor, were not available.

Energy and Materials Demand

As discussed earlier, technology in the steel industry is embodied in the three major production processes. The dominant form of technological progress is the shift from inefficient to efficient processes. Engineering data provide the materials requirements for each process. Hence, for most materials, the demand for inputs by a particular process becomes:

$$\text{CINPUT}_i = \alpha_i * X\,\text{RAWS} * X_i \qquad i = 1, \ldots, 3$$

where

CINPUT_i = consumption of factor input by process i.

Table 6–10
Relative Uses of Materials in Each Process

Process/Input	Pig Iron	Scrap	Fluxes	Oxygen	Fuel Oil	Electricity
Basix oxygen (BO)	1.0	1.0	1.0	1.0	1.0	1.0
Open hearth (OH)	.773	1.514	.717	.839	15.004	.915
Electric (E)	0.0	3.038	.503	.167	1.0	11.596

Source: John F. Elliott, "Uses of Energy in the Production of Steel," in J. Szekely, ed. *The Steel Industry and the Energy Crisis* (New York: Marcel Dekker, 1975).

α_i = amount of input required per unit of output in process i.

X RAWS   = total raw steel production.

X_i = share of total production by process i.

Total demand for a material is calculated by summing over processes:

$$\text{CINPUT} = \sum_{i=1}^{3} \text{CINPUT}_i$$

Labor Requirements

Labor is treated as a special case since data are not available for employment by production process. The manner in which labor is treated is to specify a production function, which is then inverted to give a labor-requirements function, or the optimal amount of labor needed to produce a given level of raw steel, given the level of capital stock.

In the model, a Cobb-Douglas production function is assumed, and it is inverted to give the labor-requirements function. The following specification was obtained:

$$\ln L_t = a + b \ln X_t + c \ln K_t + \lambda \ln L_{t-1} + u_t$$

where

L = labor input in man-hours.

X = raw steel production.

K = productive capital stock.

t = time subscript.

u = random error.

The following results were obtained:

b = .5491.

c = $-.7798$.

λ = .5786.

The b and c values are interpreted as follows: With capital stock held constant, a 1 percent rise in output will raise employment by 0.55 percent, whereas a 1 percent rise in capital stock with output unchanging will lower employment by 0.78 percent.

Investment Block

Investment is likely to be the impact point of much of government policy. It is particularly relevant for the efficiency and modernization of the industry.

It was our original intent to implement two approaches to investment functions: the Jorgenson approach, based on the neoclassical theory of investment and the cash-flow approach. A reason for considering the latter is that the steel industry has traditionally been suffering from a shortage of cash and has had imperfect access to capital markets, so that its investment decisions may well have been influenced by cash shortages, and the effect of compliance with environmental or OSHA regulations may well have been to divert investment from so-called productive uses. We discuss both approaches here, although, as explained later, the simulations use the Jorgenson form of the equation.

Jorgenson Investment Function

One of the goals of this model is to determine the impacts of fiscal and financial variables on investment decisions. The key variable in this specification is the user cost of capital. This variable compares the price of an investment good with the discounted revenue stream associated with it. This concept may be expressed (following the derivation in Preston (1972)):

$$R = P_I \, \delta \, (r + \delta) \, (1 - s - tb)/(1 - t)$$

where

R = user cost of capital.

P_I = price of investment good.

r = interest rate.

δ = depreciation rate.

s = investment-tax-credit rate.

t = corporate-profits tax rate.

b = depreciation method used.

Note that many investment incentives schemes such as tax credits can readily be introduced here.

Following Jorgenson's argument, we then assume a firm computes desired capital stock as that value which maximizes profits subject to a CES technology. This assumption yields the relation:

$$K^* = (P/R)^\sigma Y$$

where

K^* = desired level of capital stocks.

P = price of output.

R = user cost of capital.

Y = real output.

σ = elasticity of substitution.

Because of inherent lags in the investment process, the adjustment of the capital stock toward optimality takes place with a distributed lag. The equation to be estimated is hence:

$$I_t = a_0 + a_1 \sum_{i=0}^{n} L_{t-i}(P/R)^\sigma Y + a_2 K_{t-1}$$

where I_t = investment. Investment itself, I_t, is defined by the identity:

$$I_t = K_t - (1 - \delta) K_{t-1}$$

where δ is the depreciation rate.

An additional policy consideration we wish to address in this context is the issue of pollution-control expenditures. In principle, firms choose the optimal *productive* capital stock. Any additional expenditures are then made subject to government mandate. Hence, if INET is total investment net of pollution-control expenditures, and KNET is the productive capital stock, we can estimate a variant of the investment equation given earlier:

$$\text{INET}_t = b_0 + b_1 \sum_{i=0}^{n} L_{t-i}(P/R)^\sigma y + b_2 \text{KNET}_{t-1}$$

Total investment is then obtained by adding pollution-control expenditures to INET.

Several different lag lengths and substitution elasticities were tested during the course of estimating the parameters of this equation. A value of σ = .04 and a six-year lag on the user-cost term were chosen to be used in this model. Despite the large swings in this series (investment moves from 2.4 in

1968 to 1.5 in 1972 to 2.0 in 1977, in billions of 1972 dollars) a significant user-cost term (t-statistic over 3.0) results in a regression with $\bar{R}^2$ of almost 0.70.

Investment as Function of Cash Flow

The alternative investment specification relates new capital expenditures to the financial state of the industry, as measured by cash flow. Cash flow is defined:

$$\text{CASHFLOW\$} = \text{NETINCOMES\$} - \text{DIV\$} + \text{DEP\$}$$

where

NETINCOMES\$ = after-tax profits.

DIV\$ = dividends paid.

DEP\$ = depreciation.

Cash flow is computed by the financial sector of the model. Constant-dollar cash flow is determined by dividing nominal cash flow by the U.S. GNP deflator. Investment then responds to current and past real cash flow, and a time distribution of output:

$$I_t = C_0 + C_1 \sum_{i=0} L_{t-i} (\text{CASHFLOW}) + C_2 \sum_{i=0} L_{t-i}(\text{XRAWS}) + C_3 I_{t-1}$$

where

CASHFLOW = constant-dollar cash flow.

X RAWS = steel output.

L is the lag operator. Note that, in contrast to the user-cost based model, this investment function computes *total* investment. In this case net productive investment is computed as the difference between total investment and mandated pollution-control investment.

This equation fits significantly better than the user-cost-based specification, with an $\bar{R}^2$ of .825. An additional *real* dollar of cash flow results in an additional 22¢ of real investment within one year, 50¢ more within two years and $1.41 more in the long run. Cash flow is a significant determinant of investment.

Capital Stock

Once total investment has been computed, the capital stock is determined on the basis of the accumulation identity:

$$K_t = (1 - \delta) K_{t-1} + I_t$$

where δ = depreciation rate, which is assumed to be 10 percent.

Capacity and Capacity Utilization

Capacity measures the potential supply of steel the industry is capable of producing. This equation is specified:

$$\text{CAPRAWS} = d_0 + d_1 \sum_{i=0}^{n} L_{t-i} K$$

where L is the lag operator. Capacity utilization measures the intensity of activity in the steel industry and is computed using the identity:

$$\text{CAPUR} = \text{XRAWS}/\text{CAPRAWS}$$

Financial Sector

Table 6–11 presents a sample income statement based on AISI data for the steel industry for the year 1979. The equations used to determine the items in that table, as well as prices, are specified as follows:

Employment Costs
Employment costs are expressed:

$$\text{EMPCOST\$}_t = F(\text{WR\$}_t \cdot L_t)$$

where

$\text{WR\$}_t$ = wage rate (\$/hour).

L_t = labor demand (hours).

Other Costs
Materials costs represent spending on all energy and raw-materials inputs:

$$\text{MAT\$}_t = F(\text{TOTCOST}_t \cdot \text{XRAWS}_t)$$

Table 6–11
Steel Industry Income Statement, 1979
(billion $)

Revenues		57.35
Costs		56.16
Employment	19.09	
Materials	32.40	
Interest	.84	
Depreciation	1.88	
Income taxes	.42	
Other taxes	.81	
Flight	.71	
Net income		1.20
Dividends		.61
Retained earnings		.59
Depreciation		1.88
Cash flow		2.47

Source: Adapted from AISI, *Annual Statistical Report* 1979.

where

$TOTCOST_t$ = materials costs weighted by production process.

$XRAWS_t$ = raw steel production.

Total steel production serves as a proxy for all materials inputs in the equation since most of the raw-materials inputs are essentially determined by fixed-coefficient production functions.

Interest costs are a function of past borrowing and interest rates. The exact specification appears:

$$INT\$_t = F\left[\sum_{i=0}^{n} L_{t-i}(r_t \cdot K\$_t) \right]$$

where

r_t = long-term interest rate.

$K\$_t$ = value of capital stocks in current $.

Depreciation (in the accounting sense) is related to the value of capital stock as well as to its life expectancy. This equation is specified:

$$DEP\$_t = F\left[\sum_{i=0}^{n} L_{t-i}(K\$_t / LNT_t) \right]$$

where LNT_t = average life expectancy of capital stock (years).

Income taxes are computed from corporate income and credits for investments:

$$INCTAX\$_t = F(TAXR_t * INC\$_t, ITCR_t * I\$_t)$$

where

$TAXR_t$ = corporate-profits tax rate.

$INC\$_t$ = before-tax corporate profits = $REV\$ - EMPCOST\$ -$ $MAT\$ - DEP\$.$

$ITCR_t$ = investment-tax-credit rate.

$I\$_t$ = capital expenditures, billions $.

Total costs are calculated as the sum of seven components:

$$COSTS\$ = EMPCOST\$ + MAT\$ + INT\$ + DEP\$ + INCTAX\$ +$$
$$OTHTAX\$ + FLIGHT\$$$

where

$OTHTAX\$$ = state and local (primary property) taxes (exogenous).

$FLIGHT\$$ = losses due to discontinued operations.

Prices

Pricing in the steel industry has long been controversial. Making no judgment here about the dominance of competitive or oligopolistic elements in the industry's price behavior, there is evidence of considerable price leadership, which appears to reflect cost markup behavior. Such a pricing pattern may have been constrained by competitive forces, particularly when there was substantial excess capacity or foreign competition, and may have been limited by explicit and sometimes implied government interventions. We have not made elaborate efforts to test alternative hypotheses of price determination here.

Prices are obtained as a markup over costs, subject to market constraints:

$$P_t = F\left(\sum_{i=0}^{n} L_{t-i}(COSTS\$), CJ_t \right)$$

where

P_t is the wholesale price index for steel.

CJ_t is the unit cost of Japanese steel in U.S. dollars.

Estimation of this equation showed that foreign markets as represented by the Japanese cost variable are a significant factor in pricing decisions.[8] In addition to this specification, many attempts were made to include capacity utilization in order to capture domestic market conditions. No such term proved to be significant, however.

Prices of individual steel products are obtained in the model through regression relationships to the general steel price variable (P), typically with elasticity coefficients very close to unity.

Other Financial Variables

Prices and output generate revenues:

$$REV\$_t = F(P_t \cdot X\,RAWS_t)$$

This equation is not a strict identity because the revenues measure used here includes items other than steel operations revenues.

Net corporate income is the difference between revenues and costs:

$$NETINC\$ = REV\$ - COSTS\$$$

Dividends are a function of both net income and the change in net income:

$$DIV\$_t = F(NETINC\$_t, NETINC\$_t - NETINC\$_{t-1})$$

Retained earnings are computed as net income less dividends, whereas cash flow is computed as the sum of retained earnings and depreciation:

$$RETEARN\$ = NETINC\$ - DIV\$$$

$$CASHFLOW\$ = RETEARN\$ + DEP\$$$

Although this approach offers considerable opportunity for the analysis of business conditions on pricing and investment behavior, a problem does arise. Reported cash flow is a relatively smooth series over time. Any calculation of cash flow from a model system as a residual of revenues and costs results in a gyrating series, since small errors in revenues or costs (on a percentage basis) result in quite large corresponding errors in cash flow. This in turn has undesirable implications for the accuracy of any cash-flow-based investment function in a complete model. In the next section, this problem is discussed further.[9]

Validation of the Econometric Model

There are two main aspects of validation: a *dynamic solution* of the model as a simultaneous system from fixed initial conditions in some base year, and the *multiplier analysis*.

The first aspect of validation rests simply on the ability of the model to reproduce the historical data on which it is based. This boils down to a comparison of historical actual and predicted values. The dynamic solution solves the model as a simultaneous system, and its ability to give satisfactory results is of major importance in model validation. Multiplier analysis is interesting because it examines the economic rationality of the model by checking:

1. Whether a particular segment of the model responds sensibly in terms of sign and magnitude to a given exogenous change in some variable. It does this by comparing the base dynamic solution with the dynamic solution obtained after the postulated change.
2. Whether these responses are transmitted suitably to other segments of the model in an economically meaningful way.

Thus, for example, we would expect a postulated increase in U.S. unit cost of production to increase the share of imports in domestic demand, increase domestic price, and subsequently lower domestic demand and production with consequent adverse effects on employment, cash flow, and so on. Some of the effects may be lagged, depending on the specification of the various behavioral equations. Such an analysis provides a springboard for a detailed examination of alternative policy scenarios.

Dynamic Simulation

The model was solved dynamically for the years 1970 to 1979. With the exception of the exogenous variables and *initial* values of the endogenous variables, all subsequent values of endogenous variables were model-generated.

Table 6–12 presents error statistics resulting from a dynamic solution of the basic model. The largest errors reported are for investment and imports, with root-mean-square percentage errors of 15.8 percent and 15.9 percent,

Table 6–12
Summary of Error Statistics for Dynamic Solution (Jorgenson Investment Equation Version), 1970–1979
(Percentage errors)

Variable	RMSE[a]	MAE[b]
Production	3.52	2.71
Capacity utilization	3.16	2.73
Employment	6.04	4.74
Domestic demand	5.37	3.48
Imports	15.91	11.47
Steel price	2.81	2.01
Investment	15.77	13.93
Cash flow[c]	1.33	.097

[a]Root-mean-squared error.
[b]Mean absolute error.
[c]Errors reported are *levels* (billions of dollars), not percentages. The cash flow has *not* been fed back into the investment equation.

respectively. Both series are very noisy, however, and are subject to a wide variety of outside influences. Root-mean-square errors for the remaining variables are all 6 percent or below. Of particular note, however, is the behavior of nominal cash flow in the dynamic solution. The root-mean-squared error turned out to be $1.33 billion for a series whose largest observation is $3.13 billion. The reason for this large error value is that cash flow is treated as a residual in the basic model, and error tends to accumulate there. A 5 percent error in total cost, other things being equal, results in perhaps a 50 percent error in cash flow. Consequently, the simulations do not use the cash-flow equation, and rely on the Jorgenson version of the investment equation. Figures 6–3 and 6–4 present the results of the foregoing dynamic solution for a few key variables graphically.

Validation via Multiplier Analysis

The purpose of the multiplier exercise is to test whether exogenous shocks to the model move from one sector to another in the anticipated manner. This section describes in detail the effect of two changes in assumptions. First, we analyze the impact of a reduction in the nominal wage rate of steelworkers of 5 percent as compared to historical levels over the period 1970–1979. The second scenario discussed here involves a further price increase of 5 percent in all energy inputs in the industry over the same period. In each case the dynamic solution is compared to the dynamic control solution developed in

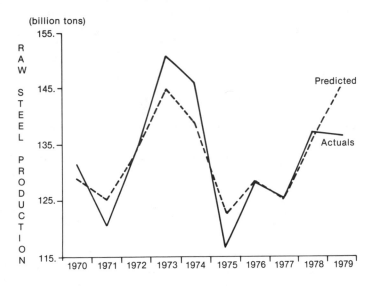

Figure 6–3. Steel Industry Basic Model: Raw Steel Production

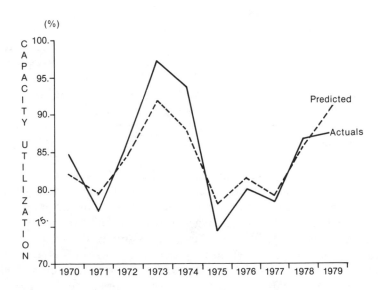

Figure 6–4. Steel Industry Basic Model: Capacity Utilization

the previous section. Tables 6–13 and 6–14 present the results of the two multiplier experiments.

Lower-Wage Simulation

First, a lower-wage-rate simulation is examined (see table 6–13). The initial impact of such a change is a reduction in industry costs, which increases cash flow and decreases the steel price. The price effect is largest after three years, when prices are 0.7 percent lower than in the base solution. After that time the impact lessens slightly each subsequent year. This price change stimulates domestic demand (eventually 0.5 percent higher than in the base solution) and reduces imports (4.5 percent lower after four years). These two changes induce an increase in domestic steel production of 1 percent after nine years. This additional output spurs an increase in domestic steel investment through the acceleration effect, which climbs slowly to 1 percent after ten years. Since the increase in output is faster than the increase in investment, additional labor is required to meet the extra demand. After nine years the industry employs 7,000 more people than it did in the base solution (an 0.8 percent increase). Finally, labor productivity rises slightly in this scenario, reaching a 0.25 percent increase after ten years.

Energy-Price Simulation

We now consider the energy scenario shown in table 6–14. The initial impact of an increase in energy prices is on costs. This increase results next in higher prices and higher imports. The combination results in lower domestic demand and depressed steel production. Factor demands (labor, capital, materials) decline proportionately. In this scenario, however, another consideration comes into play. This is because there are three production processes considered in this model: basic oxygen, electric, and open hearth. Relative costs determine the shares of each process used in total steel production. Since we assume labor was mobile among processes, labor costs do not enter the relative cost variable used here; but energy costs are a major component. Hence production in this scenario shifts to more energy-efficient processes. This in turn helps to mitigate the long-term impact of an energy price increase. Initially, the basic-oxygen process accounted for 48.3 percent of steel production in 1970, the electric process for 15.0 percent, and the open-hearth process for 36.7 percent. By 1979 these figures, in the base solution, became 61.3 percent, 25.5 percent, and 13.2 percent, respectively. Starting with the same 1970 shares, the high-energy price scenario produced corresponding figures of 62.0 percent, 24.9 percent, and 13.1 percent, respec-

Table 6–13
Multiplier Table, Lower Wage Rate Scenario

Variable	Years					
	1	2	4	6	8	10
Price	-.26	-.42	-.68	-.68	-.54	-.37
Imports	-1.84	-2.83	-4.50	-3.20	-2.22	-3.27
Domestic demand	.01	.01	.05	.17	.36	.45
Production	.23	.45	.73	.53	.89	.92
Investment	.03	.14	.10	.26	.52	1.08
Employment	.12	.31	.42	.47	.52	.68
Cash flow[a]	.15	.13	.16	.21	.30	.47
Capacity utilization	.22	.45	.72	.52	.85	.86
Productivity	.11	.14	.31	.06	.19	.24

Note: Percentage change from base solution.
[a]Level difference from base solution (billions of dollars).

Table 6–14
Multiplier Table, Higher Energy Cost Scenario

Variable	Years					
	1	2	4	6	8	10
Price	.23	.36	.29	.42	.65	.69
Imports	1.34	2.60	1.99	3.15	1.72	3.95
Domestic demand	-.01	-.02	-.02	-.12	-.19	-.24
Production	-.18	-.44	-.38	-.49	-.63	-.86
Investment	-.02	-.12	-1.11	-1.04	-.49	-.43
Employment	-.11	-.29	-.60	-.19	-.11	-.24
Cash flow[a]	-.13	-.12	-.14	-.19	-.40	-.51
Capacity utilization	-.20	-.44	-.39	-.45	-.51	-.75
Productivity	-.07	-.15	.22	-.30	-.47	-.62
Production shares:						
Basic oxygen	0.0	0.0	+.4	+1.0	+.8	+.7
Electric	0.0	0.0	-.3	-.6	-.6	-.6
Open hearth	0.0	0.0	-.1	-.4	-.2	-.1

Note: Percentage change from base solution.
[a]*Level* difference from base solution (billions of dollars).

tively, in 1979. Hence the shift in energy prices has the effect of shifting production from the electric process to the basic-oxygen process. Because of the long lags involved in such a shift, however, the effect is slow to materialize. Further, we are looking at a composite change in energy prices, rather than at individual components such as fuel oil or electricity, whose impact depends on the extent to which this specific fuel is used by a given process. Hence the multipliers produced here are much in the spirit of the labor-cost case discussed earlier. A 5 percent increase in the cost of energy inputs results in a 0.7 percent increase in prices after ten years. Imports rise by 2.5 – 3 percent after five years and stay elevated at that level over the duration of the solution. The price and import effects result in a production path that ultimately is 0.86 percent below that of the control solution. The investment multiplier declines steadily to a level of 1.2 percent after five years and then slowly recovers. Labor demand drops to a level 0.6 percent below that produced by the control solution after four years and then recovers to a level only 0.1 percent below the control after eight years.

The validation results presented in this section establish the utility of this model for purposes of policy analysis. The dynamic solution verifies that the model (with the Jorgenson investment equation) reproduces history with an adequate degree of accuracy. The multiplier analysis indicates that the model possesses dynamic features in line with historical observation and economic theory.

Policy Analysis

The purpose of this section is to use the steel model to examine the effects of a variety of policy alternatives. The steel model was designed so that the key policy issues affecting the industry—such as capital formation, import restrictions, pricing behavior, and regulatory practices—play an important and direct role in the economic decision-making process undertaken by the industry. Policy analysis can therefore proceed through the manipulation of relatively few model variables. This analysis is performed using the technique of counterfactual history; that is, over the estimation period of the model, different figures for key exogenous variables are substituted for their historical values. The model is then simulated, and the resulting values for important endogenous variables are compared to those generated by the base model solution (using actual historical data). Five broad classes of policies, some general and some industry-specific, are discussed here:

1. Fiscal policies.
2. Monetary policies.
3. Trade policies.

4. Incomes policies.
5. Policies designed to lessen government-mandated investment (pollution control).

Fiscal Policies

Slow growth in capital formation is often seen as a key reason for the lagging competitive position of American steel in international markets. In order to alleviate this problem, it has been suggested that the government offer financial incentives to the steel industry to modernize and expand their production facilities. A variety of industry-specific tools are available. Three distinct policy stimuli are considered here: a decrease in the corporate-profit tax, an increase in the investment tax credit, and an acceleration in depreciation tax lives.[10] In the context of the basic model, these changes directly affect the incentives for the industry to invest in new steel plant and equipment. This change then has an impact from one model sector to another in a way described in detail in the multiplier analysis section. The following three scenarios were run over the period 1970–1979:

1. Profits tax rate 5 percent lower than the historical level for each year of the simulation.
2. Investment tax credit rate 5 percent higher than the historical level for each year of the simulation.
3. Accelerate by five years the average depreciation tax life.

The investment impacts from each of these three policy scenarios are shown in table 6–15.

Although all three policy tools are effective, their effects take different time paths. Since the time frame over which industrial policy is to be implemented is a key policy issue, such considerations are particularly relevant in determining which tool or set of tools best meets planning objectives.

Consider first the profits-tax scenario. Historically, the effective profits tax moved from 43 percent in 1970 to 29 percent in 1979. This scenario

Table 6–15
Effect of Alternative Policies on Steel Industry Investment
(Percentage change from base solution)

Scenario	2 Years	5 Years	10 Years
(1) Profits tax	.257	6.15	3.43
(2) Investment tax credit	1.84	5.08	3.90
(3) Tax life	2.57	12.51	5.99

examines the implications of a tax rate 5 percent lower in each year of the simulation. The impact is small initially (0.8 percent in the first year), rises steadily to 6.2 percent after five years, and then drops to 3.4 percent after ten years.

A different pattern emerges from the investment-tax-credit (ITC) scenario. In this case the 5 percent increase in the ITC represents a large increase over historical levels, which peaked at near 10 percent in 1979. In this case the level of investment climbs slowly to a peak after five years, as in the profits-tax case, but subsequently drops off very slowly. During the last five years of the simulation period, the investment impact drops 2.72 percent in the profits-tax scenario while it drops only 1.18 percent in the investment-tax-credit case. Hence an increase in the ITC has a more sustained effect than impacts generated by changes in the corporate-profits tax rate.

Finally, consider the depreciation-tax-life scenario. A reduction by five years in the average allowable time in which capital may be written off represents a large change by historical standards. The actual level was 17.5 years in 1979. The time path of the effect is particularly interesting in this case. Since an acceleration of tax lives benefits the industry only with regard to capital in place, and since investment requires considerable time to install, the impact of such a policy is slow. The five-year effect in this scenario is almost five times the two-year effect; a similar computation for the profits-tax simulation yields a five-year effect less than 2.5 times the two-year impact. The dropoff of the effect after its peak occurs at about the same speed for the two simulations. Hence a change in the profits-tax structure yields the quickest impact of the three cases considered here, whereas the investment tax credit provides the most sustained effect.[11]

These proposed policies have, of course, significant impacts on other steel activity variables besides investment. These impacts arise through links within the steel model. The time pattern of these second-order effects is hence closely related to the pattern observed for investment. The effects on key variables are shown in table 6–16.

The effects of an increase in investment are transmitted to other model variables. A greater quantity of capital (given an initial level of output) results in a lower level of demand for labor. The resulting savings in labor costs influence total cost and affect the firm's pricing decisions, which in turn have an impact on both domestic and foreign demand. The level of production undertaken by the industry is then adjusted to account for these demand changes. Cash flow is computed as a residual from the total revenue and cost changes, and productivity effects are computed from the final production and employment levels reached.

Table 6–16 provides an interesting pattern of effects for key industry variables. Recall that the impact of the first scenario (lower profits tax) on investment was larger in the short run but eventually fell below the level pro-

Table 6–16
Fiscal-Policy Effects
(Percentage change from base solution)

Variable (Scenario)		2 Years	5 Years	10 Years
Price	(1)	−.42	−.52	−.25
	(2)	−.40	−.66	−.51
	(3)	.12	−.22	−.61
Production	(1)	.48	.32	.96
	(2)	.46	.37	1.25
	(3)	−.13	.03	1.28
Employment	(1)	.04	−1.65	−4.08
	(2)	.12	−1.17	−3.08
	(3)	−.33	−3.74	−9.52
Imports	(1)	−3.02	−2.44	−3.99
	(2)	−2.85	−3.02	−5.79
	(3)	0.78	−.74	−8.10
Cash flow[a]	(1)	.145	.030	.480
	(2)	.127	.214	.707
	(3)	.106	.352	1.171
Productivity	(1)	.44	1.97	5.04
	(2)	.34	1.54	4.33
	(3)	.20	3.77	10.80

Note: Profits tax, (2) ITC, (3) tax life.
[a]Values given are *changes* from base solution in billions of dollars.

duced by the second model simulation (higher investment tax credit). This pattern is reflected in the steel price variable. After two years, prices fall by 0.42 percent in the profits-tax simulation and by 0.40 percent in the investment-tax-credit (ITC) simulation. After ten years these numbers become − 0.25 percent and − 0.51 percent, respectively. Similarly, production rises by 0.48 percent in the profits-tax simulation and by 0.46 percent in the ITC simulation after two years, whereas after ten years these values rise to 0.96 percent and 1.25 percent. Employment drops, imports fall, profits rise, and productivity improves in much the same pattern over the period of simulation. Hence a change in the ITC has a more sustained effect on all key model variables than does a change in the profits-tax rate, although both are effective in stimulating industry activity.

The numbers produced by the third simulation (decrease in depreciation lives for tax purposes) provide an example of what a large change in depreciation lives, by historical standards, can have on steel industry activity. The fillip to investment is so great that a large deviation from the cost-minimizing capital/labor ratio occurs, since the labor complement is adjusted slowly. Hence, after two years, profits rise only slightly compared to the first two scenarios, and prices actually rise. By the tenth year, however, the picture has turned around. A large quantity of new capital results in higher production and productivity, and in lower prices and imports. In addition, it results in a considerable rise in the industry cash-flow position.

Monetary Policies

Monetary policy in this model is represented by the level of the interest rate (in this case an industrial bond rate). Over the period 1970–1979 the interest rate varied from a low of 7.4 percent in 1972 to a high of 9.9 percent in 1979. As in the case of the fiscal policies discussed earlier, policies designed to affect the interest rate influence steel industry activity primarily through the investment decision.[12] In addition, an industry-specific policy would take the form of government-subsidized loans made available at levels below market rates. To analyze this type of policy, the following three experiments were performed over the period 1970–1979:

1. Interest rate 2 percent lower than the historical level for each year of the simulation.
2. Interest rate 2 percent lower and profits tax rate 5 percent lower than the historical levels for each year of the simulation.
3. Interest rate 2 percent lower and investment-tax-credit rate 5 percent higher than the historical levels for each year of the simulation.

The investment impacts from each of these three scenarios are shown in table 6–17.

The time pattern of investment effects in the interest-rate scenario is similar to that provided by the profits-tax scenario. The effect rises steadily to a peak of 21.67 percent after five years and then falls off.[13]

The cumulative effects of scenarios 2 and 3, designed to test the impact of industry-specific fiscal and monetary policies working together, are quite close to the sum of the effects of the two policies working alone. We therefore concentrate on the first scenario (lower interest rates alone). Table 6–18 pro-

Table 6–17
Effect on Steel Industry Investment of Alternative Policies
(Percentage change from base solution)

Scenario	2 Years	5 Years	10 Years
1. Interest rate	6.84	21.67	8.35
2. Interest rate and reduced profits tax	8.90	24.95	10.86
3. Interest rate and increased ITC	8.78	26.21	11.83

Table 6–18
Monetary Policy Effects (Interest-Rate Scenario)
(Percentage change from base solution)

Variable	2 Years	5 Years	10 Years
Price	–.14	–.92	–1.35
Production	.17	.69	2.69
Employment	–.62	–7.35	–16.12
Imports	–1.07	–7.07	–16.43
Productivity	.79	8.04	18.81

vides these impacts for key variables. These results indicate that lower interest rates would result in a healthier steel industry. Investment by the industry lowers cost pressures on the industry, resulting in a price level 1.35 percent below that produced by the base scenario after ten years. This in turn stimulates demands and reduces imports; the cumulative effect is a level of steel production 2.69 percent higher than the base after ten years. This stimulates domestic demand, and, most important, increases industry competitiveness in international markets and increases output.

The point here is that monetary policy and fiscal policy can each affect the level of activity within the steel industry. Interest-rate policy, however, appears to be by far the more powerful.

None of the policy changes discussed up to this point are historically unprecedented. The corporate-profits tax rate dropped 14 percent over the 1970s. Accelerating that movement by 5 percent is realistic; yet such a policy at best stimulates steel industry investment by little more than 6 percent. Similarly, a drop of 2 percent in interest rates represents an average level of rates in the 1970s still about 2 percent higher than that experienced in the 1960s. Yet in this case steel industry investment increases by over 20 percent above the level produced in the base solution. Consequently, if industrial expansion and modernization are serious concerns, interest rates will have to come down.

Trade Policies

Economic arguments for protecting a domestic industry—in this case steel—are usually predicated on the belief that the protected industry has a long-run comparative advantage. There may also be a *strategic* aspect to protection, which would, for example, postulate that an industry should be maintained at a size larger than a free market would permit for national defense reasons. Social factors such as employment are frequently cited as reasons to protect the steel industry.

Assuming that a decision is made to protect the steel industry temporarily from foreign competition, two devices are usually available. The first is the imposition of a tariff, which, by raising import prices, creates an incentive to buy domestically produced steel. The second device consists of import quotas, which specify the maximum amount, or value, of an import.

We examine two scenarios: a tariff and a quota alternative:

1. Import duty of 5 percent.
2. Import share limited to 15 percent.

In the first case, a tariff of 5 percent was imposed over the period 1970–1979. This was achieved in the model by adding 5 percent to the unit cost of production for Japan, thus affecting relative unit costs of production in the United States and Japan, a prime determinant of imports. The results of the tariff scenario are shown in table 6–19.

The tariff causes a significant decline in imports, gradually reaching a peak of 19.5 percent in the last year of the simulation. This result reflects the high elasticities of import shares with respect to the relative cost variable. At the same time, the effective reduction in foreign competition enables domestic producers to raise their price, reaching a peak of about 3 percent in the fourth year of the simulation. This, of course, lowers domestic demand for steel, causing the production increase to fluctuate between about 1 percent and 2 percent over the simulation period. Employment increases for the first five years of the simulation but decreases over the next five. This is partly because domestic demand falls and partly because investment increases markedly over the first six years of the simulation, reaching a peak of 4.8 percent after five years.

The tariff scenario illustrates that prolonged protection could create improvements in some variables but deteriorations in others, such as employ-

Table 6–19
Effects of Tariff Scenario
(Percentage change from base solution)

Impact on (Domestic Variables)	2 Years	5 Years	10 Years
Imports	– 12.26	– 11.47	– 19.52
Price	2.04	2.87	1.94
Capacity utilization	1.63	.66	.25
Production	1.65	.82	.72
Employment	1.06	.11	– 2.31
Investment	1.12	4.78	1.91

ment. A tariff will be meaningful only if it gives the domestic industry breathing space to modernize plant and equipment and sharpen its competitive edge. In the simulation, technology is implicitly held constant, and wage rates are also retained at their historical levels, although wage cost is a major factor affecting the competitive ability of the U.S. steel industry relative to Japan. The major conclusion we can draw from the tariff scenario is that tariffs are effective in limiting imports for the time they are in existence. This in turn could give the domestic steel industry a chance to recoup and compete more favorably in the international sphere.

In the quota scenario, we limited import shares in domestic demand for the various steel categories to 15 percent. In the simulation, this was achieved by exogenizing imports at 15 percent or at their actual historial value, whichever was smaller. The results are shown in table 6–20.

The impact on import *levels,* as opposed to *shares,* depends on both the 15 percent import share limit and the effect of price changes on domestic demand. The constraint of 15 percent on import shares operated effectively at both the beginning and the end of the simulation periods, but was not binding during the middle of the period. Except for the fifth year of the simulation, import levels fell substantially. This in turn spurred domestic production, except for the fifth year, when it registered a marginal decline of 0.2 percent. The same was true for capacity utilization. Prices rose approximately in the same manner as for the tariff scenario. Employment increased as in the earlier scenario for the first five years and, with the exception of one year, declined in the next five. The reason is the same as before: Investment, having risen rapidly, lowered the labor requirement.

Tariffs and quotas appear, consequently, to be effective in providing temporary protection to the domestic steel industry. A choice between them would involve a host of other considerations, such as administrative convenience, welfare arguments, and the like.

Wage Policy

Incomes policies or wage givebacks are designed to break the wage-price spiral through a variety of measures, ranging from voluntary agreements to strict wage-price controls. Assuming the steel industry gets a break from its employees on wage costs, the key issue concerns the disposition of the new savings. The industry response is subject to public review and, in fact, may be considered a condition under which wage cost reductions are offered in the first place. Two alternative scenarios are considered here. First, a reduction in wage rates with no constraints is imposed on the model system. A second simulation is then performed, which includes the wage reduction of the first case and, in addition, mandates a partial pass-through of savings to steel consumers. The following two scenarios were run during the period 1970–1979:

Table 6–20
Effects of Quota Scenario
(Percentage change from base solution)

Impact on (Domestic Variables)	2 Years	5 Years	10 Years
Imports	− 18.35	2.41	− 22.28
Price	1.12	2.38	2.38
Capacity utilization	2.46	− .54	0.70
Production	2.41	− .22	1.44
Employment	1.66	.23	− 2.1
Investment	1.61	7.65	4.95

1. Wage rate 5 percent lower than the historical level for each simulation period.
2. Wage rate 5 percent lower than the historical level and steel prices 2 percent below the level produced by simulation 1.

Table 6–21 shows the profits impacts from these two scenarios. This table illuminates the differences between the two scenarios. In the first case the cost savings are passed to profits, in the second, the savings are transferred to steel consumers.

The implications of these differences for other steel industry variables are summarized in table 6–22. In both scenarios, lower wage costs result in the use of more labor and lower productivity; this effect is less pronounced in the second scenario, however, because of the partial pass-through of savings to consumers. Prices in the second scenario are uniformly 2 percent lower than in the first. This in turn stimulates demand. Without a significant increase in investment, this demand rise pushes up capacity-utilization levels. The total effect on imports is hence ambiguous, since decreased costs place pressure on domestic productive capacity. In the second scenario, imports are lower in seven of the ten years the simulation is performed. The net effect on production is 1 percent higher after ten years in the second scenario over the first.

Table 6–21
Profits Response
(Difference from base solution, billions of dollars)

Scenario	2 Years	5 Years	10 Years
1. Wage reduction	.132	.176	.473
2. Wage and price reduction	− .041	− .125	− .156

Table 6–22
Incomes Policy Impacts
(Percentage change from base solution)

Variable	(Scenario)	2 Years	5 Years	10 Years
Price	(1)	−.42	−.70	−.37
	(2)	−2.47	−2.75	−2.41
Production	(1)	.45	.36	.92
	(2)	.72	1.04	1.95
Employment	(1)	2.84	4.14	6.74
	(2)	.51	1.43	2.08
Imports	(1)	−2.83	−2.90	−3.27
	(2)	−4.06	−4.98	−1.16
Investment	(1)	.14	.19	1.08
	(2)	−.41	−.83	1.94
Productivity	(1)	−2.39	−3.78	−5.82
	(2)	.21	−.39	−.13

Note: (1) Wage reduction; (2) wage and price reduction.

This increased production is at the expense of reduced levels of investment in the near term undertaken in the second scenario. Investment in the second scenario is lower than that observed in the first scenario for the first six years of the simulation period.[14]

The conclusion that may be drawn from this comparison is that wage reduction policies are effective in inducing increased steel industry activity. If short-run demand-based industry recovery is desired, then cost reductions should be passed on to consumers. If, instead, long-run efficiency gains and modernization are of primary concern, then policies that stimulate investment are required.

Policies Designed to Decrease
Government-Mandated Investment

As a last policy option, we examine the effect of direct government intervention in the steel industry decision-making process through the vehicle of mandated pollution-control expenditures. As discussed earlier, net productive investment is determined through an optimization process, unaffected by government decree. An alternative view would state that, as a result of financial constraints, mandated levels of pollution-control investment detract from productive investment. Government-mandated investment accounted for a share of total investment that ranged from 6.8 percent in 1970 to 22.5 percent in 1979. The nominal figure was $15 million in 1979. In light of each of the views presented here, two model simulations were performed. In the first, all government-mandated investment is eliminated. Total investment is determined by efficiency criteria alone. In the second simulation, not only is all government-mandated investment eliminated, but this expenditure is then *added* to the model-produced level of productive investment on the assumption that this level of expenditures would have been put toward productive investment had the government not intervened. We have two scenarios:

1. All government-mandated investment eliminated.
2. All government-mandated investment eliminated *and* added back to productive investment.

Table 6–23 shows the price impacts from the two scenarios. Note that the price savings realized in the first scenario are quite small. If the original level of investment was the efficient level, then government-mandated pollution-control expenditures do not greatly affect steel industry activity. If, instead, such expenditures represent foregone productive investment—by levels of near 20 percent over historical values, as might be the case if financial availabilities constrained investment—then the impact may be significant. Indeed, prices in this scenario are 2.3 percent lower than those observed in the base solution after ten years. To understand the mechanism underlying these results, consider the results presented in table 6–24.

In the first scenario, cost reductions are achieved only through the direct financing reduction associated with the foregone investment. Otherwise, since the industry activity proceeds at an efficient level, other steel economic indicators do not change significantly. The ultimate result is a decrease in the steel price of less than 0.5 percent from the base value. In the second simulation, however, cost savings arise not from financing reduction but, rather, from a drop in labor costs. The new investment achieved in this scenario results in 29 percent less employment after ten years. This cost saving accounts for the relatively large price impact observed in this model solution. These combined effects, in turn, result in lower imports and higher levels of production and productivity. These scenarios are not realistic in that they eliminate all pollution-control investments. In view of the environmental impacts, this may not be desirable.

Table 6–23
Price Effects
(Percentage change from base solution)

Scenario	2 Years	5 Years	10 Years
1. No pollution control investment	0.0	−.13	−.46
2. No pollution control investment and more productive investment	−.14	−1.20	−2.34

Table 6–24
Pollution-Control Scenario Impacts
(Percentage change from base solution)

Variable	(Scenario)	2 Years	5 Years	10 Years
Employment	(1)	− .03	− .11	− .11
	(2)	− 2.24	− 11.83	− 28.71
Production	(1)	− .06	− .13	− .48
	(2)	.20	.72	3.33
Imports	(1)	.39	1.23	3.61
	(2)	− 1.23	− 7.48	− 21.33
Productivity	(1)	− .03	− .02	− .37
	(2)	2.44	12.55	32.04

Note: (1) No pollution-control investment; (2) no pollution-control investment and more productive investment.

Conclusions

The following policy measures were assessed through appropriately designed model similations:

1. *Fiscal policy:* Measures discussed here are a 5 percent reduction in the corporate-profits rate, an investment-tax-credit rate hiked by 5 percent, and an acceleration of five years in the average depreciation tax life. Our conclusion is that each measure does significantly stimulate steel industry investment, but with different time paths. The effects on other model variables, such as employment, price, and costs (and hence imports) are in accordance with an improved industry position.

2. *Monetary policy:* In one scenario the interest rate was reduced by 2 percent. In the other two, this monetary measure was combined with a profits-tax rate lowered by 5 percent and an investment-tax-credit rate raised by 5 percent, respectively. The results indicate a much healthier steel industry. High interest rates are an impediment to expansion and modernization in the steel industry.

3. *Trade policy:* Two main interventions are discussed in this section. The first is a tariff of 5 percent on imports from Japan. The second is a quota limiting import shares to 15 percent of domestic demand. Both measures give effective temporary protection to the steel industry. This relief enables the industry to improve capital investment and restore higher productivity growth levels.

4. *Wage policy:* Wage costs are an important aspect of comparative advantage in producing steel across different countries. The scenarios include a 5 percent reduction in wage rates and a simultaneous reduction of wages and prices in the spirit of some of the recent negotiations between labor and

management. Both measures lower both price and imports, indicating improved competitive ability. Prices are, of course, lower in the second scenario. At the same time, employment goes up.

5. *Pollution-control policies:* Government-mandated investment for meeting environmental-protection standards accounted for a significant percentage of total investment in the 1970s. The scenarios constructed first eliminate this mandated investment and then add an equivalent amount of spending to productive investment, the premise being that with no pollution-control investment, such investment would have augmented productive capital stock. The latter scenario produces a strong, positive effect on the steel industry's performance. This is largely attributable to a reduction in labor requirements, and hence, in wage costs of production. Clearly, this benefit must be examined in relation to the deleterious effects it is likely to have on the environment.

Notes

1. Defined as factory shipments + imports, *apparent* because it ignores inventory changes by users of steel.

2. See, for instance, Crandall (1981), table 2–7.

3. The so-called minimills, which operate electric furnaces feeding scrap, not included here, have done considerably better than the integrated producers in recent years. These mills represent one of the industry's adaptation to its problems.

4. Working Group on International Trade, *STAC Report.*

5. R.W. Crandall, (1980).

6. The model is fairly large, with 151 equations (56 behavioral) and 185 variables, of which 143 are endogenous and 42 exogenous. Mandated pollution control appears implicitly in the definitions of total and net capital stock. Some alternative equations for the cash-flow version of the model are discussed later.

7. The capacity-utilization variable used is defined as follows:

$$\frac{\text{Raw steel production in U.S.}}{\text{Rated capacity}} \div \frac{\text{Raw steel prodction in Japan and European Community}}{\text{Usable capacity}}$$

8. Dollar prices were obtained from "Prices and Costs in the U.S. Steel Industry," Report to the President by the Council on Wage and Price Stability, October 1977.

9. A listing of the complete equations for the steel model is available from the Economics Research Unit, University of Pennsylvania, Philadelphia, PA 19104.

10. Policy changes have been imposed here only on the steel industry. No recomputation of economywide variables entering the steel model has been carried out.

11. These results depend greatly on the form of the investment function. The alternative form based on cash flow would show considerably faster and greater im-

pacts. For example, the impact on investment after five years would be 16.4 percent, 17.5 percent, and 10.3 percent in the profits tax, ITC, and tax-life scenarios.

12. As before, no change in national economic variables other than the assumed policy change has been made.

13. In the cash-flow approach to investment, the effect of interest-rate changes is slower and smaller, amounting to only 7.4 percent after five years.

14. The cash-flow approach to investment would, however, show significantly greater increases in investment in the wage-reduction simulation.

7
Industrial Policy and the Electrical-Machinery Industry: The Case of Transformers

Vladimir Kontorovich

This chapter studies the effects of industry-specific and economywide policy measures on a segment of the electrical machinery industry—the transformer industry. The study is carried out with the help of a small-scale econometric model of the transformer industry. The model uses the output variables of the Wharton Annual and Industry Model as exogenous inputs. It allows the testing of fiscal and monetary policy impacts on investment in both the transformer industry and the electric utility industry (the main customer of the transformer industry), and also of wage policy in the transformer industry. The comparative efficiencies of such policy instruments as corporate tax rates, investment tax credits, depreciation rates and tax lives, and bond rates in achieving policy goals are assessed.

Qualitatively, stimulating utility investment leads to higher output and lower prices in the transformer industry. Investment and capital stock increase slightly, whereas labor productivity remains virtually unchanged. Stimulating investment in transformers expectedly increases capital stock, though after some delay. Labor productivity rises, prices of transformers fall, and this sets off increases in the demand for transformers. This is by far the most powerful effect of those our model is able to test. Wage restraint policy, by contrast, is not afforded a fair test in the model, with lower wage rates translating into higher demand for labor and lower labor productivity. Also, the absence of a link between lower costs and higher profits and increased investment opportunities does not allow us to test the effects of these policies on the industry's competitiveness through increased productivity of labor.

The chapter starts with a description of an econometric model built for the purpose of policy studies. The second section outlines the structure of the model and the individual equations. The third section deals with model validation, including sample period simulation and multiplier analysis. The fourth section discusses the results of various policy simulations with the model.

The Transformer Industry

The transformer industry (SIC3612, a subsector of the electrical-machinery industry SIC36), produces several types of transformer products with different physical and economic characteristics. Distribution transformers are used to convert transmission voltages to the end-use voltages and are located at the outlying ends of the electric utility network. Instrument transformers are devices used in the measurement of voltages and currents. Power transformers are used to step up voltage for long-distance transmission and then to reduce it at a substation for local distribution. Distribution and instrument transformers are produced according to standard ratings and are often carried in stock by producers and delivered on demand. This segment of the transformer industry is relatively less capital-intensive. Power transformers are very large units. Economies of scale in power generation and transmission have forced the industry to strive for higher voltages and to concentrate enormous power in single units. Before the 1950s, the maximum commercial alternating-current transmission voltage was 220KV; in the 1960s this was raised to 400–500KV, and in the early 1970s efforts were made to obtain 765KV.

Power transformers are designed according to the individual purchaser's specifications and are custom built. Manufacturing and engineering cycles are four to six months, and both the large size of individual orders relative to a plant's capacity and the irregularity of orders render the programming of overall production extremely difficult. Large orders and long lead times require large amounts of working capital.

There were 229 companies in the industry in 1977, up from 168 in 1972, 150 in 1967, and 134 in 1947. Industrial concentration has been falling over time: The shares of the four and eight largest firms of the total value of the industry's shipments in 1977 were 56 percent and 70 percent, respectively, down from 73 percent and 84 percent in 1947.

Transformer industry output primarily represents other industries' investment goods (67 percent in 1972), with the bulk of it going to electrical utilities (60 percent). Intermediate use accounted for 30 percent in the same year, with electrical machinery being the largest single intermediate consumer, taking in 14 percent of total output. Most of the intermediate use of transformers goes to the investment goods-producing sectors.

Though highly dependent on electrical utilities, the U.S. transformer industry is relatively independent of foreign markets, which absorbed only 3 percent of total domestic output in 1972. Similarly, foreign competition has relatively little impact on the domestic market, supplying 4 percent in the same year. These characteristics of the industry suggest that investment incentives, both economywide incentives and those aimed at the industry itself and/or at its main consumers, electric utilities, should present a powerful policy tool.

The Structure of the Model

The model of the transformer industry is designed to provide a framework for industrial-policy analysis. It is a small model, estimated on annual time-series data. The model can be operated in conjunction with the Wharton Annual and Industry Model, which provides exogenous inputs. The model is demand-driven. Demand is generally determined by the level of activity in the sectors consuming transformers and by transformer price. Demand then determines output, from which input requirements are derived. The latter determine costs. Costs explain sector price, and price feeds back into demand equations, closing the model. The individual equation specifications and estimation results are described here.

The two demand equations have similar specifications, with purchaser activity level and own price being the main explanatory variables.

Domestic Demand

Domestic demand for transformers (DEM12) is a function of a synthetic demand measure in sectors using transformers (DD12) and of the price of transformers (PIIS12):

$$DEM12 = 238.173 + 29.7193 * DD12 + 30.9717 * DD12(-1)$$
$$(2.3) \qquad (2.5) \qquad\qquad (2.1)$$

$$- 6.75564 * PIIS12$$
$$(-1.2)$$

$$\bar{R}^2 = .964 \qquad SEE = 30.24 \qquad DW = 2.416$$

Period: 1967–1977

The synthetic demand measure (DD12) is defined as a weighted sum of gross products originating in the sectors using transformers as an intermediate input, and of investment volumes of sectors using transformers as an investment good. The shares of the respective sectors in total shipments of transformers, as reflected in 1972 input-output tables, serve as weights.

$$DD12 = .302 * [.452 * XVGMFD36 + .146 * XVGMFD33$$
$$+ .136 * XVGMFD35 + .158 * (XVGMFD - XVGMFD36$$
$$- XVGMFD33 - XVGMFD35) + .013 * XVGMG13$$
$$+ .042 * XVGRGU491] + .698 * [.856 * IARGU491$$
$$+ .106 * (IBF-IARGU491) + .028 * GVPFD + .01 * GVPFO]$$

Export Demand

Export demand (EXP12) is a function of activity level abroad, relative prices (PIIS12/PTIMW) and own lagged value:

$$EXP12 = .42118 * ZWAIP7 - .203235 * \frac{PIIS12}{PTIMW} + .680858 * EXP12(-1^{\circ}$$
$$\quad\quad (3.8) \quad\quad\quad\quad (-3.3) \quad\quad\quad\quad\quad (5.7)$$

$$\bar{R}^2 = .725 \quad\quad SEE = .07969 \quad\quad DW = 2.813$$

Period: 1967 – 1976

where ZWAIP7 is a weighted average of industrial production indexes in seven foreign countries, and PTIMW is the world export unit value index.

Shipments

Shipments (SHIPI2) and value-added (VA12) are determined by the identities:

$$SHIP12 = DEM12 + EXP12$$

$$VA12 = SHIP12 - CMAT12$$

Man-Hours Worked

Man-hours worked by all employees (HOUR12) are determined by inverting the sector's Cobb-Douglas production function:

$$\log(VA12) = -5.51215 + 1.28733 * \log(KAP12) + .949734 * \log(HOUR12)$$
$$\quad\quad\quad\quad (-2.3) \quad\quad (4.8) \quad\quad\quad\quad\quad (3.5)$$

$$\bar{R}^2 = .725 \quad\quad SEE = .07969 \quad\quad DW = 2.813$$

Period: 1967–1976 where KA12 is capital stock

Capital Stock

Capital stock should theoretically be determined in a recursive fashion as a sum of last period's capital stock and current period gross investment, (NEW12) adjusted for depreciation in the current period. However, the capital stock measure available to us is too imprecise to make this approach fit well. Consequently, we ignore the depreciation of capital accrued in the current period. Depreciation has been estimated by means of regression. The resulting relation is:

$$KAP12 = INEW12 + .979977 * KAP12(-1)$$
$$(57.1)$$

$$\bar{R}^2 = .731 \qquad SEE = 25.21 \qquad DW = 2.882$$
$$\text{Period: } 1968–1976$$

Capital Expenditures

The equation for new capital expenditures in the transformer industry (INEW12) uses the Jorgensonian specification of the investment equations as in the Wharton Annual and Industry Model. Value-added appears on the right-hand side in recognition of the accelerator principle. The ratio of own price to user cost of capital (IIS12/UCKMFD36) is derived from a discounted present value assumption (neoclassical investment function). Lagged capital-stock terms represent the speed of adjustment to the equilibrium level of capital stock from the initial level.

$$INEW12 = .115.727 + .0324309 * VA12 + 10.9925 * \frac{PIIS12(-2)}{UCKMFD36(-2)}$$
$$(-2.4) \qquad (2.3) \qquad\qquad (5.3)$$

$$- .0992742 * KAP12(-1) + .179105 * KAP12(-2)$$
$$(1.5) \qquad\qquad (3.7)$$

$$\bar{R}^2 = .873 \qquad SEE = 3.64 \qquad DW = 2.237$$
$$\text{Period: } 1969–1977$$

Hourly Wage Rate

The hourly wage rate for all employees (WRE12$) is a function of compensation per man-hour in the electrical-machinery industry (WRCMFD36$), of which the transformer industry is, of course, a part:

$$WRE12\$ = .709139 + .746719 * WRCMFD36\$$$
$$(21.5) \qquad (105.6)$$

$$\bar{R}^2 = .998 \qquad SEE = .046157 \qquad DW = 1.731$$
$$\text{Period: } 1958–1977$$

Payroll

The payroll for all employees (PROL12$) is then defined as follows:

$$PROL12\$ = HOUR12 * WRE12\$$$

Demand for Intermediate Inputs

The demand for intermediate inputs equation is specified as a function of the activity level in the transformer sector (measured by SHIP12) and own price (PMAT12):

$$CMAT12 = 259.395 + .2631 * SHIP12 - .57402 * PMAT12$$
$$(5.6) \qquad (8.4) \qquad\qquad (-3.9)$$

$$\bar{R}^2 = .885 \qquad SEE = 15.947 \qquad DW = 2.097$$
$$\text{Period: } 1967\text{--}1977$$

where PMAT12, the price index for transformer sector intermediate consumption, is a weighted sum of implicit gross output deflators for sectors supplying intermediate inputs to the transformer industry. Shares of these sectors in total transformer industry intermediate consumption, derived from the 1972 input-output table, serve as weights:

$$PMAT12 = K/K(1967) * 100;$$

$$K = .1235 * PXGGMFD36 + .2399 * PXGGMFD331 + 332$$
$$+ .0303 * PXGGMFD3334 + .168 * PXGGMFD330T$$
$$+ .06 * PXGGWR + .0604 * PXGGFI$$
$$+ .0153 * PXGGMFD24 + .0273 * PXGGMFN26$$
$$+ .0246 * PXGGMFN29 + .0283 * PXGGMFD32\text{--}324$$
$$+ .0324 * PXGGMFD34 + .19 * PW$$

Cost of Materials

Cost of materials is defined by an identity:

$$CMAT12\$ = CMAT12 * PMAT12/100$$

Price Index

The price index for the transformer industry (PIIS12) is explained in accord with usual industrial-modeling practice as a markup on variable unit cost

(ULCM12). A capacity-utilization variable that might serve to measure demand pressure is not available. It is interesting to note that a rate of change of shipments variable $[SHIP12/SHIP12(-1)]$ carries a negative sign. Imports account for only a small part of total sales, so import prices do not appear to be relevant to price determination in a significant way.

$$PIIS12 = \underset{(24.6)}{1.05428} * \frac{ULMC12}{ULMC12(1967)} * 100$$

$$- \underset{(-1.9)}{.0787366} * \frac{SHIP12}{SHIP12(-1)*100}.$$

$$\bar{R}^2 = .975 \qquad SEE = 3.3124 \qquad DW = .995$$

Period: 1967–1977

where ULMC (unit labor and material costs) is defined as:

$$ULMC = \frac{PROL12\$ + CMAT12\$}{SHIP12}$$

Real magnitudes are converted into nominal values through a series of identities:

$$DEM12\$ = DEM12 * PIIS12/100$$

$$SHIP12\$ = SHIP12 * PIIS12/100$$

$$EXP12\$ = EXP12 * PIIS12/100$$

$$INEW12\$ = INEW12 * PDIBFN/PDIBFN(1967)$$

Finally, to facilitate policy analysis, the model includes an equation and two identities borrowed from the Wharton Annual and Industry Model. Determining electric utility investment in plant and equipment (IARGU491), user cost of capital in the utility sector (UCKRGU49), and electrical machinery (UCKMFD36) within the model, rather than treating them as exogenous, allows us to conduct policy simulations in terms of changes in tax, depreciation, and credit market variables, rather than directly changing user costs and utility investment. The former treatment appears to be more precise than the latter. These three relations, borrowed from the Annual Model, have the following structure:

Investment in Plant and Equipment,
Electric Utilities (IARGU491)

$$\text{IARGU491} = -60.616 - 2.243 * \text{D75} + \sum_{i=0}^{6} \alpha_i * \text{XGGUT491}(-i)$$

$$+ \sum_{j=0}^{6} \beta_j * \text{RACPUT491}(-j) + \sum_{k=0}^{6} \gamma_k$$

$$* [\text{WRCRGU49\$}(-k)/\text{UCKRGU49}(-k)/\exp(.02$$

$$* (\text{DUMTIME46}(-k) - 72))]/\exp(.02$$

$$* (\text{DUMIME46} - 72))$$

where α_i, β_j, γ_k are regression coefficients, and the right-hand side variables are described in the glossary.

User Cost of Capital, Utilities (UCKRGU49)

$$\text{UCKRGU49} = \text{PDIBFN} * (\text{FRMCSU}/100. + \text{CCARNTRGU49}/100.)$$

$$* (1. - \text{ITRARGU49}/100. - \text{TXRITEFRGU49}/100.)$$

$$* (1. - \text{ITRARGU49} * \text{DUMITL}/100.) * 2.$$

$$* (\text{FRMCSU} * \text{LNTRGU49}/100.) * * (-1)$$

$$* [1. - 1/(\text{LNTRGU49} * \text{FRMCSU}/100.)$$

$$* (1. - \text{EXP}(-\text{LNTRGU49} * \text{FRMSCU}/100.))]$$

$$* (1. - \text{TXRITEFRGU49}/100.) * * (-1)$$

User Cost of Capital, Electrical Machinery (UCKMFD36)

$$\text{UCKMFD36} = \text{PDIBFN} * (\text{FRMSCI}/100 + \text{CCARNTMFD36}/100.)$$

$$* \{1. - \text{ITRAMFD36}/100 - \text{TXRITEMFD36}/100.$$

$$* (1. - \text{ITRAMFD36} * \text{DUMITL}/100.)\}$$

$$* (\text{FRMCSI} * \text{LNTMFD36}/100) * * (-1)$$

$$* [1. - 1/(\text{FRMCSI} * \text{LNTMFD36}/100.)$$

$$* (1. - \exp(-\text{LNTMFD36} * \text{FRMCSI}/100.))]$$

$$* (1. - \text{TXRITEMFD36}/100.) * * (-1)$$

Model Validation: Baseline Simulations and Multiplier Analysis

In order to check whether the model captures the dynamic characteristics of the transformer industry, sample period simulation and multiplier analysis were conducted. The model was solved over the years 1970–1976, (that is, a part of the period over which the model parameters were estimated). Table 7–1 summarizes the accuracy of simulation for several variables, as well as the accuracy of corresponding regression fits. It shows that the simulated trajectories of the endogenous variables closely track the historical values. It can be seen that the accuracy is highest for shipments and domestic demand. This is analogous to the performance of the economywide models, which show comparatively better results for the aggregate income and product output than for the other variables.

The wage rate is also simulated with high accuracy. This is due to the tight fit of the regression estimation, which is reproduced in simulation, since the only explanatory variable in the wage-rate equation is exogenous. The least accurate is the simulation of investment (see figure 7–1) because of the extraordinary volatility of investment. A relatively large error in the simulation of man-hours worked is due to the use of an inverted production function, rather than a relation fitted to historical man-hour series. For all the variables, simulation errors stay quite close to the errors of corresponding regression estimates (for example, figure 7–2: DEM12).

Table 7–1
Error Statistics in the Simulation of the Transformer Industry Model, 1970–1976

Variable Level	Mean Absolute Percentage Error: Simulation	Root-Mean-Square Percentage Error	
		Regression[a]	Simulation
CMAT12	2.9	2.4	3.4
DEM12	1.8	1.8	2.4
EXP12	4.4	5.8	5.4
HOUR12	6.1	—	7.0
INEW12	10.3	9.3	12.9
KAP12	4.5	5.0	4.7
PIIS12	4.2	2.9	5.0
PROL12$	5.4	—	6.6
SHIP12	1.6	—	2.2
VA12	2.3	—	2.6
WRE12$	1.0	1.1	1.1

[a]Calculated for a period longer than that of the simulation.

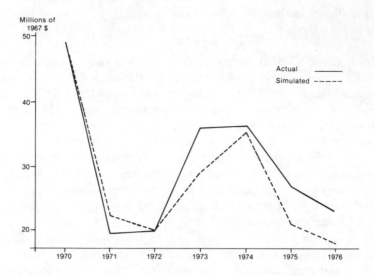

Figure 7–1. Capital Expenditures, Sample-Period Simulation

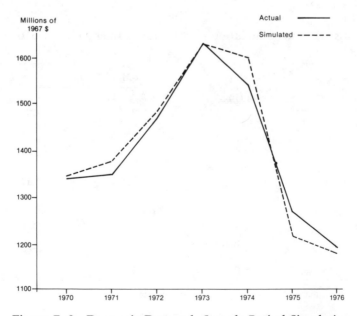

Figure 7–2. Domestic Demand, Sample-Period Simulation

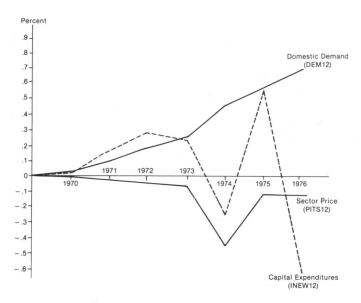

Figure 7–3. Percentage Effect (Relative to Baseline Solution) of 1 Percent Increase in Demand for Electricity

In order to check the model's reaction to the external shocks, two multiplier analysis experiments were carried out.

In the first experiment, electricity output (variables XVGRGU491 and XGGUT491) was increased by 1 percent over historic levels for the whole simulation period. This increases the domestic demand for transformers, both directly, through the increase in the utilities' intermediate demand, and through the increase in electric utility investment. From the domestic demand, the impulse is propagated throughout the rest of the industry (see figure 7–3).

The increase in domestic demand through the period is closely followed by an increase in shipments, which drives up costs of materials and value-added, at slower and faster rates, respectively, than that of shipments. Man-hours increase in roughly the same proportion as does value-added. The same is true for payroll, since the wage rate remains unchanged. Unit costs decline because material cost increases lag behind the rise of shipments, whereas payroll increases only proportionally. A decrease in unit costs drives down the price index for transformers. Lower domestic price further stimulates domestic demand and also brings about an increase in exports.

The investment multiplier has a complicated shape; it fluctuates between positive and negative values with increasing amplitude. This is explained by the interaction of a positive accelerator effect (rising value added) and a negative present discounted value effect (falling own price).

Another multiplier experiment involved cutting effective corporate tax rates in half over the simulation period. Corporate tax rates affect the user cost of capital in the utility and electrical-machinery industries, and these costs in turn are explanatory variables in the investment equations for electric utilities and transformers, respectively. A cut in the corporate tax rates raises the discounted present value of the future stream of profits and, hence, increases incentives to invest. In our model this results in larger electric utility investment, fueling domestic demand for transformers, with a simultaneous investment increase in the transformer industry. Two forces are at work here. On the one hand, exactly as in the previous experiment, an increase in the domestic demand for transformers drives up shipments. Value-added and costs of materials follow the shipments, at faster and slower rates, respectively. Higher output leads to higher demand for labor. On the other hand, sharp increases in transformer industry investment result in the rapid buildup of capital stock. Consequently, capital is substituted for labor in the production function. The result of the two forces is a decline in demand for labor, and also a decline of payroll. This means that investment, induced by fiscal stimulus, raises labor productivity to the extent that it is possible to satisfy higher (due to a fiscal stimulus in the consuming industry) domestic demand with less labor. Unit labor and material costs fall, and prices decrease (see figure 7–4).

The model's reactions to exogenous shocks appear to conform to theoretical expectations.

Policy Analysis

The model allows us to simulate the following policy options:

1. Fiscal and monetary stimulation of investment by the main consuming sector (electric utilities).
2. Fiscal and monetary stimulation of investment by the transformer industry proper.
3. Wage and price policy.

1. Policies affecting investment in the electric utility sector: As already noted, the main use of transformers is for investment by electrical utilities. Therefore, fiscal and monetary measures that influence the volume of investment by electric utilities also exert a strong influence on the transformer industry. Electric utility investment can be influenced by one of the components of user cost of capital in the regulated-utilities sector: effective

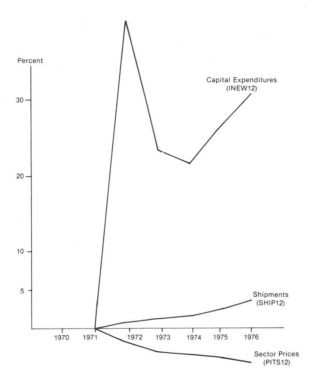

Figure 7–4. Percentage Effect (Relative to Baseline Solution) of 50 Percent Cut in Corporate Tax Rate on Electrical-Machinery Industry

corporate tax rate (TXRITEFRGU49), bond rate (FRMCSU), tax life, (LNTRGU49), investment tax credit (ITRARGU49), or depreciation rate (CCARNTRGU49).

In our model, each of these policy tools produces the same qualitative effects as the others, since all of them act through user cost of capital. The amount of change required in each of these policy variables to achieve a 1 percent change in user cost (UCKRGU49) in the utility industry are shown in table 7–2. Since user cost is nonlinear in the policy variables, the elasticities and absolute changes are estimated as averages over the 1970–1976 period for 10 percent decreases in the policy variables. Small relative changes in the bond rate and the corporate tax rate produce the same effect on user costs of capital as does a relatively large change in the investment tax credit, with depreciation rate and tax rate being of intermediate strength.

Table 7–2
Changes in Policy Variables Necessary to Bring About a 1 Percent Change in User Cost of Capital in Electric Utilities

Variable Label	Percentage Change	Absolute Change
CCARNTRGU49	3.16	0.1264 percentage points
FRMCSU	1.18	0.1023 percentage points
ITRARGU49	– 16.67	– 4.4 percentage points
LNTRGU49	5.56	1.945 years
TXRITEFRGU49	1.92	0.88 percentage points

The effect of applying certain combinations of these policy tools would be to increase the discounted value of future profits for investors, through lowering the user cost of capital, thus stimulating adjustments in capital stock, that is, investment. This would translate into a change in demand for transformers. Estimated average elasticities over the 1970–1976 period are: investment (SIC 491) with respect to user cost of capital: – .17; demand (SIC 3612) with respect to investment (SIC 491) – .83. The effects of a demand increase are identical to those described above: an increase in output, a price decline due to a unit cost decrease, a fluctuating pattern of change in investment. The time paths of the changes in model variables under the impact of the policy are presented in table 7–3.

2. *Policies effecting investment in the transformer industry:* Policy variables available for stimulating investment in the transformer sector are analogous to those for electrical utilities: depreciation rate (CCARNTMFD36), investment tax credit (ITRAMFD36), tax life (LNTMFD36), corporate tax rate (TXRITEFMFD36) in the electrical machinery industry (SIC 36), and industrial bond rate (FRMCSI). The average estimated magnitudes of impact of these variables on user cost of capital in the electrical machinery sector (UCKMFD36) is shown in table 7–4. It can be seen that the bond rate is the most potent instrument in terms of relative change, with depreciation rate and corporate tax rate exerting less impact.

User cost of capital enters the investment equation with a two period lag. The direct elasticity of investment in the transformer sector with respect to user cost of capital was estimated as – 2.4. The effects of this policy are as follows. Starting in the third period, higher investment augments capital stock. More abundant, cheaper capital replaces labor in the production process. Man-hours worked decline at an increasing rate, as flow effects (change in investment) are translated into stock effects (change in capital). Payroll reductions lead to a decrease in labor component of unit costs, causing the price of transformers to decline. This stimulates demand for transformers,

Table 7-3
Effects of an Investment Stimulus in the Electric Utility Sector on Transformer Industry (Stimulus: 10 Percent Cut in the Tax Life of Investment over 1970–1976)
(Percentage difference between policy simulation and sample-period simulation)

Variable	1970	1971	1972	1973	1974	1975	1976
CMAT12	.004	.019	.038	.059	.088	.129	.158
DEM12	.008	.030	.058	.087	.128	.199	.249
EXP12	.001	.004	.009	.011	.012	.016	.020
HOUR12	.009	.035	.064	.089	.126	.202	.249
INEW12	.005	.047	.092	.081	.111	.168	.223
KAP12	.000	.002	.006	.011	.018	.025	.033
PIIS12	−.002	−.007	−.015	−.023	−.031	−.048	−.059
PROL12$	.009	.035	.064	.089	.126	.202	.249
SHIP12	.008	.029	.057	.084	.122	.188	.233
Unit labor and material costs	−.001	.004	−.008	−.013	−.019	−.034	−.043
VA12	.010	.036	.069	.099	.142	.224	.279

Table 7–4
Percentage and Absolute Changes in Policy Instruments Resulting in a 1 Percent Change in User Cost of Capital in the Electrical Machinery Sector

Variable Label	Percentage Change	Absolute Change
CCARNTMFD36	2.64	0.132 percentage points
FRMCSI	1.29	0.107 percentage points
ITRAMFD36	− 12.52	− 0.64 percentage points
LNTMFD36	6.03	1.03 years
TXRITEFMFD36	3.18	1.29 percentage points

both domestic and foreign, so that constant-dollar shipments increase, as do value-added and material costs, at rates higher and lower than shipments, respectively. Higher productivity results in lower prices and higher real output. Shipments and demand in nominal terms decline somewhat. The time paths of the changes in the variables under the impact of the policies are presented in table 7–5. Unfortunately, the model does not allow us to test the cash-flow effects on investment of the policies we have analyzed in the two preceding sections.

3. *Wage policy:* This section explores the effects of different patterns of growth in the hourly wage rate on the performance of the transformer industry. The question is: What are the benefits of negotiating wage-increase postponements or cuts for the growth of a sector? The hourly wage rate in the transformer sector was increasing at a 6.7 percent average annual rate in the 1970–1976 period, with year-to-year percentage rates of change being 6.7, 7, 3.4, 3.7, 10.1, 12.4, and 4.3. For policy-simulation purposes, the wage rate was exogenized and assumed to increase at a uniform rate of 4 percent per annum.

The effect of the slower wage-rate growth in the model is to decrease the price of transformers through smaller increases in payroll and unit cost. The lower price stimulates both domestic and foreign demand for transformers. The effects of higher demand, as already described, are higher output (shipments, value-added) and, consequently, higher demand for labor. The latter counteracts the initial impact of the lower wage rate on the payroll (and hence on unit cost and the price of transformers). On the other hand, since material costs trail shipments, there is a reinforcement of the initial downward pressure of unit cost and prices.

Investment in the transformer industry experiences conflicting influences. Increased output, through the accelerator effect, induces higher investment. The decrease in the price of transformers relative to the user cost of capital depresses the discounted present value of the future profit stream and, conse-

Table 7-5
Effects of an Investment Stimulus within the Transformer Industry on the Industry Variables (Stimulus: 10 Percent Cut in the Tax Life of Investment over 1970–1976)
(Percentage difference between policy simulation and sample-period simulation)

Variable	1970	1971	1972	1973	1974	1975	1976
CMAT12	0.	0.	.052	.094	.132	.208	.275
DEM12	0.	0.	.076	.132	.138	.352	.479
EXP12	0.	0.	.067	.119	.140	.173	.207
HOUR12	0.	0.	-.250	-.483	-.686	-.720	-.811
INEW12	0.	0.	5.729	3.434	3.427	4.277	4.999
KAP12	0.	0.	.254	.474	.671	.854	1.038
PIIS12	0.	0.	-.161	-.303	-.391	-.477	-.573
PROL12$	0.	0.	-.250	-.483	-.686	-.720	-.811
SHIP12	0.	0.	0.076	.132	.186	.341	.460
Unit labor and material costs	0.	0.	-.140	-.261	-.345	-.429	-.519
VA12	0.	0.	.091	.154	.217	.423	.575

Table 7-6
Effects of Wage Policy on the Industry Variables (Uniform 4 Percent Per Year Growth in Hourly Wage Rate over 1970–1976)

(Percentage difference between policy simulation and sample-period simulation)

Variable	1970	1971	1972	1973	1974	1975	1976
CMAT12	.548	.791	.541	.715	1.351	2.598	3.219
DEM12	.830	1.140	.753	.979	1.895	3.852	4.809
EXP12	1.015	1.815	1.715	1.537	1.558	2.027	2.393
HOUR12	.974	1.275	1.032	1.599	2.763	5.178	6.607
INEW12	.801	1.785	-4.469	-3.809	-1.460	-1.857	-5.793
KAP12	.080	.153	-.032	-.277	-.353	-.426	-.644
PIIS12	-1.720	-2.386	-1.630	-2.311	-3.867	-6.412	-7.099
PROL12$	-3.814	-3.667	-2.509	-3.716	-6.693	-11.782	-12.509
SHIP12	.835	1.160	.785	.999	1.880	3.722	4.642
Unit labor and material costs	-1.501	-2.080	-1.410	-1.983	-3.386	-5.735	-6.386
VA12	1.027	1.406	.939	1.167	2.183	4.402	5.508

quently, equilibrium capital stock and, thus, investment. The net result of these two influences is that investment decreases, though at a fluctuating rate, and capital stock also decreases. Cheaper labor substitutes for capital in production; lower labor productivity results. Time paths of the changes in the model variables under the impact of the policy are presented in table 7–6.

How should the results of this policy be judged? The policy of restraining wage-rate increases may have two conceivable goals. First, the reining in of labor costs may serve as a price competition weapon with foreign producers. Our model captures the effect of labor cost on price of transformers, and shows improvement in the sector's international competitiveness as reflected by the decrease in imports.

Second, it may be that by holding down labor cost increases, the sector's ability to finance investment in equipment modernization and research and development is improved. In the long run, this should improve the sector's price and product competitiveness and is likely to increase labor productivity. Our model cannot capture this effect. In the model a lower wage rate, translated into lower transformer price, depresses investment in the sector (through the present discounted value of profit); both capital stock and labor productivity decline. To be able to provide the full test of the wage-restraint policy, the model should allow lower costs to translate into higher profits, the latter improving the sector's ability to finance investment from both internal and external sources. As noted in the previous chapter, this link is difficult to introduce into the model.

Conclusion

The policy simulations conducted with this model of the transformer sector demonstrated that the sector is highly sensitive with respect to fiscal and monetary stimuli to its own investment and to investment by electric utilities. The effects of wage-restraint policy on the sector's price competitiveness could be tested only partially, because of the structure of the model. Developing the model to include additional aspects of the sector's economy might improve the accuracy of analysis of these policies and make possible the testing of still others.

Appendix 7A
Mnemonics and Definitions of Variables

Table 7A-1
Endogenous Variables from the Original Sources

Label	Description	Unit of Measurement	Source of Data
CMAT12$	Cost of Materials, SIC3612	billions of $	Census of Manufactures
EXP12$	Exports, Domestic Merchandise	billions of $	FT610, Bureau of the Census
IARGU491	Investment in Plant and Equipment, Electric Utilities	billions of 1972$	Wharton Annual Model
INEW12$	Capital Expenditures, New, SIC3612	billions of $	Census of Manufactures
PIIS12	Industrial Sector Price Index, SIC3612	Index, 1967 = 100	Handbook of Labor Statistics
PROL12$	Payroll, All Employees	billions of $	Census of Manufactures
SHIP12$	Value of Industry Shipments		
UCKMFD36	User Cost of Capital, SIC36		Wharton Annual Model
UCKRGU49	User Cost of Capital, SIC49		

Table 7A–2
Endogenous Variables: Transformations

Label	Description	Unit of Measurement	Transformation
CMAT12$	Cost of Materials, SIC3612	billions of 1967$	CMAT12$/PMAT12 * 100
DEM12	Domestic Demand, SIC3612	billions of 1967$	SHIP12 − EXP12
EXP12	Exports, SIC3612	billions of 1967$	EXP12$/PIIS12 * 100
HOUR12	Manhours, All Employees, SIC3612	millions	HOUR12W + (EMPL12 − WORK12) * 1.9
INEW12	Capital Expenditures, New SIC3612	billions of 1967$	INEW12$/(PDIBFN/PDIBFN (1967)) * 100
KAP12	Capital Stock (Gross Value of Fixed Assets (GVFA) with deflated annual changes)	billions of 1967$	GVFA (1967) + $\sum_{j=1967}^{k}$ (GVFA$(j+1)$ − GVF)
PMAT12	Price Index, Cost of Materials, SIC3612	Index, 1967 = 100	$\sum_{i=1}^{11} \alpha_i$ PXGG&$_i$/(PDIBFN/ PDIBFN (1967) * 100) $\sum_{i=1}^{11} \alpha_i$PXGG&$_i$ (1967) * 100
VA12	Value Added, SIC3612	billions of 1967$	SHIP12 − CMAT12
WRE12$	Hourly Wage Rate, All Employees, SIC3612	$ per hour	PROL12$/HOUR12

Table 7A–3
Exogenous Variables

Label	Description	Unit of Measurement	Enters the Equation or Identity for:
CCARNTMFD36	Depreciation Rate, Electrical Machinery	percent	UCKMFD36
CCARNTRGU49	Depreciation Rate, Utilities	percent	UCKRGU49
DUMITL	Dummy, User Cost, Long Amendment		UCKMFD36, UCKRGU49
DUMTIME46	Time Trend		IARGU491
D75	Dummy = 1 in 1975, = 0 otherwise		IARGU491
FRMCSI	Bond Rate, Industrial	percent	UCKMFD36
FRMCSU	Bond Rate, Utilities	percent	UCKRGU49
GVPFD	Government Purchases of Goods and Services, Federal, Defense	billions 1972$	DEM12
GVPFO	Government Purchases of Goods and Services, Non-Defense	billions 1972$	DEM12
IBF	Investment, Fixed	billions 1972$	DEM12
ITRAMFD36	Investment Tax Credit Rate, Electrical Machinery	percent	UCKMFD36
ITRARGU49	Investment Tax Credit Rate, Utilities	percent	UCKRGU49
LNTMFD36	Tax Life, Investment, Electrical Machinery	years	UCKMFD36
LNTRGU49	Tax Life, Investment, Utilities	years	UCKMFD36
PDIBFN	Implicit Deflator, Fixed Investment, Nonresidential	Index, 1972 = 100	UCKMFD36, UCKRGU49
PTIMW	Unit Value Index, World Exports (in U.S.$)	Index, 1972 = 100	EXP12
PW	Wholesale Price Index, All Commodities	1967 = 100	PMAT12

PXGGMFD36	Implicit Deflator, Gross Output with IBT, Electrical Machinery	Index, 1972 = 100	PMAT12
PXGGMFD331 + 2	Implicit Deflator, Gross Output with IBT, Iron and Steel	Index, 1972 = 100	PMAT12
PXGGMFD3334	Implicit Deflator, Gross Output with IBT, Primary Aluminum	Index, 1972 = 100	PMAT12
PXGGMFD330T	Implicit Deflator, Gross Output with IBT, Primary Nonferrous Metals, Excluding Aluminum	Index, 1972 = 100	PMAT12
PXGGWR	Implicit Deflator, Gross Output with IBT, Wholesale and Retail	Index, 1972 = 100	PMAT12
PXGGFI	Implicit Deflator, Gross Output with IBT, Real Estate, Finance, and Insurance	Index, 1972 = 100	PMAT12
PXGGMFD24	Implicit Deflator, Gross Output with IBT, Lumber and Wood Products	Index, 1972 = 100	PMAT12
PXGGMFN26	Implicit Deflator, Gross Output with IBT, Paper and Allied Industries	Index, 1972 = 100	PMAT12
PXGGMFN29	Implicit Deflator, Gross Output with IBT, Petroleum Refining and Related Industries	Index, 1972 = 100	PMAT12
PXGGMFD32 – 324	Implicit Deflator, Gross Output with IBT, Other Stone, Clay, and Glass Products	Index, 1972 = 100	PMAT12
PXGGMFD34	Implicit Deflator, Gross Output with IBT, Fabricated Metal Products	Index, 1972 = 100	PMAT12
RACPUT491	Ratio, Capacity Utilization of Electric Power Plants	fraction	IARGU491
TXRITEFMFD36	Effective Corporate Tax Rate Electrical Machinery	percent	UCKMFD36
TXRITEFRGU49	Effective Corporate Tax Rate Utilities	percent	UCKRGU49

Table 7A–3 (continued)

Label	Description	Unit of Measurement	Enters the Equation or Identity for:
WRCMFD36$	Compensation per Manhour, Electrical Machinery	current $/hour	WRE12$
WRCRGU49$	Compensation per Employee per Week, Electric, Gas and Sanitary	current $/week	IARGU491
XGGUT491	Gross Output, with IBT, Public and Private Electric Utilites	billions of 1972$	IARGU491
XVGMFD	Gross Product Originating, Manufacturing, Durables	billions of 1972$	DEM12
XVGMFD33	Gross Product Originating, Primary Metals	billions of 1972$	DEM12
XVGMFD35	Gross Product Originating, Machinery, Except Electrical	billions of 1972$	DEM12
XVGMFD36	Gross Product Originating, Electrical Machinery	billions of 1972$	DEM12
XVGMG13	Gross Product Originating, Mining, Crude Petroleum and Natural Gas	billions of 1972$	DEM12
XVGRGU491	Gross Product Originating, Utilities Electric	billions of 1972$	DEM12
ZWAIP7	Weighted Average, Industrial Production Index in 7 countries	1972 = 100	EXP12

Source: Wharton Annual Model Databank.

Table 7A–4
Variables Used in Transformations

Label	Description	Unit of Measurement	Transformation
EMPL12	Number, All Employees, SIC3612	thousands	HOUR12
GVFA12	Gross Value of Fixed Assets, SIC3612	millions of $	KAP12
HOUR12W	Plans Hours, Production Workers, SIC3612	millions	HOUR12
WORK12	Number, Production Workers, SIC3612	thousands	HOUR12

Source: Census of Manufactures.

8
Quantity and Quality of Capital Impacts on Productivity in the Chemical Industry: An Empirical Study

Menahem Prywes

Has productivity growth in U.S. manufacturing been restrained by the quantity or by the quality of capital? Government regulations introduced since the late 1960s may have held back growth in the quantity of capital used directly in production. Firms invested large quantities of capital to meet these new regulations, especially in the heavily environmentally regulated chemical industry. Furthermore, this capital may have been diverted from directly productive capital.

The quality of capital, in terms of the cost of producing a unit of output using capital put in place, was probably set back by the energy price jump. Growth in the quality of capital might also have been held back by insufficient investment in research and development (R&D). This slowed development of capital that can operate with reduced costs per unit of output or that can produce new products. Firms might have underinvested in R&D because they underestimated the yield on such investments or did not foresee the problems brought on by the energy crisis.

The appropriate industrial-policy response depends on whether quantity or quality was the primary factor limiting productivity growth, since very different policies increase the quantity of capital than improve the quality of capital. The quantity of capital can be expanded by relaxing government regulations that restrain its growth. The quantity of capital can also be expanded by building incentives into the tax system. For example, the investment tax credit can be increased or tax depreciation can be accelerated. Policy can also work through the corporate tax system to improve the quality of capital. For instance, it can increase the R&D tax credit or allow faster depreciation of capital used in R&D. Government agencies can also carry out more industrial research or can fund more private research. If the quality of capital is poor because it cannot be used to lower energy input per unit of output, the government may want to create special tax cuts for R&D into energy-efficient capital or to focus its own R&D funds in this area.

The chemical industry is a good subject for a case study of the problems suffered by capital in U.S. manufacturing in the 1970s. It is a very capital-intensive industry and is heavily burdened by regulation—especially environmental regulation. The chemical industry is also very dependent on energy as both a fuel and a raw material, and it conducts a substantial amount of R&D.

This study focuses on productivity growth in the U.S. chemical industry. The first section briefly describes the data set and the production function. The second section estimates the lost labor productivity resulting from capital investments to meet the two main types of new regulations introduced since the late 1960s: environmental and occupational safety and health regulations. The next section computes a measure of the ability of capital to substitute for energy over 1971–1976. The last section estimates a relationship between technical knowledge accumulated through R&D and productivity.

The results suggest more striking problems with the quality of capital than with its quantity in assessing the restraints on productivity growth. Environmental and occupational safety and health regulations lowered labor productivity by between about 1.0 to 2.3 percent during 1971–1976. The energy crisis and weak growth of R&D expenditures, however, seem to be more important factors in retarding productivity growth.

Estimates show that existing vintages of capital could not be substituted for energy during 1971–1976. Thus increased capital investment could not reduce the increase in costs of production per unit of output. This increase in unit cost is equivalent to a decrease in total factor productivity. Furthermore, slowed growth of technical knowledge accumulated through R&D appears to explain part of the productivity-growth slowdown and decline of the mid-1970s. There seems to be an effective remedy for the quality problem, however. Estimates show a very high return in terms of increased productivity for investments in R&D in the chemical industry.

Data and the Production Function

All our empirical work relies on the very disaggregated Census-SRI-Penn (CSP) data set, which was designed for analyzing production. A chemical industry production function is estimated from the CSP data set. This is the most important analytical tool in the analyses of productivity growth.

The CSP data set covers all 450 four-digit standard industrial classification (SIC) industries within U.S. manufacturing. It consists of observations on real gross output (X); the capital stock (K); labor (L); energy (E); other intermediate materials (M); their price indexes (which are respectively, P, P_K, P_L, P_E, and P_M); and other variables.[1] The CSP data set includes observations on all 28 four-digit SIC industries within the U.S. chemical industry for the years 1971–1976, a period spanning the initial energy crisis and the recession that followed.

This production function is estimated from a pooled time series of cross-sections. Thus an observation on output and the inputs for each four-digit SIC industry in each year is treated as an observation on the overall industry production process. This assumes that all four-digit SIC industries use the same production process. However, this assumes far less than do studies that are conducted at the aggregate business sector or manufacturing level and such studies implicitly assume that all industries within the relevant aggregate use the same production process.

The production function models the maximum amount of output X that can technically be produced from each combination of K, L, E, and M.

$$X = F(K, L, E, M)$$

The particular functional form of the general production function chosen here is the nested constant elasticity of substitution (CES) production function. The nested CES function emphasizes the role of energy in restricting capital use. It also effectively models the relationship between cuts in energy use and the productivity of labor and the other factors. Therefore, the nested CES function is appropriate for modeling the 1971–1976 data period, when energy cutbacks may have restricted capital use and productivity. Appendix 8A presents and explains the nested CES function.

The Effect of New Regulation on the Quantity of Capital and Productivity

This section estimates the reduction in the quantity of capital in the chemical industry caused by major new government regulatory programs begun in the late 1960s and early 1970s. It then estimates the effect of this cut in the quantity of capital on labor productivity.

These estimates depend on the approach used to measure the connection between capital invested to meet new regulation and labor productivity. This connection occurs because extra output could be produced if the funds invested in capital to meet new regulation were invested in directly productive capital, holding all other inputs constant. This study estimates the loss of labor productivity caused by the capital invested to meet new regulation as the difference between actual labor productivity and what labor productivity would be if the capital invested to meet new regulation were invested in directly productive capital.

There is no guarantee that funds invested in capital to meet new regulation would actually be invested in productive capital in the chemical industry if there were no new regulation. This is a balanced assumption, however, since this study excludes the possibility that any of the substantial noncapital costs of new regulation would be invested in conventional capital.

This study focuses on the two main types of new regulation imposed since the late 1960s: environmental and occupational health and safety regulation. These new regulations follow from legislation such as the Water Quality Act of 1965, the Water Pollution Act Amendments of 1972, the Air Quality Act of 1967, the Clean Air Amendments of 1972, and the Williams-Steiger Occupational Safety and Health Act of 1970.

Firms would most likely direct some capital expenditure toward environmental and occupational health and safety even without regulation. Therefore, this study focuses on new regulations introduced after 1966, for it is regulatory capital created after the introduction of new regulation, not the level of regulatory capital that existed all along, that may restrain productivity growth.

This approach parallels the approach in the classic studies by Denison (1978 and 1979) in many ways. It follows the same opportunity cost approach in measuring the cost of new regulation on output and productivity. Like Denison, it focuses on incremental costs of environmental and occupational health and safety regulation introduced after 1966.

However, this study differs significantly from Denison's in its method of measuring what output firms would produce if funds devoted to capital to meet new regulation (regulatory capital) were invested in directly productive capital. Denison uses an accounting method that values output at factor cost. Therefore, the lost output is the current-period depreciation of regulatory capital plus what the return on the funds invested in regulatory capital would be if they were invested in directly productive capital. He calculates this return as the product of the stock of regulatory capital times the ratio of earnings net of depreciation to the capital stock in the business sector.

An estimated production function makes an alternative to Denison's approach possible. The production function relates the value of the capital stock with and without new regulation to values of output, for fixed labor and other inputs. After computing these alternative values of output, alternative values of labor productivity are computed by dividing through by labor manhours.

In order to carry out this calculation, it is necessary to develop a measure of the stock of regulatory capital (K_{reg}). Measured capital in the CSP data set (K_m) consists of both directly productive (K) and regulatory capital. Having an estimate of K_{reg} makes it possible to estimate K by subtracting K_{reg} from K_m ($K = K_m - K_{reg}$).

An estimate of K_{reg} is developed by the perpetual-inventory method. Since only capital invested to meet regulation introduced after 1966 is considered, K_{reg} equals zero in 1966. Afterwards K_{reg} is computed by adding 1972-dollar capital expenditures for environmental and occupational health and safety purposes and depreciating the previous year's value of K_{reg}. Appendix 8B describes the estimation of K_{reg} in detail.

To recapitulate, this experiment compares labor productivity using the actual inputs

$$\hat{F}(K,L, E, M)/L \qquad (8.1)$$

to labor productivity using what capital would be if there had been no new regulation after 1966.

$$\hat{F}(K + K_{reg},L,E,M)/L \qquad (8.2)$$

Table 8–1 shows the results of this experiment.

Table 8–1 lists the percentage point difference between (8.1) and (8.2) for each of the four-digit SIC industries within the chemical industry, and for the aggregate chemical industry, for each of the years 1971–1976. As expected, there is a loss of labor productivity because labor has less capital to work with when there is new regulation. The loss of productivity tends to grow from 1971 to 1976 because the capital used to meet new regulation increases over time as firms make further investments in regulatory capital. However, the loss in labor productivity can fall over time if E or M—which increase labor's productivity—rises sufficiently.

The estimated loss of labor productivity caused by capital invested to meet new regulations rose from 1.0 percent in 1971 to 2.3 percent in 1976 for the entire chemical industry. This is not a shockingly large loss, especially for such a heavily environmentally regulated industry. It is, however, large enough for policymakers to take notice. They can combat this shortfall in labor productivity either by relaxing regulations or by using traditional policies that tend to increase the quantity of capital.

Energy and the Quality of Capital

An unforeseen change in the relative price of an input decreases the quality of capital because it increases the costs of producing a unit of output. Firms can be thought of as choosing a technical process that minimizes input costs given current and expected input prices. Furthermore, this technical process is usually built into the capital stock. Thus when relative input prices change unexpectedly, the capital stock may not be able to adjust quickly to the new cost-minimizing ratios of input to output. Costs per unit of output increase, increasing the real resources necessary to produce a unit of output. This is equivalent to a decrease in total factor productivity.

Table 8–1
Estimated Changes in Chemical Industry Labor Productivity Due to Diversion of Capital to Meet New Regulations
(*In percentage points*)

	SIC	1971	1972	1973	1974	1975	1976
Alkalines & chlorine	2812	-.5	-0.4	-0.6	-.7	-.8	-1.1
Industrial gases	2813	-.0	-.0	-.1	.1	-.1	-.2
Inorganic pigments	2816	-2.5	-3.5	-4.1	-4.4	-5.8	-5.9
Industrial inorganic chemicals	2819	-.9	-1.0	-1.2	-1.5	-1.2	-.9
Plastics materials & resins	2821	-1.1	-1.4	-1.8	-2.0	-2.5	-2.7
Synthetic rubber	2822	-.5	-.7	-.8	-1.0	-1.3	-1.6
Cellulosic man-made fibers	2823	-1.0	-1.5	-1.5	-2.1	-2.9	-3.2
Organic fibers, noncellulosic	2824	-.5	-.7	-.9	-.9	-1.1	-1.2
Biological products	2831	-.1	-.0	-.0	-.1	-.1	-.1
Medicinals & botanicals	2833	-.7	-1.0	-1.1	-1.2	-1.5	-1.6
Pharmaceutical preparations	2834	-.2	-.3	-.4	-.4	-.6	-.7
Soaps & detergents	2841	-.8	-1.0	-1.3	1.5	-1.7	-1.8

	Code						
Polishes & sanitation goods	2842	-.1	-.1	-.2	-.2	-.2	-.2
Surface & active agents	2843	-2.7	-3.4	-3.7	-4.0	-4.3	-4.1
Toilet preparations	2844	-.1	-.1	-.2	-.2	-.3	-.3
Paint & allied products	2851	-.3	-.4	-.6	1.7	-.8	-.9
Gum & wood chemicals	2861	-.1	-.1	-.5	-.6	-.7	-.8
Cyclic crudes intermediates	2865	-1.7	-2.3	-3.0	-3.4	-3.8	-4.2
Industrial organic chemicals	2869	-1.1	-1.5	-1.9	-2.1	-2.6	-2.9
Nitrogenous fertilizers	2873	-.6	-.3	-.4	-.5	-.6	-.9
Phosphatic fertilizers	2874	-3.2	-4.4	-4.8	-5.4	-6.2	-7.0
Fertilizers, mixing only	2875	-.7	-1.0	-1.8	-2.1	-2.4	-2.5
Agricultural chemicals nec.	2879	-3.9	-5.1	-6.2	-7.0	-7.4	-7.3
Adhesives & sealants	2891	-.4	-.5	-1.0	-1.1	-1.3	-1.3
Explosives	2892	-.8	-1.1	-1.2	-1.4	-2.4	-3.9
Printing ink	2893	-.1	-.2	-.5	-.5	-.8	-.8
Carbon black	2895	-4.5	-5.9	-9.5	-10.9	-9.4	-7.6
Chemical preparation nec.	2899	-.8	-1.2	-1.5	-1.8	-2.4	-2.8
Chemicals	28	-1.0	-1.2	-1.6	-1.9	-2.1	-2.3

Of course, relative energy prices increased unexpectedly in the mid-1970s. The substitution of capital for energy helped to limit the increase in real costs per unit of output. Capital could be substituted for energy by making investments to replace capital in place with new capital that uses less energy. Capital can also be substituted for energy by making capital investments to retool or to better maintain capital in place in ways that save energy. The more capital firms substitute for energy when the relative price of energy rises, the less costs per unit of output rise.

The engineering elasticity of substitution between capital and energy measures the rate at which capital can be substituted for energy. The engineering elasticity holds the joint contribution to output of capital and energy working together constant. The engineering elasticity does not count cuts in capital and energy use that firm undertake because their budget buys less after an input price rise. Thus the engineering elasticity focuses on the purely technological capacity of cost-minimizing firms to save energy by adding capital.

Estimation of the nested CES production function produces an estimate of the engineering elasticity. The estimated elasticity of -0.4 is problematic since economic theory requires that engineering elasticities be positive. However, the equation from which the engineering elasticity is estimated has a very low $\bar{R}^2$. This suggests that the true value of the capital-energy elasticity may actually be zero.

An engineering elasticity of zero means that capital and energy were in fixed proportions over the 1971–1976 period, allowing no possibility for saving energy by substituting capital for energy. Thus all energy savings must come from proportional reduction in capital and output. Capital may well have been taken out of operation to reduce energy costs, and this may have set back labor productivity.

Thus the rise in the relative price of energy reduced the quality of capital in terms of the costs of producing a unit of output. However, the roughly zero rate of capital-energy engineering substitution probably did not continue long after the data period. There probably was not enough time to design and build new energy-efficient capital between the onset of the energy crisis at the end of 1973 and the end of the data period in 1976. By the early 1980s new energy-saving capital-investment projects begun in the mid- and late 1970s may well have come into operation. This sort of improvement was undoubtedly the result of intensive research and development efforts.

R&D and Productivity

R&D efforts often aim to reduce the costs of production per unit of output by improving technical knowledge. This is a reduction in the real factor inputs necessary to produce a unit of output and thus means an increase in total factor productivity. So productivity can be increased by increasing technical knowledge through R&D. Policymakers then decide how much to increase R&D through direct expenditures and by tax incentives for business. These measures can be costly for the government. Therefore, policymakers may want to know the return in terms of increased productivity of improvements in technical knowledge brought about by increased expenditures on R&D before recommending R&D promoting tax cuts.

A relationship between total factor productivity and technical knowledge is estimated in two steps. The first step develops an index of technical knowledge accumulated since 1960 through both private and government expenditures on R&D within the chemical industry (KR&D). The second step expands the part of the production function that models productivity change to include KR&D. One of the parameters of the expanded productivity term is, approximately, the percentage change in total factor productivity associated with a 1 percent increase in the rate of growth of KR&D.

This study defines the index KR&D along the lines of a perpetual inventory measure of the capital stock. The perpetual inventory method starts with a base-year value of the capital stock, adds current-year real investment, and depreciates the previous year's stock.[2] This index must build on a base of zero (which is 1959) because of the difficulty of valuing all the technical knowledge in the chemical industry in any base year. The index values the current-year addition to (investment in) technical knowledge as equal to expenditures on R&D.[3] That is, the index values additions to technical knowledge at cost. This is necessary because of the difficulty of directly valuing each firm's useful new technical knowledge in the absence of markets for such knowledge.

The perpetual-inventory method of estimating each year's KR&D subtracts depreciation from the previous year's KR&D. This is done by multiplying the previous year's KR&D by one minus the rate of depreciation. This procedure incorporates the idea that some technical knowledge ceases to be useful to firms as it is superseded by knowledge of more cost-efficient production processes (or of more profitable products that supersede similar products).[4]

The use of this depreciation procedure makes it possible to interpret KR&D as a weighted average of current and past expenditures on R&D. This perpetual-inventory type of depreciation procedure implicitly weights each year's expenditures on R&D with geometrically declining weights. This can be thought of as modeling the tendency of expenditures on R&D to influence productivity long after they have been undertaken. It is this current accumulated stock of effective technical knowledge that moves productivity.

This analysis evaluates the degree to which KR&D affects productivity by estimating and comparing two alternative specifications of productivity change in the production function. The first specification makes productivity change depend exclusively on a time trend term (with separate time dummy variables for each year of the sample after the base year, 1971). The second specification makes productivity depend on the same time trend *and* a term that includes KR&D. The parameter of the KR&D term should measure the response of productivity to increases in the growth of KR&D. The estimated parameters of the time dummies may be smaller in the second specification than in the first. This would mean that fluctuations in KR&D explain some of what appears to be simple year-to-year changes in productivity in the first specification.

The first specification fits a productivity change time trend term $D(t)$ into the production function in the following way.

$$X = G(K,L,E,M)D(t) \tag{8.3}$$

G is part of the production function, which explains output by changes in inputs.[5] Total factor productivity is $X/G(K,L,E,M)$. Changes in total factor productivity are essentially changes in output that are not explained by changes in the inputs. $D(t)$ models the change in total factor productivity associated with each year.

Mathematically, the productivity change time trend term is

$$D(t) = A\exp(d_{1972}D_{1972} + \ldots + d_{1976}D_{1976}) \tag{8.4}$$

A is a constant term. The Ds are time dummy variables for each year. The ds are their coefficients. The ds are defined in such a way that each d times 100 can be interpreted as the year-to-year percentage-point change in total factor productivity associated in that year. Appendix 8A more fully defines and explains the ds.

Estimation of $D(t)$ preceeds easily after estimation of G. Taking logs of equation 8.3 and then subtracting the log of estimated G from both sides produces the regression equation

$$\ln X - \ln \hat{G} = \ln A + \sum_{t=1972}^{1976} d_t D_t + u \tag{8.5}$$

where u is an independently normally distributed error.

The first row of table 8–2 shows estimates of the d_ts that result from estimating equation 8.5 by the ordinary-least squares (OLS) method. Productivity rises in 1972 through 1974 but falls by a substantial 15.1 percent in 1975 before recovering a bit in 1976. The 1975 setback of productivity is striking, so its source deserves investigation.

This setback might be caused by a fall in the utilization of measured capital. However, adjustment of measured capital by a measure of capital utiliza-

Table 8–2
Estimated Coefficients of Time Dummy and R&D Capital Variables

	D_{1972}	D_{1973}	D_{1974}	D_{1975}	D_{1976}	KR&D/KR&D$_{-1}$
Eq. 8.5	.026	.063	.012	−.151	.031	—
Eq. 8.7	.047	.087	−.039	−.079	.059	7.26

Note: The estimated parameters of the time dummy variables (times 100) can be read as year over year percentage changes in total factor productivity.
[a]T-Statistic

tion—the ratio of census actual to preferred hours of operation of plants—does not result in substantially different estimates of the d_ts.[6] It is possible that R&D play a role in explaining the fall of productivity in 1975 and its weak growth over the entire data period.

The second specification investigates this possibility by including the ratio of current to lagged KR&D as an explanatory variable in the production function, alongside the time dummy variables.

$$X = G(K,L,E,M)D(t) \qquad (\text{KR\&D}/\text{KR\&D}_{-1})^{\eta} \qquad (8.6)$$

The ratio of current to lagged KR&D rather than the level of KR&D appears in equation 8.6 because this ratio is a measure of the change in KR&D. The change in KR&D is more meaningful than the level of KR&D, because KR&D is not based on a benchmark value for all technical knowledge within the chemical industry. Hence its absolute level is unknown.

η is the elasticity of total factor productivity with respect to a change in KR&D/KR&D$_{-1}$. This means that η multiplied by 100 approximately equals the percentage change in productivity associated with a 1 percent rise in the growth rate of KR&D.

η and new values of the d_ts are estimated by taking logs of equation 8.6 and subtracting estimated G from both sides.

$$X - G(K,L,E,M) = \ln A + \sum_{t=1972}^{1976} d_t D_t \qquad (8.7)$$

$$+ \eta(\ln\text{KR\&D} - \ln\text{KR\&D}_{-1})$$

Estimating equation 8.7 using OLS yields estimates of the d_ts, which are shown in the second row of table 8–2.

The estimated value of η is a surprisingly high 7.26. Furthermore, its T statistic of 7.07 is highly significant, given the pooled cross-section–time-series sample size of 168. This high value of η means that a 1 percent increase in the ratio of current to lagged KR&D is statistically associated with more than a 7 percent increase in productivity.

Including the KR&D term in the production function also substantially changes the estimated d_ts. The estimated 1972, 1973, and 1976 d_ts show much stronger growth under this second specification. Apparently, KR&D statistically explains a good deal of what appears to be productivity growth associated with the time dummy variables in the first specification. The only exception is in 1974, when d_t rises under the first specification but falls under the second. Including KR&D in the production function has a striking affect on d_{1975}. Productivity falls an estimated 7.9 percent in 1975 instead of the originally estimated 15.1 percent. This means that the large estimated contraction of productivity in 1975, which could have been caused entirely by a drop in capital utilization, seems to have been caused partly by a drop in the growth of technical knowledge as measured by KR&D.

Conclusion

This study concludes that events in the early and mid-1970s had more apparent effect on the quality than on the quantity of chemical industry capital. Thus productivity growth was probably restrained more by the quality than by the quantity of capital. One of the main events that probably limited the quantity of capital was the imposition of new regulations.

The chemical industry devoted a substantial part of its gross investment to meeting new environmental and occupational safety and health regulations imposed since 1966. This study estimates that labor productivity was between 1.0 and 2.3 percent lower over 1971–1976 than it would have been without these new regulations. This is a substantial but not surprisingly large loss of potential productivity. This loss could be reversed by relaxing government regulations or by building further investment tax incentives into the corporate income tax.

The quality of capital was probably reduced by the energy crisis. Improvement in the quality of capital was probably also held back by falling real expenditures on R&D within the chemical industry. The 1973 jump in energy prices reduced the quality of capital by increasing the costs of producing a unit of output using existing capital. The estimated engineering capital-energy elasticity of substitution implies that cost-minimizing firms could not reduce these increased energy costs by substituting existing energy-efficient capital.

The behavior of the estimated index of technical knowledge in the chemical industry (KR&D) appears to explain a good part of the slowed and sometimes falling estimated total factor productivity growth over 1971–1976. This suggests that reduced real expenditures on R&D growth limited improvement in the quality of capital and restrained productivity growth. The high estimated elasticity of total factor productivity with respect to increases in KR&D suggests that increased real expenditures on R&D can significantly improve productivity growth. Public policy could be used to improve productivity through the quality of capital by building an improved R&D tax credit into the corporate income tax.

Notes

1. *X* is real shipments adjusted for changes in inventories so that it measures production. *K* is the real capital stock, constructed using the perpetual-inventory method. *E* is a measure of energy used for power and heat. *M* is all nonenergy intermediate materials, including both raw materials and parts. *M* includes petroleum used as raw material rather than as a fuel. For a fuller description of the CSP data set, see Prywes (1983), pp. 7–10.

2. KR&D is computed from the following equations:

$$\text{KR\&D}_{t,i} = (1 - \text{DEP})\text{KR\&D}_{t-1,i} + \text{ER\&D72}_{t,i}$$

which can be written

$$\text{KR\&D}_{t,i} = \sum_{t=1960}^{1976} (1 - \text{DEP})^k \ \text{ER\&D72}_{t,i}$$

$t = 1960, \ldots, 1976$

$k = 1976 - t$

i is an index running across four-digit SIC industries, ER&D72 is 1972 dollar expenditures on R&D within the chemical industry, and DEP is the depreciation rate.

3. Data on expenditures for private plus government expenditures on R&D within the chemical industry (ER&D) come from the National Science Foundation (1979), table B–2. ER&D is broken down into three parts within chemicals: industrial chemicals (SIC 281–282), drugs and medicines (SIC 283), and other chemicals (SIC 284 – 289). ER&D is disaggregated to the four-digit SIC level using each industry group's share of output in 1974. ER&D is deflated to ER&D72 by a price deflator for the overall U.S. economy developed by Batelle Columbus Laboratories, *Probable Levels of R&D Expenditures in 1977: Forecast and Analysis,* December 1976, Table 4, p. 12.

4. This study adopts the depreciation rate of 1/10 which was adopted by Grabowski and Mueller (1978) after they experimented with alternative rates.

5. *G* consists of all of equations 8A.1–8A.3 in appendix 8A except for *D*(*t*) in equation 8A.3. The estimation method for the entire production function proceeds in steps, estimating *G* before *D*(*t*). See Prywes (1981, 1983).

6. Census preferred hours of operation are a measure of the economically desirable maximum hours of operation rather than technically feasible (practical) hours. See U.S. Census Bureau, *Survey of Plant Capacity, 1975 Supplement,* Current Industrial Reports (Washington, D.C.: U.S. Government Printing Office, March 1977), for full definitions.

Appendix 8A: The Three-Level Nested CES Production Function

The advantage of the three-level nested CES production function is that it models the relationship between capital and energy, so important in the early 1970s. Another advantage of the nested CES function is that it is relatively simple to estimate. Moreover, its parameters can be used to construct useful estimates of the elasticities of substitution within the chemical industry. The nested CES production function was developed by Sato (1967) following closely related work on consumption by Brown and Heien (1972). The particular form of the nested CES estimated here originates with Sheinin in (1980).

The mathematical form of the nested CES function is[7]

$$X_{KE} = (\delta_0 K^{-\rho 0} + (1 - \delta_0) E^{-\rho 0})^{-1/\rho 0} \qquad (8A.1)$$

$$X_{KEL} = (\rho_1 X_{KE}^{-\rho 1} + (1 - \rho_1) L^{-\rho 1})^{-1/\rho 2} \qquad (8A.2)$$

$$X = A(\rho X_{KEL}^{-\rho} + (1 - \rho) M^{-\rho 0}) D(t) \qquad (8A.3)$$

where

$$A > 0; \rho_0, \rho_1, \rho \geq -1$$

$$0 \leq \delta_0, \delta_1, \delta \leq 1$$

$$\sigma_0 = \frac{1}{1 + \rho_0} j; \quad \sigma_1 = \frac{1}{1 + \rho_1} j; \quad \sigma = \frac{1}{1 + \rho}$$

X_{KE} is the intermediate input produced by K and E working together. X_{KEL} is the intermediate input produced by X_{KE} and L. The ρs are the substitution parameters, which determine the engineering (gross) elasticities of substitution. The σs are the elasticities of substitution between inputs in a particular level CES function holding the intermediate inputs produced by that level CES function constant. The ρs are the share coefficients, which determine the relative weights of the factors within a particular level CES function.

$D(t)$ is a total factor productivity-change term. It is Hicks neutral for X_{KE} and M. The productivity-change time trend term has the form

$$D(t) = \exp\left(d_{72}D_{72} + \ldots + d_{76}D_{76}\right)$$

The subscripted Ds are dummy variables for the years 1972–1976. They are defined so that their coefficients, the subscripted ds, have the interpretation of percentage annual changes in total factor productivity.

The economic elasticities of substitution depend on the engineering elasticities and input shares, as the preceding example suggests. The Allen elasticities of substitution (AES), which follow, are one type of economic elasticity. Their advantage is that they have a simple form that shows the interaction of engineering elasticities and cost shares.

$$AES_{KL} = AES_{LE} = \sigma + \frac{P_j X_j}{P_{K_j} K_j + P_{E_j} E_j + P_{L_j} L_j} \, (\sigma_0 - \sigma)$$

$$AES_{KE} = + \frac{P_j X_j}{P_{K_j} K_j + P_{E_j} E_j} \, (\sigma_0 - \sigma_1) + \frac{P_j X_j}{P_{K_j} K_j + P_{E_j} E_j + P_{L_j} L_j} \, (\sigma_1 - \sigma)$$

$$AES_{KM} = AES_{EM} = AES_{LM} = \sigma$$

j is an index running over the observations.

Appendix 8B: Estimation of the Regulatory Capital Stock

T
he stock of capital devoted to meeting new regulation imposed after 1966—that is, regulatory capital—is estimated by the perpetual-inventory method. Total regulatory capital (K_{reg}) is the sum of pollution-abatement capital (KPA) and occupational safety and health capital (KOSH), which are estimated separately. This calculation requires data on current-dollar capital expenditures on pollution abatement (CPA) and occupational safety and health (COSH), their deflators, and the depreciation rates of these sorts of capital goods. This appendix develops these data series and uses them to compute an estimate of K_{reg}.

The census publishes four-digit SIC data on CPA but, unfortunately, only for 1973 on. Estimation of KPA requires CPA data for 1967–1976. McGraw-Hill data on CPA for the aggregate chemical industry form a basis for extending the census data back to 1967.

The census data on CPA consist of separate series on air, water, and solid-waste pollution abatement. The McGraw-Hill data consist of series on only air and water pollution abatement. An estimate of aggregate chemical industry CPA on solid waste for 1967–1971 is calculated by multiplying the sum of the McGraw-Hill air and water CPA series in those years by the (aggregate chemical industry) ratio of solid waste to air and water CPA in the 1974 census data.

However, the 1967–1976 air, water, and solid waste CPA data still exist only at the aggregate chemical industry level. Estimates of the four-digit SIC industry CPA series are computed by multiplying the 1967–1976 aggregates by the 1974 distribution of CPA over four-digit SIC industries in the census data. (1974 instead of 1973 data are used because the 1973 sample was poor.)

The CPA data are put on a 1972-dollar basis using Bureau of Economic Analysis (BEA) price deflators. Air, water, and solid-waste CPA are divided by separate deflators and then summed to produce 1972 dollar CPA (CPA72).

The BEA unofficially estimated the mean life of pollution-abatement capital equipment at twenty-five years. The depreciation rate is then $1/25$.

This completes the development of data necessary to calculate KPA by the perpetual-inventory method. KPA is calculated from the following equation with a base of zero in 1966:

$$KPA_{t,i} = KPA_{t-1,i}(1 - 1/25) + CPA72_{t,i}$$

which can be rewritten as

$$KPA_{t,i} = \sum_{t=1967}^{1976} CPA72_{t,i}\, 0.96^k$$

where

$t = 1967, \ldots 1976.$

i is an index of four-digit SIC industries.

$k = 1976 - t.$

The KOSH series measures the extra capital needed to meet new occupational safety and health regulations. Therefore, KOSH begins in 1971 when the major relevant new legislation—the Williams-Steiger Act—became effective.

McGraw-Hill publishes aggregate chemical industry data on COSH from 1972 on. 1971 COSH is interpolated by assuming that the 1971–1972 growth rate of COSH was the same as the 1972–1973 growth rate. 1971 COSH is then 1 minus the 1972–1973 growth rate times 1972 COSH.

No four-digit SIC data on COSH are available, so the aggregate McGraw-Hill data were disaggregated to the four-digit SIC level by multiplying by the 1973 distribution of real output over four-digit SIC industries. Unfortunately, this procedure eliminates any statistically meaningful variation of KOSH in the four-digit SIC cross-section part of the pooled cross-section–time-series data set. Since KOSH is small compared to KPA, however, this probably does not much affect the meaningfulness of cross-section variation in K_{reg}.

No deflators are available for occupational safety and health capital goods, so COSH is put on 1972 dollar terms (to form COSH72) by dividing by the BEA's investment price deflator for manufacturing. Following Denison (1979), a $1/10$ depreciation rate is used.

This completes the development of data necessary to calculate KOSH by the perpetual inventory method. KOSH is calculated from the following equation with a base of zero in

$$KOSH_{t,1} = KOSH_{t-1,i}(1 - 1/10) + COSH72_{t,i}$$

$$KOSH_{t,i} = \sum_{t=1971}^{1976} COSH72_{t,i}0.9^k.$$

where

$t = 1971, \ldots , 1976.$

i is an index of four-digit SIC industries.

$k = 1976 - t.$

K_{reg} is then the sum of KOSH and KPA. The final estimates of K_{reg} comprise a full time-series of cross-sections. An estimate of K_{reg} exists for each of the twenty-eight four-digit SIC industries within the chemical industry for each of the years 1967–1976.

9
Industrial Policy and Optimization in the Coal Industry

Robert F. Wescott

T he primary resource industries have been a particular focus of industrial policies in most countries. This chapter analyzes quantitatively how government policies might affect the U.S. coal industry over the next twenty-five years. Specifically, we consider how the competitiveness of the U.S. coal industry might be influenced by a number of possible government actions—from policies designed to stimulate demand, to those that might promote supply, to those that might reduce the industry's transportation costs. This analysis is accomplished through the simulation of a world coal model featuring eleven international supply and demand regions. The model uses a maximization procedure to determine regional demand, supply, and price levels as well as interregional coal trade flows; it is a suitable tool for studying the effects of government policies.

The study's main conclusion is that the competitiveness of U.S. coal could be affected, but not strongly, by U.S. government policies over the twenty-five-year horizon. The long-run prospects for U.S. coal are favorable. After world demand reaches a certain level, major alternative suppliers ultimately will face production constraints. Large quantities of U.S. coal will be consumed, no matter what the competitive factor. In the near term, the United States will be the marginal coal supplier to world markets after Europe. Because U.S. coal will be the most expensive to produce and ship outside Europe, however, marginal improvements attributable to industrial policies will not alter efficient trade-flow routes or quantities.[1]

In many ways the competitiveness of U.S. coal is more a function of foreign industrial policies aimed at coal than of domestic industrial policies. If a large number of foreign governments decided to buy only domestic coal, no matter what the price, or imposed stiff protectionist measures against U.S. coal, U.S. exports could be sharply reduced. If many foreign governments decided to forsake coal for large nuclear electric power plants, the future of U.S. coal exports could be radically altered.

This study has four main parts. The first section describes the international trade flow model that is used to perform the policy analysis. The second section describes the baseline forecast against which industrial policy scenarios are compared. The third part details alternative scenarios developed to analyze the effects of government policies on the competitiveness of the U.S. coal industry. In addition to analyzing aggregate effects, it also examines the relative effects on the coal industry. Finally, a concluding section summarizes the study's major findings.

An Overview of the International Trade Flow Model for Coal

The international trade-flow model for coal used in this study is a welfare-maximizing model. It is fed by two submodels—a coal-supply submodel and an electric utility interfuel-substitution submodel. The supply and demand modeling take process-analysis approaches. The trade-flow model solves the Cournot-Enke classical transportation problem employing a quadratic programming optimization framework. It focuses on the maximization of Samuelson's (1952) notion of net social payoff. Because this welfare concept is linked to efficiency through duality assumptions, the trade-flow model's predictions represent optimal production levels, prices, and trade flows.

Modeling the Supply of Coal

A process-analysis approach is taken in modeling supply, following a procedure first described by Newcomb and Fan (1980). This approach begins with detailed coal reserve data for each of eleven supply regions and transforms these data into supply curves via a number of adjustments.[2] The basic idea is to:

1. Collect detailed information on from twenty-five to forty coal deposit categories in each region.
2. Develop model mine-type costing functions via process analysis to determine how mining costs are affected by the available deposit variables.
3. Use these cost functions to rank the order of exploitation of the different coal categories in each region.
4. Develop a supply curve for each region based on the assumption that the coal category that is cheapest to exploit will be mined first, that the second-cheapest category will be mined second, and so on.

Keeping track of the quantities of coal available in each category, each supply curve is determined by fitting a function (linear or piecewise linear) through the midpoints of each region's supply categories when they are ranked from least-cost category to highest-cost category. The effects of depletion are implicitly accounted for with this integrated approach, as are certain dynamic factors affecting supply prices.

In order to develop good cost functions, many factors affecting the cost of mining coal in a particular category are taken into account—whether the coal is surface minable or not, seam thickness, seam depth, sulfur content, beneficiation characteristics, miners' wage rates, capital equipment costs, government black lung exposure insurance taxes, reclamation fees, and so forth. Unfortunately, econometric approaches to modeling coal supply have had poor success in describing behavior accurately. To avoid the econometric problems, this submodel systemizes the cost-supply information via a modified index number approach. Three factors are conceptually defined as contributing to total cost: technical factors, economic factors, and government policy factors. All technical factors affecting coal production costs are transformed from real-world dimensions—for example, tons of output per manshift or percentage of sulfur content—into index number values that represent the cost impacts of these variables. This general weighting function approach, suggested by Newcomb and Fan (1980), has the advantage of collapsing reams of technical data into a vector of index numbers that summarize cost effects.

The underlying cost of producing a standardized ton of coal is determined by model-mine or cost-engineering analysis and is referred to in this study as the economic component of the total cost function. Katell (1978) provided a framework for the basic cost analysis. This underlying cost includes such cost elements as wages and salaries, capital equipment costs, supplies, power costs, and a fair return on equity. Technical factors show how the cost of mining coal in a particular category differs from the cost of producing a standardized ton of coal, assuming standardized productivity. Suppose a certain category of coal could be mined with the standardized productivity, but the coal was dirtier than standard coal and therefore required more thorough cleaning. This coal would cost the standardized (economic cost) amount, plus an additional premium to cover the coal's technical disadvantage of being dirty.

Finally, costs resulting from government policies are added into the cost function. Most of these—for example, black lung taxes, severance taxes, and reclamation fees—are additive in nature and are appropriately summed together with the other cost components to produce total costs. Adjustments are made, however, to reflect the tax effects of such policy-related cost components. By varying these cost assumptions, supply-side industrial-policy actions can be simulated by the model. Table 9–1 summarizes the supply modeling framework.

Table 9–1
Factors Affecting the Long-Run Cost of Production

Economic Factors	*Technical Factors*	*Government Policy Parameters*
Summarized by K	Mainly Summarized by I	Summarized by G

A. Reflect standardized costs of producing a standardized ton of coal, including:
  1. Labor costs
  2. Maintenance costs
  3. Capital costs
  4. Provision for income taxes
  5. Provision for normal profit
  6. Normal depreciation, depletion, etc.
	A. Direct technical adjustments
	  1. BTU content
	  2. Recovery factors
	B. Components of the index
	  1. Productivity in mining
	    a. surface
	    b. deep
	  2. Yield in beneficiation
	  3. Sulfur content
	  4. Ease-of-development factors
		A. Reflect direct cost impacts of government policies, including:
		  1. Reclamation costs
		  2. Abandoned mine reclamation fees
		  3. Severance taxes
		  4. Royalties
		  5. License fees
		  6. Black lund taxes and insurance

B. Determined by Katell-Type model mine-costing simulations	C. Index weights determined by model mine/preparation plant costing simulations	B. Determined directly from data from each region/country
C. Vary from region to region, country to country, depending on data	D. Basic technical relationships constant across regions, while data, of course, vary	

Note: Assumed functional form: $C = K + \gamma \ln(I) + G$.

Modeling the Demand for Coal

Demand-side modeling also takes a process-analysis approach. Although demand levels in regions outside the U.S. are exogenously determined, an electric utility interfuel substitution model endogenously determines the demand for coal by U.S. electric utilities. Like several other models—ICF (1980a); Van Horn, Large, and Smith (1980); and Cazalet (1977)—the interfuel substitution model is based on the assumption that utility managers are cost minimizers in the short run, and optimal investors (minimizing present value cost) in the long run, while always seeing that total demand is met. Conceptually, this study concentrates on the interfuel substitution question, and posits the hypothesis, suggested by Griffin (1979), that there are three substitution effects over time: a utilization effect (short run), a technical-adjustment effect (intermediate run), and a capital-turnover effect (long run). The analysis begins with the realization that capital stock and energy consumption are related by a function such as:

$$E_{ij} = e_{ij}K_j^*$$

which says that for each hour of capital services by a particular stock of generating capacity (K_j^*) there is a fixed technical energy coefficient (e_{ij}) showing the energy requirements (E_{ij}) for fuel i by plant type j. Aggregating over time, K_j can be thought of as the product of the magnitude of capital, K_j, and its utilization, u_j:

$$K_j = u_j K_j^*$$

Aggregating over an individual fuel type and over time, the total demand for fuel i would be:

$$E_i = \sum_j e_{ij}(u_j K_j^*)$$

From this simple equation, all three effects can be described. In the short run, both technology and the magnitude of capital stock are assumed to be constant. Thus, e_{ij}, the technical heat rate, and K_j are fixed. The only possible response to a change in relative fuel prices or in the institutional environment is a change in the utilization level, u_j. In the intermediate run, capital stock is still considered fixed, but certain technical changes are allowed. For example, perhaps the technical heat rate, e_{ij}, might improve reflecting an increase in efficiency. The utilization level could, of course, also vary. Finally, in the long run, K_j is also allowed to vary in response to changing economic, demand, and technological factors.

The electric utility model explicitly takes account of these three sensitivities over time: utilization effects, technical-adjustment effects, and capital-turnover effects. The first step is to determine the stock of electric utility capital, by fuel type, that will exist between now and 2004. Over the 1980–1990 period, the stock is assumed to be the existing 1980 stock, plus announced utility additions, less announced utility retirements. A technical-adjustments submodel modifies these assumptions to reflect price-induced early retirements, conversions, and so forth. After 1990 a capital-turnover submodel determines both the optimal amount of capacity and the type of new generating equipment, based on vintage structure characteristics and economic analysis. It is assumed that utilities will add sufficient new capacity to meet demand, and that they will invest in the capacity and type that are optimal from a present-discounted-value point of view. Technical adjustments are not made in this period, however, because it is assumed that in the long run (after 1990) all adjustments will have been made, and that the industry can build completely new capacity as desired.

The end result is that adjusted capital stock is derived for both time periods—1980–1990 and 1990–2004. A utilization-effects submodel then takes this generating-type capacity information and decides at what rate the capital stock of each fuel type will be operated. Cost minimization provides the mechanism for determining these utilization rates. Demands for fuel—coal, oil, and gas—are then endogenously determined through technical relationships (heat rates and the like).

The Maximization Trade-Flow Model

The international trade-flow model uses the result of the supply and demand modeling and solves what has become known as the Cournot (1838)–Enke (1951) transportation problem. It is assumed that all regions are trading a homogeneous good (Btus of cleaned coal), that each region constitutes a distinct market, that profit-seeking traders operate without restrictions in each region, that unit transportation costs are constant irrespective of quantity shipped, and that supply and demand functions are known. Takayama and Judge (1971), elaborating on the original work of Samuelson (1952), show how this problem can be expressed as an extremum problem and related to mathematical programming. They begin by assuming a Marshall-Hicks-Samuelson neoclassical world where regional supply curves are seen as being derived from aggregate regional cost functions and demand curves from regional utility functions. Samuelson's quasi-welfare function, a theoretical representation of the union of consumers' surplus and producers' surplus, is then employed. Assuming integrable supply and demand functions, this concept involves subtracting the integral of the supply function from the integral of the demand function over an appropriate domain, leaving an area that can be thought of as representing welfare. Then assuming additive regional quasi-welfare functions, a mathematical programming model can be applied to maximize the global sum of these areas or welfares. In turn this maximizes Samuelson's concept of global net social payoff. This solution would also minimize total costs and yield the equilibrium prices and trade flows that would result from the natural forces of competitive markets, as Takayama and Judge show. Based on this theoretical work, a solution algorithm using quadratic programming is employed to actually solve the model.

At Takayama and Judge (1971) demonstrate, the solution involves specifying the appropriate objective function and maximizing it using standard Lagrangian techniques. The Kuhn-Tucker conditions require that:

1. The imputed demand prices and imputed supply prices exactly equal the actual regional demand and supply prices.
2. Locational price equilibrium exists; that is, if a trade flow occurs, the difference between the price of the good leaving the supply region and the price of the good arriving in the demand region must exactly equal the transportation cost.
3. Market equilibrium exists, that is, no excess supply or demand exists.
4. Total consumer spending exactly equals the sum of total production costs and total transportation costs.

Figure 9–1 uses a two-region two-period gains-from-trade type diagram to illustrate how an optimization process focusing on consumers' surplus and producers' surplus can lead to the maximization of net social welfare. Figure 9–1 shows two regions' supply and demand situations. Before trade is allowed, each region is at equilibrium (E_1 and E_2) with prices of p_1 and p_2 and equal demands and supplies, $y_1 = x_1$ and $y_2 = x_2$. Consumers' surpluses are represented by the areas BE_1p_1 and AE_2p_2, while producers' surpluses are p_1E_1D and p_2E_2C respectively for regions 1 and 2. Now imagine that trade is allowed between the two regions at a transportation cost of t_{12}. Because of profit-seeking traders, price in region 1 rises leading to a contraction of domestic demand (to y_1) but an expansion of production (to x_1) while just the opposite occurs in region 2.

The question, then, is: What area can be used to guide prices to their optimal levels (which is where $p_1 + t_{12} = p_2$ due to standard arbitrage-type arguments), and consequently to lead to the maximization of welfare? An examination of the consumers' surplus and producers' surplus areas shows that it is areas MNE_1 and QRE_2, the sum of which Samuelson calls net social payoff, that play the critical role. In region 1, as price rises to p_1, consumers' surplus falls to BMp_1, but producers' surplus increases to p_1ND—with area MNE_1 being the net addition to regional welfare resulting from trade. In

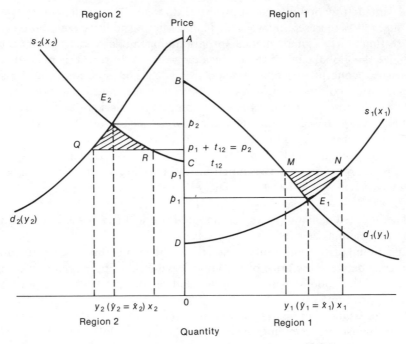

Figure 9–1. Samuelson's Net Social Payoff Concept

region 2, as price falls to p_2, consumers' surplus increases to AQp_2 while that of producers falls to p_2RC—a net gain of QRE_2.

Transportation Costs

Finally, the trade-flow model requires good transportation cost estimates to predict future coal trade flows and prices. All costs are based on trade flows between selected regional supply and demand centroids and are exogenous to the model. Transportation costs are broken down into three segments where appropriate: (1) mine-mouth to export port, (2) oceanic shipping, and (3) final distribution. In all cases the cheapest, most efficient modes of transport are selected, given appropriate (that is, most likely) technical constraints. Since all transportation data are developed on a per ton basis, all costs are adjusted by the average Btu content of the coal from each supply region; that is, final transport costs are expressed 1981 dollars per million clean Btu.

The Baseline Forecast

Simulating the coal trade-flow model without any adjustments produces welfare-maximizing or efficiency-maximizing trade flows, based on the theoretical construction of the model and its reliance on the Samuelson-Takayama-Judge theory. In such a simulation, all buyers are pure welfare maximizers and purchase their coal from the least-cost supplier, no matter who it is; and all sellers ship their coal to the regions willing to pay the highest price. In the real world, however, some countries consciously subsidize the production of domestic coal and often require that utilities purchase domestically mined coal, even if it is considerably more expensive than imported coal. For this reason, the pure welfare-maximizing solution was deemed inappropriate as a baseline against which to compare industrial-policy simulations. Instead, a real-world baseline was developed by assuming that the four major European producers—the United Kingdom, France, Germany, and Poland—continue to subsidize roughly 38 percent of their production costs, as they have historically, and by assuming that these four countries give preferential purchase contracts to domestic coal—buying 85 percent of all steam coal produced locally, regardless of price. For more minor producers—for example, Spain, Japan, Korea, and Turkey—it was assumed that all domestic production would always be used locally, and these amounts were subtracted from domestic demand to yield effective demand levels.

Tables 9–2 through 9–6 display the results of the maximization simulations for five-year periods from 1980 to 2004. They show that U.S. steam coal should flow basically eastward, with the East Coast shipping to Europe, the Central U.S. shipping to the Southeast and Midwest, and Northern Great Plains coal quenching demand in the whole middle part of the country, from Minnesota to Texas. The natural market for U.S. Rockies, Canadian, and Australian coals should be the Pacific Rim. South Africa should be a more efficient supplier to Europe than the Pacific Rim; when world coal demand really starts growing in the 1990s, these trade flows should become important. Latin America's production should continue to satisfy regional demand, and its small excess steam coal capacity should flow to Europe.

By the final forecast period, 2000–2004, the dominant coal trade flows will quite logically still be intraregional and between contiguous regions. The vast bulk of U.S. coal, for example, will eventually be consumed either in the region where it is produced, or in a bordering region. Virtually all European coal will be consumed domestically. The largest flows will be from the U.S. Central Basin to the Southeast, 46.0 quads, and from the Northern Great Plains to the Central and Western regions, 40.4 quads and 43.3 quads. The major international trade flows will be from the U.S. Rockies to the Pacific Rim, 21.5 quads; from Canada to the Pacific Rim, 20.0 quads; and from South Africa to Europe, 20.5 quads. More minor flows should occur from

Table 9–2
Coal Trade Flows and Prices, 1980–1984, Real-World Baseline Scenario

To: From:	US NE	US SE	US Central	US N. Plains	US West	Canada	Australia	Africa	Europe	Pacific Rim	South America	Total Supply	Supply Price
North Appalachia	14.6					3.6						18.1	$1.70
Central/South Appalachia	13.3	3.3							7.5			24.1	1.60
Central U.S. (Ill. Basin)		12.7	2.0									14.7	1.58
Northern Great Plains U.S.			9.0	4.8	5.2							19.0*	0.99
Rockies/West U.S.					6.9					0.7		7.6	1.41
Canada										2.4		2.4	0.94
Australia							6.3					6.3	1.56
South Africa								10.6				10.6	1.19
Europe (Hard coal)									35.2			35.2	1.95
Europe (Lignite)									5.3			5.3	1.92
South America									0.5		3.0	3.5	1.63
Total demand	27.9	16.0	11.1	4.8	12.1	3.6	6.3	10.6	48.5	3.1	3.0	147.2	
Demand price	$1.89	1.82	1.73	1.49	1.61	1.99	1.86	1.33	2.33	2.14	1.88		

Note: Units: Trade flows in quads ($10^{**}15$ Btu), Prices in 1981 U.S. dollars per million Btu, Type of coal: steam.

Table 9-3
Coal Trade Flows and Prices, 1985–1989, Real-World Baseline Scenario

To: From:	US NE	US SE	US Central	US N. Plains	US West	Canada	Australia	Africa	Europe	Pacific Rim	South America	Total Supply	Supply Price
North Appalachia	20.1					0.6						20.7*	$1.88
Central/South Appalachia	13.7								11.2			24.9*	1.78
Central U.S. (Ill. Basin)		21.1				0.7						21.8	1.69
Northern Great Plains U.S.			16.3	6.5	11.4							34.2	0.96
Rockies/West U.S.					7.0					3.3		10.3	1.39
Canada										3.9		3.9	0.92
Australia							9.8					9.8	1.58
South Africa						3.9		14.2				18.1	1.17
Europe (Hard coal)									37.1			37.1	2.13
Europe (Lignite)									7.5			7.5	2.10
South America									2.6		4.7	7.2*	1.81
Total demand	33.8	21.1	16.3	6.5	18.4	5.2	9.8	14.2	58.4	7.1	4.7	195.6	
Demand price	$2.07	1.93	1.71	1.47	1.59	2.17	1.88	1.31	2.51	2.12	2.06		

Note: Units: Trade flows in quads (10**15 Btu), Prices in 1981 U.S. dollars per million Btu, Type of coal: steam.

Table 9-4
Coal Trade Flows and Prices, 1990–1994, Real-World Baseline Scenario

To: From:	US NE	US SE	US Central	US N. Plains	US West	Canada	Australia	Africa	Europe	Pacific Rim	South America	Total Supply	Supply Price
North Appalachia	21.8											21.8*	$1.98
Central/South Appalachia		14.4							13.8			28.2*	1.88
Central U.S. (Ill. Basin)	4.9	26.8										31.8	1.78
Northern Great Plains U.S.			23.3	8.7	21.4	0.6						53.9*	1.03
Rockies/West U.S.					9.8					8.9		18.6	1.46
Canada										7.3		7.3	0.99
Australia							13.4			0.5		13.9	1.52
South Africa						7.6		16.8	3.8			28.2	1.25
Europe (Hard coal)									38.3			38.3	2.23
Europe (Lignite)									9.3			9.3	2.20
South America									3.2		6.4	9.7*	1.91
Total demand	41.1	26.8	23.3	8.7	31.2	8.2	13.4	16.8	68.5	16.7	6.4	261.0	
Demand price	$2.17	2.02	1.78	1.54	1.66	2.25	1.82	1.39	2.61	2.19	2.16		

Note: Units: Trade flows in quads (10**15 Btu), Prices in 1981 U.S. dollars per million Btu, Type of coal: steam.

Table 9-5
Coal Trade Flows and Prices, 1995–1999, Real-World Baseline Scenario

To: From:	US NE	US SE	US Central	US N. Plains	US West	Canada	Australia	Africa	Europe	Pacific Rim	South America	Total Supply	Supply Price
North Appalachia	23.4											23.4*	$2.09
Central/South Appalachia	17.3								15.4			32.7*	1.99
Central U.S. (Ill. Basin)	10.3	34.6										44.9*	1.89
Northern Great Plains U.S.			30.0	11.2	30.5	7.1						78.8*	1.14
Rockies/West U.S.					13.9					15.9		29.8*	1.57
Canada										11.6		11.6	1.10
Australia							19.0			2.8		21.8	1.63
South Africa						3.8		20.6	14.1			38.5*	1.36
Europe (Hard coal)									40.2			40.2	2.34
Europe (Lignite)									11.7			11.7	2.31
South America									3.1		8.8	11.9*	2.02
Total demand	50.9	34.6	30.0	11.2	44.4	10.9	19.0	20.6	84.5	30.3	8.8	345.3	
Demand price	$2.28	2.13	1.89	1.65	1.77	2.36	1.93	1.50	2.72	2.30	2.27		

Note: Units: Trade flows in quads ($10^{**}15$ Btu), Prices in 1981 U.S. dollars per million Btu, Type of coal: steam.

Table 9-6
Coal Trade Flows and Prices, 2000–2004, Real-World Baseline Scenario

To: From:	US NE	US SE	US Central	US N. Plains	US West	Canada	Australia	Africa	Europe	Pacific Rim	South America	Total Supply	Supply Price
North Appalachia	25.5											25.5*	$3.54
Central/South Appalachia	24.5								14.2			38.7*	3.44
Central U.S. (Ill. Basin)	13.8	46.0										59.7*	3.34
Northern Great Plains U.S.			40.4	15.3	43.3	14.3						113.2*	2.57
Rockies/West U.S.					15.9				6.7	21.5		44.1*	3.00
Canada										20.0		20.0*	2.53
Australia							26.0			9.7		37.7*	3.06
South Africa								25.0	20.5			45.5*	2.81
Europe (Hard coal)									42.6			42.6	3.79
Europe (Lignite)									17.6			17.6*	3.76
South America									3.7		11.5	15.1*	3.47
Total demand	63.7	46.0	40.4	15.3	59.2	14.3	26.0	25.0	105.3	51.2	11.5	457.7	
Demand price	$3.73	3.58	3.32	3.08	3.20	3.79	3.36	2.95	4.18	3.74	3.72		

Note: Units: Trade flows in quads ($10^{**}15$ Btu), Prices in 1981 U.S. dollars per million Btu, Type of coal: steam.

the Central Appalachian region to Europe, 14.2 quads, and from Australia to Europe, about 10 quads. The U.S. Rockies region should also ship a small quantity of coal to Europe.

Many of these predicted steam coal trade flows do in fact appear to be beginning. New supply contracts are being reported for southeastern U.S. mines to supply Europe, for U.S. Central Basin mines to supply the Tennessee-Carolinas-Georgia region, for Northern Great Plains coal to supply the middle part of the United States, and for U.S. Rockies coal (especially from Utah) to be shipped to the Pacific Rim. Other routes for which contracts are being signed include South African steam coal to Europe, western Canadian coal to the Pacific Rim, and Australian steam coal to the newly industrialized Asian countries. Initial contracts for Colombian El Cerrejon coal have been signed with the Spanish national electric utility. Again, the model predicts essentially all of these flows.

About the only trade flow predicted by the model that does not appear to be occurring yet is the small South Africa to Canada flow. This flow could be very reasonable, especially if it were to supply electric utilities in the Canadian Atlantic provinces, which are rapidly switching from oil to coal.

Analyzing the Impact of Potential U.S. Coal Policies

This section seeks to analyze the impact of potential U.S. coal policies over the twenty-five-year horizon both qualitatively and quantitatively through the development of alternate scenarios. Three main types of coal policies are discussed:

Those designed to influence the demand for coal.

Those that aim to affect coal supply (either cost competitiveness or production capacity).

Those designed to influence coal transportation economics.

In addition, this section examines the potential impact of some quasi-policy-determined factors—for example, an appreciation of the U.S. dollar.

Table 9–7 summarizes the results of the baseline simulations and four alternative simulations. In presenting U.S. shares of the total world export market for steam coal for the 1990–1994 period—the middle period of the five time blocks simulated—the table suggests that the competitiveness of U.S. exports is insensitive to policy factors such as demand-stimulating policies or supply-enhancing policies. A major exception is policies affecting transportation cost. In the less-competitive United States scenario, in which U.S. exports were assumed to be shipped in smaller ships than competitors'

Table 9–7
Steam Coal Export Market Shares: Real-World Baseline, Less Competitive United States, Polish Cutback, Higher Synfuels, and Severance Tax Cap Scenarios, 1990–1994 Period
(*Percentage of world exports*)

	Real World Baseline	Less Competitive U.S.	High Synfuels	Polish Cutback	Severance Tax Cap
United States	51.0	33.9	43.9	45.8	51.0
Canada	16.0	19.3	16.7	15.3	16.0
Australia	1.1	5.0	1.0	0.6	1.1
South Africa	24.9	34.7	31.6	32.0	24.9
Latin America	7.0	7.1	7.1	6.5	7.0

Note: Assumes Europe subsidizes coal production and imposes buy-domestic policies.

coal, the U.S. market share dropped dramatically—from 51.0 percent to 33.9 percent in the 1990–1994 period. In quantity terms, for example, this would represent a drop of roughly 8 quads a year in U.S. coal exports.

Demand Policies

U.S. demand for coal is largely determined by economic factors, not policy factors.[3] Coal demand is mainly a function of the rate of economic growth and the rate of electricity demand growth—two factors that are outside the direct purview of U.S. policymakers. Within the limits set by these two parameters, coal demand, especially for electricity production, is potentially affected by policies designed to steer utilities toward or away from certain types of generating capacity. However, analysis suggests that U.S. utilities make decisions based mainly on economic variables. Oil-fired power is economically unattractive, policy considerations aside, for example, so government exhortations not to burn oil are essentially moot. In the industrial sector, the story is basically the same. Demand is largely a function of economics and new technological developments, especially fluidized bed combustion (FBC) technology, and not of policy variables. Although the government has supported some research in such areas as fluidized bed combustion and coal-water mixtures, its overall impact on industrial coal demand cannot be considered significant.

The main possible exception to these arguments about the importance of U.S. coal demand policies is the area of synthetic fuels (synfuels). Even if, as is likely, only a fraction of the $88 billion Synthetic Fuels Corporation becomes reality, this program could have an important impact on U.S. coal demand. The baseline demand projections assume rather low synfuel demand levels, with the first demands appearing in the 1985–1989 period. These figures were deemed to be consistent with the present situation of depressed oil prices and plentiful oil supply. This could change, however, and U.S. policy could support a much stronger synfuel program.

In order to assess the impact of such a move on world coal markets, a high U.S. synfuels scenario was developed with the underlying assumption that U.S. steam coal synfuel demand would be twice as high as in the baseline case, starting with the 1990–1994 period. This scenario shows higher coal prices, both in the United States and in the rest of the world, and slightly decreased U.S. exports. This last fact is expected because more U.S. coal must flow to the Northern Great Plains and U.S. West regions to satisfy synfuel demands. Decreased U.S. exports to the Pacific Rim are offset by increased shipments from Canada and Australia, and slightly decreased exports to Europe are replaced by more shipments from South Africa. In addition, Europe satisfies a little more of its demand with its extremely inefficient and expensive domestic production. Still, the magnitudes of these decreases are not very great. In fact, the main conclusion that could be reached is that, given sufficient lead time (and appropriate policy signals), U.S. suppliers could be expected to gear up to higher production levels and greatly mitigate the effects of such a program on aggregate U.S. exports.

Another point about U.S. coal demand policy concerns environmental control policy. This study recognizes that it would be theoretically possible for policymakers to have a major impact on U.S. coal demand by either greatly reducing regulations like the Alternate New Source Performance Standards, or by greatly strengthening them. However, both alternatives now seem to be extremely unlikely. Even the conservative Reagan administration has been unable to roll environmental regulations back to any substantial extent. On the other hand, our modeling work here explicitly assumes that all new coal plants will use washed coal and will abide by the stringent Alternate New Source Performance Standards.

Supply Policies

Other U.S. coal policies could try to make U.S. coals more price-competitive or could try to expand U.S. productive capacity. According to the model's supply structure, supply price is a function of three forces: economic factors, technical factors, and government policy factors. There are seven direct government policy cost components: black lung taxes, black lung exposure insurance premiums, abandoned mine reclamation fees, severance taxes, federal royalties, reclamation fees, and licensing fees. In this study's process-analysis approach, these government policy costs are recognized on a per million Btu basis and can easily be modified for investigating alternative scenarios. Once again, however, U.S. policies in this area are very constrained by institutional forces. For social and political reasons, for example, it seems extremely unlikely that substantial cuts in such categories as black lung taxes or reclamation fees could be achieved. Mine owners today accept these charges as a cost of doing business and no longer seriously lobby to have them changed. Federal royalties are due only on coals mined on federal lands and are only in the 8–12 percent range anyway. A complete phasing out of such royalties is quite unlikely and in any case would have only a small impact on aggregate U.S. cost competitiveness. Likewise, licensing fees at only about 14¢ per ton have little effect on U.S. coal supply prices.

One significant cost element that could reasonably be changed by government policy is severance taxes. These are set by individual state governments and range all the way up to 17 percent of selling price in Wyoming and 30 percent in Montana. Emphasizing the policy nature of the tax, legislation is currently pending in the U.S. Congress to establish a federal severance tax cap of 12 percent. For this reason, a 12 percent cap scenario was developed and simulated. In virtually all scenarios, however, the Northern Great Plains supply region (the only region with states whose severance taxes exceed 12 percent), is a very efficient supply region, even with the taxes, and is generally the first domestic region the trade-flow model orders to produce at full capacity. This means that production from the region cannot be pushed harder through such a cap because the region should optimally produce at capacity anyway. Therefore, the cap was shown to have virtually no effect on optimal regional production levels or trade flows. Interestingly, this suggests that high severance taxes might be a very rational revenue policy for the state governments of Wyoming and Montana.

In no scenario does the trade-flow model call for Northern Great Plains coal to be exported outside the United States. This includes the severance cap scenario. In all cases, the combination of high transport costs for the low-heat-content coal and the existence of closer domestic demand centers is sufficient to insure that Northern Great Plains coal goes no further than the central U.S. demand regions.

Another possible price-competitiveness issue for U.S. policymakers might be making better coal reserves available to mine operators through more favorable coal deposit leasing programs. This is not really an issue in this study, however, because the supply modeling explicitly assumes that the best possible reserves are always available for mining. Generally speaking, this seems to be a realistic assumption, especially in light of the U.S. government's recent generous leasing policies. In fact, in recent leasing rounds, the government has had difficulty attracting bidders for some very attractive coal deposits in Montana and Wyoming. In such a context, it is not appropriate to think of U.S. policy as advancing supply competitiveness further.

Transportation Policies

A third main focus for U.S. coal policies is transportation infrastructure and shipping cost issues. On the domestic front, the main transportation modes are railroad, barge, and potentially slurry pipeline. All are influenced to a rather high degree by U.S. government policy—railroads through Interstate Commerce Commission (ICC) regulation; barges through waterway construction programs (for example, Tennessee-Tombigbee) and ICC regulation; and slurry lines, potentially through the federal right of eminent domain. The most interesting potential government policy change over the forecast period would be a federal right of eminent domain for slurry pipelines. Currently there is one operating slurry line in the United States, and one pipeline is nearly in the construction phase—a line from Gillette, Wyoming, to Little Rock, Arkansas. Others—from the Powder River Basin to Minneapolis and Chicago, for example—would probably be built were eminent domain to be granted to pipeline companies.

Analysis with a slurry pipeline scenario, which assumes lines running from the Northern Great Plains supply region to the Central U.S. and Northern Great Plains demand regions (one large line to each), suggests that the overall impact of slurry pipelines would be insignificant compared to the baseline estimate. Interregional trade flows both inside and outside the United States and prices are essentially unaffected. There are two reasons for this. First, slurry pipelines are not expected to be significantly cheaper than the unit trains they would replace. Typically, costs are projected to be only 10 or 20 percent lower than unit rail costs. Second, a slurry pipeline will naturally move coal on only one trade route. This means that slurry routes would be determined by careful economic analysis, like the efficiency analysis in this study, and would be built only along expected trade-flow routes anyway.[4]

Slurry pipelines from the Powder River Basin are not expected to have any effect on U.S. coal exports. In addition to the low-heat-content characteristics of coals from this area, slurries impose a type of technical constraint that works against exports. The powderized coal-water mixtures can be used directly by electric utilities after dewatering, but are not conveniently stored and loaded on ships because the coal is ground too finely. Thus slurries have a comparative advantage in immediate and direct domestic uses rather than for export.

The other main transportation topic is government support of oceanic shipping infrastructure, from the aggregate quantity of export capacity, to questions of harbor dredging, wharf or embankment construction, and loading pier length and capacity expansion. Conceptually, there are three main policy factors that affect U.S. exporting costs:

1. Those that affect harbor costs directly—for example, the burden the government transfers to coal shippers for habor dredging, breakwater construction, and so on.
2. Those that have to do with aggregate annual U.S. export capacity, which affect demurrage costs or other costs of not having adequate overall capacity.
3. Those that affect the maximum ship sizes that U.S. ports can accommodate, thereby affecting oceanic shipping costs.

The first issue—harbor costs—has been the subject of much recent debate because the Reagan administration has decided to shift U.S. policy to try to make shippers pay for the actual cost of services they have been receiving from the U.S. Army Corps of Engineers and other government agencies. In fact, however, harbor fees are typically a small component o total shipping costs—only about 70¢ per ton according to the IEA (1978) out of a $40 or $50 delivered ton of coal. As a result, even a policy shift calling for their doubling would have little overall effect.

The second issue, aggregate U.S. export pier capacity, has also been discussed at length. In 1980 and early 1981, many looked at the long lines of ships backed up in the Hampton Roads harbor, and, extrapolating into the future, claimed that high demurrage costs due to insufficient U.S. port capacity would leave the United States out of the future coal export boom. Many called for the U.S. government to step in to help. Over the past two years or so, however, virtually dozens of capitalists have announced plans to build new coal export piers and terminals and to enlarge existing ones, in cities on the east coast from Wilmington to Charleston and Savannah, on the Gulf Coast from Mobile to Galveston, and on the west coast from San Diego to Seattle. The planned expansions are so great that most recent analysis suggests that if most of the projects are actually built, the United States will have far too *much* export pier capacity. In fact, by 1982, in large part because of innovative ship arrival-loading scheduling contracts and, of course, the world recession, waiting lines at the main U.S. ports had virtually disappeared. For these reasons, this study assumes that U.S. export capacity, built by private initiative, will not present an obstacle to U.S. exports over the twenty-five-year horizon. This policy consideration is assumed moot.

It is the third issue in oceanic shipping—maximum future U.S. ship size accommodation—that is most uncertain at this time. In addition, of all three issues, ship size will probably have the greatest impact on total coal transport costs. According to ICF (1980a), for example, shipping from the U.S. Gulf Coast to Europe in 110,000 dead weight ton ships instead of 60,000 ton ships could save almost $5 per ton, or almost one-third of the shipping cost. For these reasons, alternative ship-size assumptions were chosen in developing the alternative scenario dealing with U.S. transportation policy. This scenario asks what happens if U.S. ports are not able to accommodate larger ships, while ports in Australia, South Africa and Latin America are able to. Actually this scenario goes one step further and combines this assumption with an assumption of a 10 percent long-term appreciation of the U.S. dollar. Together they create a less competitive U.S. scenario.

Most of the impact on the steam coal markets from this scenario comes in the early periods, 1985–1989 and 1990–1994. In the 1985–1989 period, for example, aggregate U.S. production falls by about 10 percent, and U.S. exports drop by a drastic 56 percent from the baseline estimate. In fact, U.S. exports to Europe disappear completely and are replaced by shipments from South Africa. Exports from the U.S. Rockies region to the Pacific Rim are slashed in half and are replaced by Canadian shipments. By the last two forecast periods, there are much smaller differences from the baseline projection. This is because of the tighter world coal markets expected by the late 1990s, which should be mainly the result of fast-growing world demand. As the world scrambles for coal in the 2000–2004 period, for example, chief competitors of the United States—Australia, Canada, and South Africa—will be unable to satisfy European and Pacific Rim demand, even at full capacity. Therefore, U.S. exports, even delivered in expensive small ships and bought with expensive U.S. dollars, should find ready markets. Such U.S. coal would still be much cheaper than underground—mined European coal in European markets.

Table 9–8 summarizes the trade effects of this higher U.S. transportation cost scenario for the middle forecast period, 1990–1994. Output drops in three of the five U.S. production regions—the Central region, the Northern Great Plains region, and the Rockies West region—but increases for competing suppliers. Canada's production jumps 21 percent, Australia's is up 13 percent, and South Africa's increases 16 percent. The biggest coal trade-flow shift is that South Africa replaces the Central Appalachian region as the primary supplier to Europe. Canada and Australia both pick up significant market share in the Pacific Rim, at the expense of the U.S. West region. Canadian exports to the region jump up 21 percent, and Australian exports jump 360 percent; U.S. West exports fall 37 percent in the 1990–1994 period, relative to the baseline projection. The price effects are completely as expected. U.S. domestic prices increase marginally, but the rest of the world faces roughly 5 percent higher delivered prices because of the higher U.S. oceanic shipping costs. Foreign suppliers also exact somewhat higher producer prices—about 5 percent higher—because their coals face relatively more demand as a result of the diminished competitiveness of U.S. coal.

Other Scenarios

Over a twenty-five-year forecast horizon a number of production-constraint scenarios could be envisioned. In view of the economic and political difficulties in Europe's major supply country, Poland, a Polish cutback scenario was developed. This scenario simulates the effects on world markets if Polish production were 15 percent lower than in the baseline projection, starting in 1985. The cutback is assumed to strike both lignite and hard coal production. One complicating factor is any such scenario is how production capacity in other supply regions will respond to such news. In this scenario, no production-capacity response is assumed until the 2000–2004 period. The Polish cutback is assumed to be a surprise; and, given the long lags associated with opening up new mines, a capacity response probably could not result until the 1995–1999 period at the earliest, anyway. For the 2000–2004 period, a total world coal capacity factor equal to the baseline capacity factor is

Table 9-8
Coal Trade Flows and Prices, 1990–1994, Higher U.S. Transport Costs Scenario

To: From:	US NE	US SE	US Central	US N. Plains	US West	Canada	Australia	Africa	Europe	Pacific Rim	South America	Total Supply	Supply Price
North Appalachia	14.7					7.1						21.8*	$1.99
Central/South Appalachia	26.4								1.8			28.2*	1.89
Central U.S. (Ill. Basin)		26.8										26.8	1.82
Northern Great Plains U.S.			23.3	8.7	20.3	1.0						53.3	1.06
Rockies/West U.S.					10.9					5.6		16.5	1.49
Canada										8.8		8.8*	1.14
Australia							13.4			2.3		15.7*	1.63
South Africa								16.8	15.8			32.6*	1.45
Europe (Hard coal)									38.3			38.3	2.24
Europe (Lignite)									9.3			9.3	2.21
South America									3.2		6.4	9.7*	2.01
Total demand	41.1	26.8	23.3	8.7	31.2	8.1	16.8	68.5	16.7	6.4	261.0		
Demand price	$2.18	2.06	1.81	1.57	1.69	2.28	1.93	1.59	2.62	2.22	2.26		

Note: Units: Trade flows in quads (10**15 Btu), Prices in 1981 U.S. dollars per million Btu, Type of coal: steam.

assumed, with regional capacity increases above the baseline projection weighted by baseline 2000–2004 over 1995–1999 capacity increases.

The results of the simulation show that South African steam coal shipments to Europe mainly make up for the Polish shortfall. Overall, South African production would increase by about 16 percent over the baseline level. U.S. production levels and exports would increase, but only marginally—up by less than 1 percent in most periods, and up by less than 3 percent in the 2000–2004 period. Table 9–9 summarizes the results of the Polish cutback scenario for the 1990–1994 period. South Africa's production and export increases, relative to the baseline estimate, are apparent. World coal prices actually decrease slightly with the Polish cutback, because more world production occurs in lower-cost supply regions like the United States and South Africa, and less in the marginal supply region, Europe. That is, Europe is not producing quite as far out on its upward-sloping supply curve.

Other hypothetical scenarios that could be simulated can be broken down into three main categories: demand side, supply side, and trade-flow overrides. On the demand side, alternative economic growth rate assumptions could be used. The elasticities developed by Wescott (1983), would be used to produce revised demand projections, and these would be directly substituted into the trade-flow model. Generally speaking, electric sector coal demand to GDP elasticities are significantly greater than one, as are overall steam coal demand to GDP elasticities. This means the trade-flow model is quite sensitive to economic-growth assumptions. This is especially true when GDP growth assumptions are varied for regions shifting rapidly to coal—for example, the Pacific Rim region. It is even more true when such regions are heavily dependent on coal imports.

Another demand-side scenario could be a high-nuclear case. It is highly unlikely that there will be many changes from the baseline projection before the early 1990s, because of ten-year nuclear plant construction lags. Thereafter, however, certain countries conceivably could rejuvenate their nuclear programs. Assuming that nuclear power and coal are effectively the only choices today for large new operating capacity, and using the fact that a typical 1.2 GW nuclear plant would substitute for approximately 2.5 MTCE of coal per year, revised electric sector coal demands could be developed. Again, these revised projections would be substituted directly into the trade-flow model.

The trade-flow model would respond rather significantly to a major new nuclear building program. The low nuclear capacity additions presumed in the baseline case, however, are consistent with current mainstream thinking, since recent economic analysis has shown that in most cases coal-fired electric plants should be cheaper than nuclear plants when total costs per kilowatt-hour are compared. For this reason, a high-nuclear scenario might more logically be driven by an assumption that significant coal-based sulfur-

Table 9-9
Coal Trade Flows and Prices, 1990–1994, Polish Production Setback Scenario

To: From:	US NE	US SE	US Central	US N. Plains	US West	Canada	Australia	Africa	Europe	Pacific Rim	South America	Total Supply	Supply Price
North Appalachia	14.2					7.7						21.9*	$1.95
Central/South Appalachia		26.9							1.2			28.1*	1.85
Central U.S. (Ill. Basin)		26.8							4.6			31.4	1.77
Northern Great Plains U.S.			23.3	8.7	21.5	0.5						54.0*	1.02
Rockies/West U.S.					9.7					8.7		18.4	1.45
Canada										7.6		7.6	1.02
Australia							13.4			0.3		13.7	1.51
South Africa								16.8	15.8			32.6*	1.34
Europe (Hard coal)									35.0			35.0	2.13
Europe (Lignite)									8.6			8.6	2.10
South America									3.2		6.4	9.6*	1.90
Total demand	41.1	26.8	23.3	8.7	31.2	8.2	13.4	16.8	68.5	16.7	6.4	261.0	
Demand price	$2.13	2.01	1.77	1.53	1.65	2.24	1.81	1.48	2.51	2.10	2.15		

Note: Units: Trade flows in quads (10*15 Btu), Prices in 1981 U.S. dollars per million Btu, Type of coal: steam.

dioxide pollution by the 1990s forces the world to look for alternatives to coal.

A lower world oil price scenario could also be implemented on the demand side. Two coal demand sectors—electric utilities and synthetic fuels—would be affected the most by such an assumption. As far as electricity generation is concerned, cost analysis performed for U.S. utilities by Wescott (1983) showed that unless oil prices were to drop to the $12–$16 per barrel range (in 1982 dollars), new coal plants would be preferred by rational managers. This analysis included coal beneficiation costs and flue gas desulfurization costs. In the long run, therefore, no new oil-fired electric units will probably be built unless oil prices drop drastically. If one did want to assume $14 per barrel oil, one could assume that new oil units would be built and would substitute for coal capacity. Since $14 is roughly the U.S. utility oil-coal breakpoint, one could assume that half of all new plants would be coal-fired and half oil-fired at that price (with nuclear and hydro contributions continuing to be exogenous). For Europe and Japan the breakpoint for utilities is roughly $18 per barrel of oil. In addition, in the short to intermediate run, coal consumption in existing burners would be affected by $14 ($18 in Europe) oil. All oil-to-coal conversion plans would be scrapped, and accelerated oil retirement plans would be shelved. Also, because coal burners usually can be converted to oil fairly easily, it is probably reasonable to assume that some coal burners would be converted to oil. Most would not switch, however, because of the predominance of twenty-year coal supply contracts in the utility industry.

Synthetic fuel demands would be sensitive to much smaller changes in the oil price assumption. In fact, an assumption of $28 per barrel oil (in 1982 dollars) would probably mean the end of most synthetic fuel coal demands if it were projected into the future with no real increase. South Africa would probably continue its very significant SASOL program for political reasons, however, and there might be a few other exceptions. The main point, however, is that if one wanted a long-run simulation with an only slightly lower oil price assumption than the $34 per barrel price (in 1982 dollars) assumed for the baseline case (with 1 percent per year real increase), then a scenario that dropped most synfuel demands (except South Africa's) would be very reasonable. Note that by the later time periods, when baseline synfuel demands represent a significant portion of some regions' total steam coal demands, the effects on world production, prices, and trade flows would be very significant. The long-run effects of a 12 percent lower oil price assumption (say, $34 to $30) on the electric sector would be quite small.

On the supply side, it would be easy to envision pro-export policies in Canada, Australia, or South Africa. As with the United States, however, the underlying upward slopes of the supply curves are determined by technical and economic factors generally considered to be beyond the reach of policymakers. These include such factors as average coal seam characteristics, coal sulfur content, relative wage levels, and capital costs. Government policies such as lower export levies, royalties, or reclamation fees could easily be implemented in the model, however, by changing the intercept terms of the supply curves. The end result would be lower supply prices.

Production-capacity estimates could also be revised. A late 1970s coal reserve reestimation in South Africa, which roughly doubled the official recoverable reserves estimate, led policymakers to increase production quotas significantly, for example. One could assume another reestimation in the late 1980s, with a 30 percent increase in production constraints by the late 1990s, for instance. Among other possibilities, one could assume and implement: higher European production subsidies; a phase-out of domestic production by minor country suppliers such as Japan or Spain; significantly greater (or cheaper) Colombian El Cerrejon region production; or a political revolution in South Africa in 1985, with production only at 1980 levels thereafter.

A final category of alternative scenarios could be called trade-flow override simulations. These types of situations could arise when—for political, social, or even secondary economic reasons—a country or region might decide to ignore efficient market price signals and open up an inefficient trade flow. Historical supplier relationships and importer diversification schemes would fall into this category. These types of assumptions could all be inserted into the trade-flow model without too much difficulty. Required price discounts or acceptable premiums would be integrated into the model by modifying the transportation cost assumptions on particular trade routes. Mandatory trade flows (set at either zero or a fraction of some variable) could be imposed directly as additional constraints on the model.

Conclusions

U.S. coal will play an extremely important role in world coal markets over the next twenty-five years, mainly because the United States is the only supplier country not expected to face significant production constraints. Western surface-mined U.S. coals can be produced as cheaply and efficiently as coal anywhere; logistically, however, the coal is poorly situated. It requires expensive rail shipping to get to major demand centers or even export ports. Eastern U.S. coal, on the other hand, is much more expensive to mine because underground techniques are required and the labor force is heavily unionized and expensive. However, the coal is located near major demand centers and export ports. Overall, this analysis suggests that policymakers in the United States have relatively little scope for influencing future coal markets. The biggest potential effect would occur if European policymakers would agree to phase out production subsidies and buy-domestic policies, and allow more efficient world producers to fill the production gap. This study shows that world welfare could be significantly improved by such a shift. Otherwise, policy levers have relatively small effects. This is because coal markets are demand driven, and coal demand is mainly a function of the rate of economic growth and the rate of growth of electricity demand—two factors considered to be outside the direct purview of government policymakers.

There is some scope on the demand side for governments to better coordinate energy policies and programs to help the coal industry get over some of its planning uncertainties. International uncertainty surrounding nuclear energy, for example, is hurting the coal industry. Government synfuel programs, tentative at best, have led to several false starts. Realistic programs by policymakers, based on long-run oil price assumptions, could be very useful to the coal industry. Industrial demand will be mainly a function of fluidized bed combustion economics. This technology, developed largely with public-sector support, now exists; its success will depend mainly on capital cost and reliability considerations.

The analysis showed that government policymakers can affect the supply side, at least in theory. As far as price is concerned, the vast bulk of production cost results from basic economic and technical factors—wages and salaries, the cost of materials and power, a fair return on capital, taxes, and so forth. Direct government-policy-related costs however—reclamation fees, licensing fees, black lung taxes and insurance, and severance taxes—are significant. In fact, they account for up to 40 percent of production cost in the U.S. Northern Great Plains region—compared to roughly 15–21 percent in most U.S. regions and Canada, less than 10 percent in Australia, and less than 5 percent in South Africa. The analysis suggested, however, that most of these government-related costs were more or less institutionalized and were not likely to be changed dramatically. In the United States, for example, a significant cutback in black lung taxes or reclamation fees is regarded as politically infeasible. Licensing fees and most royalties are shown to be not very significant.

Finally, policymakers can influence transportation costs. On the inland front, it was assumed that rail and barge shipping costs were factors policymakers could not directly influence. Slurry pipelines were shown to have surprisingly small effect on world coal trade. On the oceanic shipping front, government policies could affect harbor costs, aggregate national export capacity, and the maximum ship sizes that ports accommodate. Alternative trade-flow scenarios were run assuming that Canada, Australia, and South Africa expanded berth sizes and dredged ports in order to accommodate large ships, while the United States did not. These simulations showed that the competitiveness of U.S. coal exports could be seriously reduced by the failure of the United States to respond with similar measures.

Notes

1. Western U.S. coal is surface mined as efficiently and cheaply as anywhere in the world, but it is expensive to ship it to major demand centers. Eastern U.S. coal, though nearer major demand centers, is fairly expensive to produce because of a combination of technical factors and high labor costs. European deep-mined coal, however, is much more expensive to produce than either type of U.S. coal.

2. The basic sources of coal reserve data were ICF (1980a) for the United States and ICF (1980b) for South Africa, Australia, and Canada. European data came from the U.S. Department of Energy (1978).

3. Except, of course, government regulations limiting the use of alternative fuels, natural gas or atomic energy, or policies limiting use of coal for environmental reasons.

4. In principle, though perhaps not in practice, these can be different from existing routes.

10
Empirical Evaluation of Industrial Policy: An Appraisal

F. Gerard Adams

Establishing a sound quantitative basis for considering policy alternatives is a problem, particularly with respect to industrial policy. In contrast to macroeconomic policy, which has a fairly clear theoretical basis and offers an extensive record of experience, in today's United States an industrial policy would represent almost a new policy frontier. In a clear break with the postwar policy tradition, the focus of concern would be with industrial structure rather than with aggregate output. Which industries, if any, should have priority? How can new, frequently technologically advanced, industries be encouraged? How can old industries be rejuvenated or phased out? To be sure, not all industrial policies would be new or narrowly industry-specific: The Kennedy tax cut policies of the 1960s or the recent changes in depreciation tax lives can be seen as a form of industrial policy broadly favoring investment. The concern of industrial policy, however, is clearly more disaggregated and sectoral than has been customary in U.S. policy in recent years.

Moreover, most industrial-policy proposals call for supplementing or overriding the free market. As noted in chapters 1 and 3, even if these interventions are non-industry-specific—that is, if they are available to all comers on an equal basis—they are likely to benefit some sectors more than others. In fact, however, many industrial-policy initiatives call for targeted policies directly seeking to advance certain industrial sectors, certain firms, or certain types of technology. Such policies may be ad hoc—as they have frequently been in the past—or part of a coherent development plan or vision, as in Japan. In any case, they introduce new relationships between business and government. They may call for a broad range of new policy measures:

Tax incentives.

Tariffs and import quotas.

Loan guarantees or government contracts.

Preferential financing.

Administrative guidance.

Changes in antitrust regulations.

Research and development financing.

Accelerated depreciation.

Public enterprises.

These measures may need to be administered by new institutions, which may include:[1]

Information-gathering or coordinating agencies.

New financial institutions.

New forms of public or private enterprise.

Evaluating industrial-policy proposals poses formidable difficulties, but the industrial-policy debate need not (and must not) be simply a matter of conflicting economic philosophies. Like the physician who consults with his patient about the merits of various potential treatments, the political economist advises the administrative and legislative branches of government about the probable consequences of alternative policies. However, whereas the physician can find in his medical books countless records of past treatments and controlled experiments, the economist offers advice on the basis of a much slimmer body of evidence. He may consider similar experiences in other countries or in economic history, but the circumstances of such examples seldom fit.[2] He may draw on economic theory, but theory seldom offers information on quantitative impacts. That leaves empirical research and model simulation—with simple or complex systems—as a way to determine the nature and dimensions of the effect of policy. This approach has much to offer toward resolving some, though not all, the points under dispute.

This book is concerned with the quantitative approach to analyzing industrial policies. This chapter summarizes and evaluates what we have learned from empirical models and simulation studies. It ends with a discussion of the remaining gaps and their implications for needed research.

First, it is useful to consider some general guidelines.

Industrial policy, even if industry-specific, is ultimately concerned with the well-being of the entire economy. This statement reflects a broad judgment about the role of economic policy—that it is intended to benefit the society rather than certain industries, sectors, regions, or social groups. Once one accepts such a premise, it goes almost without saying that looking at particular industries is not enough. Industrial-policy proposals must be evaluated in a macroeconomic context. Suppose, for example, that there are problems in the steel industry. Industrial-policy directives may be aimed toward protecting the steel industry, toward providing the means for modernizing or restructuring it, and/or toward compensating or retraining its laid-off workers. In the end, however, such a policy should not be evaluated only in terms of whether the steel industry has become profitable or whether its workers are better off. The evaluation must take into account national as well as sectoral impacts, although benefits may well be greater for some sectors than for others and may well involve transfers between various parts of the economy.

Although we emphasize the macroeconomic implications, industrial policy cannot be appraised adequately without recognizing its implications for particular industries and for industrial structure. The concern is with the performance of various *critical* industries and with the composition of production. There is an underlying assumption that some forms of industrial structure are better, in some sense, than others.

Quantitative studies of industrial policy thus call for both macro and sectoral models. The sectoral model should be sufficiently detailed to show the industry's reactions to policy alternatives. For example, it should show the responses of investment to tax incentives and the consequences for productivity, costs, prices, and international competitiveness. The national model, too, should show policy responses (particularly if it is to be used without separate industry models). Preferably it should show the interactions between sectors through input-output relationships or through competition of the same limited resources, for example. In the ideal case the national model is linked directly to sector models or includes an elaborate sectoral breakdown.

Although some of the work in this book uses such a model system, considerable progress can be made with relatively simpler models. Indeed, sometimes there is a trade-off between model size and operational effectiveness. Larger models are not necessarily better models. Given the limited resources of the researcher, there is undoubtedly an optimal mix between model-building effort, simulation studies, and interpretation. In that case, somewhat smaller, more limited models may well represent a more effective research approach than large, highly complex, expensive model systems. This is illustrated by the variety of approaches in this book.

The structural integrity of the model is, however, a crucial consideration. The results can be no better than the model. The purpose is simulation of policy alternatives, rather than forecasting. In simulation applications the structural integrity of the model—its realistic recognition of behavioral relations and structural linkages—is essential. Models are by their very nature simplifications of the real world. The question of their accuracy or realism is thus not one of whether they are an exact replica of reality. Rather, it is a question of whether the model structure adequately describes the principal relevant aspects of the industry and of the economy. Do the behavioral equations measure accurately the behavioral responses and the technical relations of the industry? Are the linkages between the sectors of the economy elaborated and properly specified? Does the model system describe the historical development of the sector and of the economy with accuracy? Does it respond realistically to exogenous shocks? These approaches to model validation have been illustrated in the work described earlier.

It is important to emphasize at this point that industrial-policy applications of models often emphasize properties and behavior that are different from those emphasized in business-cycle models. The central questions of industrial policy are longer-term: the impact of changes in relative factor costs, the effect of increased capital stock, changes in production processes, new technology, improvements in labor productivity, and so on. Although there has been much recent work on some of these questions, they are considerably closer to the frontiers of econometric research than the traditional forecasting and macro policy applications of econometric models. We will consider some of these questions further in the following discussion of outstanding gaps.

Experience with Empirical Studies of Industrial Policy

Despite the long experience with industrial policies abroad—and, to a lesser extent, in the United States—the record shows few formal empirical or econometric studies of industrial policy. There are, of course, many empirical studies of particular structural elements, the studies of the production function,[3] or of particular policy problems, energy policy, for example.[4] There is also a vast body of historical and qualitative evaluations.[5] The uniqueness of the studies reported in this book is that they are specifically addressed to evaluating industrial policy and that they are broadly empirical, covering entire industrial sectors, the national economy, and even the world.

The studies considered in this book fall into two broad classes:

1. Those concerned with the macro economy—that is, those considering industrial policies and industrial structure in a model of the entire economy.
2. Those focused on particular industries and sectors.

We will consider these approaches in turn. First, however, it is appropriate to draw some general conclusions. A great deal can be learned from econometric model simulation of policy alternatives. It appears, first of all, that industrial policies can have significant aggregate impacts. These impacts, however, can differ greatly with respect to amplitude and timing and industrial and regional impact. Not all alternatives have been examined—nor, for that matter, would it be possible to examine all alternatives, since in many respects they are specific to the particular setting to which they are to be applied. But there is clearly a need to examine in detail how specific policy possibilities affect the economy—with what timing, with what magnitude, and where they have their impact. It is also important to recognize the longer-run consequences of policies. We will note later in more detail how the effects of policies sometimes appear to fade away if there are no other adjustments in the economy such as appropriately increased money supply or even demand-side stimulus.

Industrial policies also clearly have important international implications. These can be measured in world model systems or for one country in a separate country model. It is important to take into account the impacts of the so-called international adjustment process as well as the responses of trade policies and industrial policies of other countries. A crucial issue is what happens when a country goes it alone, when it meets foreign industrial policy, or when it goes cooperatively with other countries in the world economic system.

On the industry level, also, it is possible to discern the effect of industrial policies. It is particularly interesting to observe the behavioral reactions of industries not only to the special incentives provided, but also, throughout the entire sector model, with respect to capacity utilization, modernization, pricing, investment, and the like. There are some questions, to be considered in more detail later, about the ability of industry models to capture fully some of the effects of policy measures, particularly those affecting technological change and worker incentives. Unfortunately, industrial modeling is not sufficiently far developed to fully capture some of these effects. The modeling exercise point to the additional important point: that industry effects must be followed through at the macro level in order to measure secondary effects, both positive and negative, that may have important implications for the overall effect of the proposed policy.[6]

Macro Model Simulations

The macro model simulations presented in chapters 2 and 5 of this book represent progressively more disaggregated simulations.

Chapter 2 deals entirely with aggregated macro economies in the world scale of Project LINK. The results of the simulation exercises are clear and can easily be summarized. Investment incentive policies have impact on real economic activity and unemployment at relatively small cost in inflation. The models leave unclarified the question of how much of this impact is attributable to the demand-side effect of the investment stimulus, and how much of it occurs through supply-side improvements in productivity or productive capacity. The implications for increased world trade and for international transmission of the impulses (although that turns out to be relatively small) are also traced out. The interesting result is the somewhat greater impact, particularly on international trade, of the convoy as compared to the locomotive scenario. Apparently there are some benefits to coordinated stimulus policy. Indeed, had the exchange rate and international financial dimensions of the model been more elaborate, the importance of policy coordination might well have been more apparent.

Chapters 3 and 4 are concerned with alternative stimulus policies within a much more detailed macro model of the U.S. economy, including a flexible input-output scheme. This model makes possible examination of the impact of alternative general investment incentives, as well as the examination of the impact of policies that are somewhat sector-specific. Again, the results are fairly clear. Among the policy alternatives considered, investment-tax-credit policies appear to be the most effective per dollar of initial Treasury cost.[7] Ultimately, the effects of the measures increase the revenue stream to the Treasury so that the ex post cost is less than what has initially been computed as revenue loss. Policies also vary significantly with respect to the timing of their effects and, to a lesser extent, with respect to industrial impacts. In all cases, however, it is clear that a nonspecific policy will have diverse industry-specific impacts.

The second dimension, that of specific policies, suggests that if investment tax incentive policies are focused, particularly on high-technology and to a lesser extent on metals-using industries, they will have greater impact than if they are nonspecific and available to all industries. Since the marginal product of investment appears to differ between industries, perhaps this is not a surprising result. Nevertheless, it is clearly one that policymakers may want to take into account. On the other hand, it is not clear that the full potential difference between industry-specific efforts and more general policies is captured in these studies, since there is, in the macro model, little allowance for potential new-technology effects.

Another important dimension of these simulations is the question of whether the effects of industrial policies are durable, at least in the absence of other policy actions. In these simulations, it appears that industrial policy impacts fade away after some time, reflecting perhaps the inability of the demand side of the economy to keep up with the supply side in the absence of demand-side adjustment policy. The result is that improved productivity shows up in the form of somewhat greater unemployment. This is true of all the alternatives; but, of course, the greater the impact on productivity, as in the investment tax credit oriented toward high-technology industries, the greater the adverse effect on unemployment.

The simulations presented in chapter 4 are regional disaggregations of the work shown in chapter 3. The disaggregation is accomplished with a sophisticated regional model that recognizes intraregional demand effects and allows for differences in relative input costs in various regions. As anticipated, the impacts of the policies vary between the regions. It is striking, however, that the differences between the regional effects are considerably greater than the differences between the policies, even between the policies focused on different industries. Some regions are evidently more strongly benefited than others by policy, in the sense of improvements of regional product. Nevertheless, it is also clear that certain types of policies—particularly policies with an industrial focus—tend to be of greater value to specific regions. Much more needs to be done with regional breakdowns and regional modeling, to determine the regional impacts of policies and to evaluate the interactions between industrial and regional policy.[8]

The final macro chapter uses the same disaggregated macro model of the U.S. economy as before, the Wharton Annual and Industry Model, but looks at the problem from a somewhat different dimension. The impact of foreign industrial policies is a concern even of people who do not believe in industrial policy as an appropriate prescription for the U.S. economy. The question, then, is what the effect is of imports into the United States from industries that benefit from foreign export aids. This question is particularly associated with imports into particular industry categories. These simulations measure the effect of introducing substantial additional imports of machinery and transportation equipment to the disadvantage of the output of the corresponding domestic industries. Not surprisingly, the output and employment of the corresponding U.S. industries is reduced, as is the output of industries that feed into them through input-output relations. The greater imports also appear at first glance to be disadvantageous to the U.S. economy at the macro level. There is greater unemployment and a lower level of GNP, with a multiplier effect. The deficit in the trade balance and on current account is greatly increased, though not by quite as much as the assumed increase in imports. These effects continue as long as the extra foreign imports are continued, throughout an eight-year simulation period.

Clearly, however, in the real world this is not the end of the story. We would presume that the international adjustment process would provoke some adjustment in exchange rates—a readjustment of the value of the dollar with respect to other currencies. Tests showed that the balance on current account in current dollars could be brought back to equilibrium within three years through depreciation of the dollar. Imposing the dollar depreciation on the economy, in addition to the initial increase in imports, produces a readjustment of the economy largely back toward its original growth path. Even those industries disadvantaged by foreign imports largely return to their base paths. This is not to say that there is no cost from foreign imports: The dislocation is considerable both in terms of lost industrial output and employment and in terms of the ultimate terms of trade. On the other hand, there is also substantial adjustment—a strong testimonial for the value of free trade with exchange-rate adjustment.

Sector-Level Simulations

Chapters 6 to 9 illustrate the application of industrial policies at the level of specific sectors of the economy. These represent sector-model simulations, which are linked to the national model of the U.S. economy. However, it is important to note that there is no attempt here either to integrate the sectoral model with the national model or to provide a simultaneous or iterative joint solution of a sector and a national model. This means that, given the national solution, the sector model is simulated; but there is no feedback. The feedbacks on the national model, if they had been considered, might somewhat alter the final results. For example, had the simulations on steel been allowed to have an impact in the national model, activity levels in some of the industries that affect the demand for steel might have been different, with consequent results in the steel industry. However, it is not likely that the omitted effects would significantly alter the results obtained.

Since the models are simulated separately, the policy inputs affect only the industries involved (except in the case of some of the transformer industry simulations). This might be visualized as somewhat similar to the impact of industry-specific policies, benefiting only one industry but not others. This would not be an entirely accurate description, however. Industry-specific policies would benefit some industries more than others, an effect on relative competitiveness with respect to other sectors that should be fully recognized in the functions of the model. Even though the policies affect only one industry in these cases, it is not likely that the full sector-specific impact is captured, since the equations typically do not show incentive effects relative to other industries.[9]

The typical approach is one of constructing an industry model and of simulating the policy impacts. In these chapters we show a variety of sectoral models—one highly detailed for the steel industry; another smaller for a smaller industry, transformers. Then we show a somewhat narrower empirical analysis of the production function of the chemicals industry to measure the nature of policy impacts on capital. Finally, we study the impact of policy in a highly detailed programming optimization model of the coal industry. No attempt has been made to standardize these exercises, since they are intended to illustrate some of the broad possibilities of policy studies through industrial modeling.

The steel model presented in chapter 6 falls into a pattern of model building for industrial models. (Adams (1973)) This model can simulate the response of steel production to demands in the domestic economy, the impact of import competition, the determination of production costs, the determination of price, and investment and capital stock. Although alternative processes of production are represented, it is not clear that the choice between production processes and the introduction of new technology is fully represented in this system, a handicap of some importance.

The steel model simulations show significant responses to investment incentives in the industry. Not only does investment increase and capital stock grow relative to the base solution, but other consequences are also largely as predicted. There is improvement in productivity, somewhat lower cost, and improved international competitiveness. These effects take time, however, and the effects are mixed, from the standpoint of social policy, in that higher productivity produces reduced unemployment. It is not within the scope of a sector model to ask whether and where the unemployed workers might be absorbed. Difficulty with the simulation treatment of cash flow in the model system causes some hesitation with respect to a version of the model that bases investment on cash flow rather than on standard Jorgensonian profitability and user cost notions. It is clear, however, that the impact of the cash-flow version is considerably stronger in cases where investment incentives favor the cash flow of the steel industry.

Trade policy—that is, protectionist—simulations also benefit the steel industry. We note that they do improve investment and capital stock but, again, at the cost of some employment. The increase in output is more than offset by the capital-labor substitution after some years. An interesting question, which we have not attempted to consider, is whether purely temporary protectionist policies would pay off in making the industry modern and competitive.

With respect to wage policy, the model shows strikingly different results when wages are reduced depending on whether or not the policy calls for holding prices in check along with wages. If prices as well as wages are constrained, the gain of wage restraint is relatively small, at least insofar as the steel industry rather than the rest of the economy is concerned. Considerably greater gains can be produced for the steel industry if wage policy is independent of price policy (except insofar as the two are linked by the normal behavior of the industry, as shown in the model). In the latter case prices are reduced, but not as much; profits improve; investment increases. Interestingly, the adverse employment effect of the increase in capital is offset by higher domestic production, so that employment is also benefited. With respect to the pollution-control expenditure alternatives, the crucial consideration appears to be whether cutbacks in the mandated investments can be transferred into productive investment. In that case the industry benefits greatly, but, as before, at the cost of some reduction in employment. The effects on the society as a whole and on the environment must also be considered.

Chapter 7 deals with a much smaller model, but also one that focuses very narrowly on the electrical transformer industry. The model is structured similarly to the steel model—recognizing, of course, that most transformers go as investment to the final users, the electrical utilities, rather than as an input into the production of other sectors. It is not necessary to repeat the results here since they are similar in general nature to those obtained in the model of the steel industry.

Chapter 8 deals with an altogether different approach. This is not a complete industry model. Rather, it consists of production function studies intended to measure the impact of alternative specifications of capital stock, and R&D investment on labor productivity. Although the approach is limited and technical, it offers numerous implications for questions that are central to policy and to other dimensions of the industry. Specifically, the model computations show that diversion of investment toward government-mandated pollution controls could have impacts, though not necessarily large ones, on labor productivity. Business tax cuts could, however, go a long way toward improving investment incentives and offsetting the damaging effect of the diversion of capital to pollution-control purposes (no judgment is made on the economywide impact of pollution-control expenditures.) The model also investigates the impact of R&D spending and reaches the conclusion that it makes a substantial contribution to productivity. On the other hand, it must be noted that the description of the chemicals industry provided in an aggregate production function is greatly simplified and the results obtained from these estimations might well be greatly modified if a more realistic production function formulation—perhaps in the form of an engineering optimization model—had been used and if other aspects of the industry's behavior were modeled.

Chapter 9 presents a large-scale maximization model of the world coal industry. The system combines an international trade-flow model, a coal supply model, and an electrical utility sector interfuel substitution model. Supply and demand take a process-analysis model approach. The trade-flow model solves the classical transportation problem by employing a quadratic programming optimization framework. This approach turns out to have great potentials for projecting the future role of U.S. coal under a variety of assumptions in the world market. Specifically in the present context it can be used to examine alternative policies with respect to facilitating U.S. exports of coal, with respect to trade barriers to U.S. coal in foreign markets, and with alternative domestic policy scenarios. In each case the model system provides a stylized, though detailed and persuasive, picture of the impact of alternative policies on coal supply from various parts of the United States, coal demand in the United States and abroad, and the movements of coal from sources to destinations. Policy measures do not have large impacts, however, and can damage as well as benefit the participation of the U.S. coal industry in foreign markets over a long-term time horizon.

We conclude this section on the note that significant information can be gained by modeling approaches. It is clear, however, that they can take various forms and must be designed to meet the specific requirements of the questions being posed.

The Gaps

Are there any limitations to these simulation studies—and, perhaps, in econometric studies of industrial policy in general—with respect to evaluating the impact of industrial policy?

Unfortunately, the answer to this question must be yes. Industrial policy poses some special difficulties to the policy analyst, difficulties that carry the analysis to the frontiers—perhaps even beyond the frontiers—of econometric analysis. These problems involve micro dimensions and macro dimensions. They are concerned with the least tractable aspects of quantitative analysis— the questions of technical change and organization of production—and, most important, they involve the dynamics of economic development and growth. It is appropriate that our discussion should include some emphasis on needs for additional research.

Is There an Optimal Industrial Structure?

A first question, which goes to the heart of industrial policy, is whether there is an optimal industrial structure. There is little doubt that industrial structure and the structure and technique of production processes can be adapted to the resource and capital base and technological development of an economy. Assuming trade and freely operating markets, economic theory would point to an industrial structure, or composition of output, which follows from principles of comparative advantage.[10] Two points need to be emphasized in this regard: (1) comparative advantage must be seen in this context in a dynamic sense, recognizing the potentials of various industries for technical progress, terms of trade, and growth over a forward time horizon; and (2) few countries have been willing to trust their economic development entirely to market forces. The case of Japan, discussed at length in chapter 13 of Adams and Klein (1983), is a good example of both these points. The aim of MITI in setting its industrial-policy objectives has been to develop industries with high potentials for capturing the gains associated with modern technology, with high elasticity with respect to the income of the consuming countries, and with long-run potential for Japanese competitiveness in export markets. Achievement of these objectives has not been simply through operation of free market forces. There have been extensive policy initiatives, although there is still debate on the relative roles of policy and of private industry. Much the same pattern is being followed in other Southeast Asian countries, with sufficient success in recent years that these countries are being termed the New Japans. Many other countries have attempted to force industrialization and technological advancement, though typically with less success. Behind most development plans there is clearly a presumption—one that is not always based on facts or sound theory—that industry is better than agriculture or services, and that high-technology industry is better than less advanced, less capital intensive industry.

The widespread acceptance of such ideas does not make them true. In fact, we have little understanding of the concept of an optimal dynamic industrial structure. Some cases have relatively straightforward answers. Certain industries are not adapted to some settings—mass production industries to countries that have small markets, and high-technology industries to countries that lack education and technology, for example. Some industries appear to be particularly suited for certain parts of the world—cattle raising and grain in Canada, the United States, and Australia. Some industries are resource-related—for example, petroleum and hydrocarbons. Aside from these cases, however, economic theorists have little of practical significance to conclude about optimal industrial structure. Nor is there much to go on with regard to empirical studies. They would encounter directly some of the difficulties with respect to measuring impacts of R&D and technological change that we will discuss later. Suffice it to say here that the question of optimal economic structure represents a gap—one that calls for theoretical and empirical work and is notable for the fact that it is seldom recognized.

Technical Development and Impact of R&D

Despite the extensive theoretical and econometric literature on technological change and on R&D expenditures, there is yet little basis for empirical relationships that would be useful or reliable in a policy-simulation-oriented model. Much of the research in this area remains qualitative, and empirical work often has been pieced together from scanty data or has been worked out by imposing powerful theoretical constraints on production function models.[11] The problem of modeling the technological-change phenomenon in industrial-policy simulation models is that causation is needed. It is not sufficient to hypothesize an exogenous rate of technological change, or to treat technological change as an unexplained residual,[12] the issue is what the impact is of policy on technological change. How can policy serve to accelerate the shifts of the production function, or how can it serve to replace an obsolete production process with one that is technologically more advanced? One should not, however, assume that what is typically seen as technical change or gains in productivity is outside the scope of most econometric treatments. In fact, what is typically called technological change or gains in productivity is captured by the models in the form of shifts between factors of production—for example, deepening of capital or shifts between energy and capital. Maximization models like the system of our coal study can also capture signficant aspects of technical change through shifts between production processes, as could the model of the steel industry. Nevertheless, it must be said that the role of technical change in the production function of most model systems, at the level of the industry as well as at the aggregate level, is still quite rudimentary. The quantitative effects are not well known; and, most important, the interrelationships between investment in research and development and the shifts in the production function are not yet well understood or accurately measured. The theory postulates a stock of knowledge on the basis of which innovations are made. It is widely accepted that R&D produces externalities that are beyond the ability of the individual R&D producer to capture in the market economy. Consequently, there is much support for government contribution toward R&D. To a lesser extent, similar arguments can be made about expenditures intended for product development. The issue then is how much such expenditures contribute to progress of knowledge for the economy, how rapidly and effectively the development of new research findings can be integrated into innovations, and how rapidly the innovations are phased into the economy's capital stock? The quantitative dimensions of these processes have been treated only in case studies of particular industries (Mansfield 1968), and there is little empirical basis for building them into model systems. This is clearly a serious handicap for modeling industrial policy or, in particular, its technological change and R&D aspects.

Organization of Production

Organizational aspects of industrial activity have turned out to be one of the most argued and most challenging questions of the industrial-policy question. The point is being made time and again—supported by little more than forceful rhetoric—that in the United States and in Europe industries have become rigid and inflexible (Reich 1983), that entrepreneurs are concerned with short-term profit targets, and that workers have lost their incentives to work. On a somewhat different scale, there are also questions about optimal industrial organization, with Americans still putting their faith in competition, whereas many Europeans talk about rationalization and optimum scale of production.

Issues related to organization of production are challenging precisely because they go far beyond the technical questions that engineers are equipped to handle. Here the concern is with incentives, worker rewards, organization structure, and so on—all questions in the realm of social science and social-management policy. Unless the robot replaces the worker altogether—and one cannot help thinking that in some industries the robot is being introduced to substitute for increasingly obstreperous workers—the problems of managing people will remain an important and still largely unsolved aspect of industrial policy. Some progress is apparently being made—quality circles and similar approaches. There is some micro evidence on the effectiveness of this type of program. However, there is no way to link measures dealing with the human dimension to the models, or to gauge their industry or macro-level effects. The challenge is not only empirical—it remains conceptual.

Investment in Human Capital

There is by now an extensive literature on the role of human capital, education, and training on income and productivity power. Much of this work is on the micro level, but some macroeconomic evaluations (Denison 1978, 1979a) have been made. It stands to reason that an advanced society using high technology requires a highly educated labor force. It is not clear in a quantitative dimension, however, what the interrelationships are between economic development and education and training. Nor, for that matter, is it clear what types of education are the most productive—at the technical level, at universities, in basic or applied science. There is not yet much basis for entering this important consideration quantitatively into evaluations of industrial policy.

Impact of Infrastructure Investment

Investment in infrastructure—roads, railroads, ports, water, and electrical supplies—represents an important aspect of investment favoring industrial development. Traditionally, infrastructure has been a function of the public sector. Without doubt, infrastructure is important, making possible industrial production and commercialization. Again, there is a question of payout. The use of infrastructure facilities represents one of the inputs into production. To the extent that these facilities are provided at a tariff near actual cost, one may argue that the economy operates as if the private market were operating. In fact, however, public facilities are seldom provided at cost. Rather, in many instances, facilities are provided below cost. Improvement in the facilities is not passed on to the private user in reduced cost. More likely, the improvement in infrastructure facilities benefits the user through improved ease of use, faster shipment, fewer capacity bottlenecks. In these cases there is undoubtedly advantage to the industry from the improvements in facilities, but the question for the econometrician is how to measure this improvement and enter it into a model.

The Role of the Public Sector

Since industrial policy is public policy, government's central role is obvious. It is less clear what that role might be and how it can be implemented optimally. What should be the institutions through which policy decisions are made and carried out? What should be the policy measures? Should they take the form of incentives, or of administrative guidance, or of government regulations? Experience with industrial policy worldwide suggests that the means for implementing industrial policy range widely, reflecting the traditional relationships between business and government in each country. There may be much to be learned from the experience of other countries and of other times, but industrial-policy mechanisms cannot readily be transferred from one setting to another.[13] Nor can one judge accurately the efficacy of industrial-policy measures or the impact of proposed measures simply by looking at other experiences.

Unfortunately, this means that empirical studies have had little to contribute to the question of how—in terms of mechanics—the public sector should intervene in imposing its industrial-policy initiatives. There may be some theoretical or psychological priors. For example, in the United States we may prefer to make maximum use of private-market decision making, using incentives as much as possible. In other countries, rightly or wrongly, confidence in public enterprises may be greater, and the development of targeted publicly owned and operated firms may be seen as the optimal device—as in France, for example.

The problem is that the effectiveness of industrial-policy steps is undoubtedly related to the way they are implemented. This poses significant problems for quantitative evaluation of their impacts. There are basically two types of problems:

1. The models do not have policy handles appropriate for certain types of policy. It is relatively straightforward to recognize in the model tax incentives for investment that modify the user cost of capital, which enters the investment equations. As noted earlier in connection with the model of the steel industry, the issue arises of whether these measures might have a somewhat different impact by way of the cash-flow mechanism. The problem is that for other forms of policy there are no mechanisms in the model. For example, a change in pollution-control regulations designed to lighten the burden on industry calls for arbitrary adjustments in investment.

2. The development of a publicy owned enterprise to take on the tasks of technological and entrepreneurial leadership, as in France or Canada, is difficult if not impossible to integrate into the model system. Does the public enterprise have behavior or effects different from those of private alternatives?

The issue of the role of the public sector thus is not simply one of finding optimal mechanisms, but also one of measuring impacts of the alternative approaches possible. This clearly remains a great unknown for many types of industrial policy.

The International Dimension

We turn finally to the international dimension of industrial policy. This is the aspect that is likely to be central to discussions both within and between countries over the next decade. The age of tariff cutting that contributed so much to postwar growth in trade and development appears to be past. The relative roles of different countries appear to be undergoing rapid change as Japan and the so-called New Japans take on an increasingly greater role in supplying high-technology manufactured goods. At the same time, the mature industrial countries, becoming more concerned about the threat of foreign industrial policies and export incentives, are responding by raising trade barriers. Alternatively, they are imposing their own industrial policies partly in direct retaliation for those of their excessively successful trade partners.

In chapters 2 and 5 we considered in a quantitative way some of the implications of industrial policies in an international setting. This represents only a small beginning to an enormously challenging and important task. What are the international linkages of industrial policies that are targeted either explicitly or implicitly on specific industries? The model frameworks now available only begin to offer some possibilities in this respect. The essential element missing so far, but now becoming available in certain model systems, is the disaggregated international input-output table, which links the country models.[14] In traditional world model systems—Project LINK, for example—the breakdown of international trade flow is into relatively few categories—food, other raw materials, fuels, and manufactures, for example. Moreover, the impact of trade on the country models is through aggregate trade balances. The model needed for international transmission of industrial policy must have highly detailed disaggregation of trade flows to show the impact of policies directed at particular industries on exports of the producing country and imports of the consumer.[15] Second, the model system must recognize the impact of imports and exports at the industry level on the production of the industries in the exporting and importing countries. Third, the model system must be able to recognize the effect of industrial policies, export-promotion policies, and trade barriers—again at the level of individual industries. There are beginning to be models available for this purpose, but the analysis of industrial policies remains a challenging task in such large-scale model systems.

Nevertheless, the challenge is worth taking. The central issue of the next decade is whether countries will seek to develop their own policies independently in an atmosphere of controversy, or whether they can determine the quantitative dimensions of the mutual advantages that could be drawn from a cooperative international industrial policy.

Notes

1. For a discussion of institutions proposed for the United States, see Congressional Budget Office (1983).

2. The uniqueness of the policy experience at various times and in various countries is amply illustrated in Adams and Klein (1983).

3. See, for example, the work of Hudson and Jorgenson.

4. For example, see Griffin (1979).

5. For example, see Trezise (1983); Shinohara (1982); Stoffaes (1981).

6. For practical purposes, an exception may be a policy directed toward an industry so small or so isolated that it would have few spillovers.

7. A mixed policy, which combines interest-rate adjustment with some tax concessions, is even more cost-effective since it was computed so as to impose zero cost on the U.S. Treasury.

8. The intersection between regional policy and industrial policy poses special problems in that there may be contradictions between regional and national objectives.

9. The flow of financing might, for example, be greater into steel if steel were the only beneficiary of industrial policy as compared to a policy benefiting many industries.

10. There is an extensive modern literature dealing with questions of comparative advantage, trade, and the composition of economic activity.

11. An example is the study in chapter 8.

12. See, for example, Denison (1979a).

13. For a discussion see Adams (1983).

14. Such tables are available; for example, the work of Almon at Maryland and the Institute of Developing Economies in Tokyo.

15. However, country-to-country flows are not necessary, only the exports by industry and the imports by industry.

Bibliography

Adams, F.G. 1973. From econometric models of the nation to models of industries and firms. *Wharton Quarterly* supplement.

Adams, F.G., and Ichimura, S. 1983. Industrial policy in Japan. In F.G. Adams and L.R. Klein, eds., *Industrial policies for growth and competitiveness*. Lexington, Mass.: Lexington Books, D.C. Heath and Company, pp. 307–330.

Adams, F.G., and Klein, L.R., eds. 1983. *Industrial policies for growth and competitiveness*. Lexington, Mass.: Lexington Books, D.C. Heath and Company.

Adams, F.G.; Klein, L.R.; and Duggal, V.G. 1984. Foreign industrial policies and the United States: Impact and response. Paper presented to the Conference on Industrial policy, Sewanee, Tennessee, March 1–3.

American Iron and Steel Institute (annual) *Annual Statistical Report*.

Ball, R.J. 1973. *The international linkage of national models*. Amsterdam: North-Holland.

Brown, M., and Heien, D. 1972. The S-branch utility tree: A generalization of the linear expenditure system.

Cazalet, E.G. 1977. Generalized equilibrium modeling: The methodology of the SRI-Gulf Energy Model. Report prepared for the Federal Energy Administration. Palo Alto, Calif.: Decision Focus, Inc., May.

Cournot, A.A. 1838. *Mathematical principles of the theory of wealth*. N.T. Bacon, trans., 1897. New York: MacMillan.

Crandall, R.W. 1981. *The U.S. steel industry in recurrent crisis: policy options in a competitive world*. Washington, D.C.: Brookings Institution.

Crandall, R.W. 1980. The economics of the current steel crisis in OECD member countries. In *Steel in the 1980s*, Paris; unpublished.

Denison, E. 1978. Effects of selected changes in the institutional and human environment upon output per unit of input. *Survey of Current Business* 58 (January): 21–44.

———. 1979a. *Accounting for slower economic growth: The United States in the 1970s*. Washington, D.C.: Brookings Institution.

———. 1979b. Pollution abatement programs: Estimates of their effect upon output per unit of input, 1975–78. *Survey of Current Business* 59 (August):58–59.

Enke, S. 1951. Equilibrium among spatially separated markets: Solution by electric analogue. *Econometrica* 10:40–47.

Federal Trade Commission. 1977. The United States steel industry and its international rivals: trends and factors determining international competitiveness. Staff report of the Bureau of Economics to the Federal Trade Commission (FTC Report) Washington.

Grabowski, H., and Mueller, D. 1978. Industrial research and development, intangible capital stocks, and firm profit rates. *Bell Journal of Economics* 9(Autumn): 328–343.

Griffin, J.M. 1979. *Energy conservation in the OECD: 1980 to 2000.* Cambridge, Mass.: Ballinger.

Hamilton, A. 1791. *Report on manufactures. Reprinted in S. Ratner, 1972, The tariff in American history.* New York: Van Nostrand.

ICF, Inc. 1980a. *Coal and electric utilities model documentation: A draft.* Provided by ICF's Ken Schweers, May.

———. 1980b. *Coal supply curves for Australia, Canada, and South Africa.* Submitted to U.S. Department of Energy, Energy Information Administration, International Energy Analysis Division. Washington, D.C.: ICF, Inc., Fall.

Jorgenson, D. 1963. Capital theory and investment behavior. *AER* 53:247–259.

Katell, S. 1978. *Economic analysis of coal mining costs for underground and strip mining operation.* Washington, D.C.: U.S. Department of Energy, Energy Information Administration, October.

Klein, L.R. 1978. The supply side. *American Economic Review.*

Klein, L.R. 1976. Five years experience of linking national econometric models and of forecasting international trade. In H. Glejser. *Quantitative studies of international economic relations.* Amsterdam: North-Holland (in press).

Klein, L.R., V. Filatov, and S. Fardoust. Long term projections of world trade, output and prices when oil prices are indexed: Link system simulations for 1981–90. *International Economic Review,* in press.

Klein, L.R., S. Fardoust and V. Filatov. 1981. Purchasing power parity in medium term simulation of the world economy. *Scandinavian Journal of Economics.*

Mansfield, E. 1968. *Industrial research and technological innovation.* New York: Norton.

McGraw-Hill, Department of Economics. 1975. Historical pollution control expenditures and related data. Mimeo. New York: McGraw-Hill.

———. 1972–1977. Annual McGraw-Hill survey of investment in employee safety and health. Mimeo. New York: McGraw-Hill.

National Science Foundation. 1979. *Research and development in industry.* Surveys of Science Resources Series. Washington, D.C.: U.S. Government Printing Office.

Naylor, T.H., ed. 1979. *Simulation models in corporate planning.* New York: Praeger.

Newcomb, R.T., and Fan, J. 1980. *Coal market analysis issues.* EPRI Report EA-1575. Palo Alto, Calif.: Electric Power Research Institute, October.

Office of Technology Assessment. 1980. *Technology and steel industry competitiveness.* (OTA Report). Washington.

Preston, R.S. 1972. *The Wharton annual and industry forecasting model.* Economics Research Unit, University of Pennsylvania.

Prywes, M. 1981. Three essays on the econometrics of production, productivity, and capacity utilization. Unpublished Ph.D. diss., University of Pennsylvania, Philadelphia.

————. 1983. A nested CES approach to capital-energy substitution. Federal Reserve Bank of New York Discussion Paper, New York, October.

Reich, R.B. 1983. *The next American frontier.* New York: Times Books.

Rutledge, G., and O'Connor, B. 1981. Plant and equipment expenditures by business for pollution abatement, 1973–80 and planned 1981. *Survey of Current Business* 61(June):19–25.

Samuelson, P.A. 1952. Spatial price equilibrium and linear programming. *American Economic Review* 42:283–303.

Sato, K. 1967. A two-level constant-elasticity-of-substitution production function. *Review of Economic Studies* 34:201–218.

Sheinin, Y. 1980. The demand for factor inputs under a three level CES four factor production function. Unpublished Ph.D. diss., University of Pennsylvania, Philadelphia.

Shinohara, M. 1982. *Industrial growth, trade and dynamic patterns in the Japanese economy.* Tokyo: University of Tokyo Press.

Stoffaes, C. 1981. The rise of industrial policies. Paper presented at Wharton EFA Conference, Oslo, Norway.

Takayama, T., and Judge, G.G. 1971. *Spatial and temporal price and allocation models.* Amsterdam: North Holland.

Trezise, P. 1983. Industrial policy is not the major reason for Japan's success. *The Brookings Review.*

U.S. Census Bureau. 1974–1977. *Pollution abatement costs and expenditures.* Current Industrial Reports. Washington, D.C.: U.S. Government Printing Office.

U.S. Department of Energy, Energy Information Administration, International Analysis Division. 1978. *Coal reserves and production in eight major non-U.S. coal producing countries—Final report.* Washington, D.C.: U.S. Government Printing Office.

Van Horn, A.; Lare, D.B.; and Smith, L.F. 1980. Modeling the economic and environmental impacts of alternative electric utility futures. In W.T. Ziemba et al., eds., *Energy policy modeling: United States and Canadian experiences, specialized energy policy models,* vol. 1. Boston: Martinu Nijhoff, pp. 331–354.

Wescott, R. 1983. World coal demand, supply and trade: A maximization analysis. Unpublished Ph.D. diss., University of Pennsylvania, Philadelphia.

Index

Index

Adams, F.G., 1, 7, 68, 218, 221
Agriculture, 1, 65, 222
Air Quality Act (1967), 164
Aircraft industry, 73
Alternate New Source Performance
    Standards, 198
Antitrust regulation, 212
Apparel industry, 39
Australia, 21, 222; coal, 189, 195,
    197, 201, 202, 206–207
Austria, 21
Automobile industry, 73, 80; and
    investment tax credits, 35, 39, 44;
    in Japan, 69–70; and steel industry,
    88, 91, 97

Bailouts, 2, 4
Barge transportation, 199
Basic industries, 33–34; growth,
    54–55; and investment tax credits,
    42, 60, 65; regional effects of
    industrial policies, 50, 64
Baseline forecasts, 9; and coal
    industry, 182, 189–195; and
    foreign industrial policy effects, 70;
    and regional effects of industrial
    policies, 49–50, 54–57; and
    transformer industry, 141; and
    world economy simulation, 18–21
Basic oxygen furnace, 87, 101–102,
    116–119
Belgium, 21
Black lung tax, 198
Bond rates, 145, 146
Brown, M., 175
Bubble concept, 90
Business cycle models, 214

Canada, 21, 28, 222, 225; coal, 189,
    195, 197, 202, 206–207
Capacity utilization, 215; and steel
    industry, 85, 87, 88–89, 97, 98,
    99, 102–103, 109, 126
Capital, return on, 7
Capital-consumption allowance, 57,
    59–60
Capital costs, 9, 34; and investment
    tax credits, 35–39, 64; regional, 49
Capital stock: and energy
    consumption, 185–186; and
    environmental regulation, 177–179;
    and perpetual inventory method,
    169, 177–179; and transformer
    industry, 136–137
Carter administration, 3
Cash flow, 108, 112–113, 114, 121,
    219, 225
Cazalet, E.G., 185
Census-SRI-Penn (CSP) data set,
    162–163, 168, 175–176
Centrally planned economies, 21
Charleston, S.C., 201
Chemical industry, 13, 161–174;
    energy costs, 162, 165–168, 172;
    environmental regulation, 162,
    163–165, 172–173, 220; growth,
    55, 60; and investment tax credits,
    35, 39, 60, 65, 161, 172, 220;
    production function, 162–163, 172,
    220; productivity, 163–165,
    168–172, 220; research and
    development, 162, 168–172, 220
Clean Air Act Amendments (1972),
    164
Coal industry, 13, 181–209, 220;

Coal industry *(continued)*
demand, 185–186, 195, 197–198, 204, 208; and electric utilities, 182, 186, 204, 206, 208; environmental regulation, 198; industrial policy effects, 182, 195–208, 220; leasing programs, 199; production costs, 183; regional effects, 189–195, 198–199, 208; supply, 182, 184, 195, 198, 206–207, 220; trade flow, 181, 182–188, 189–195, 199, 208, 220; transportation, 186, 187–188, 195, 199–202, 208; welfare function, 182, 186–188, 189
Colombian El Cerrejon coal, 195, 207
Construction industry, steel demand, 88, 91
Continuous casting, 87, 91
Convoy industrial policies, 17, 21, 28, 216
Corporate tax rate, 17; and electric utilities, 144, 148; and gross national product, 35; and output, 59; and quality of capital, 161; regional, effects, 57, 59; and steel industry, 111, 124; and transformer industry, 146–148
Cournot–Enke transportation function, 182, 186
Crandall, R.W., 91
Criteria for industrial policies, 6–8
Current account, 73, 80, 217

Defense industry, 1, 54–55
Demand: and income, 15; regional, 53
Demurrage costs, 200–201
Denison, E., 164, 178, 224
Depreciation allowance, 3, 32; and econometric modeling, 9; and electric utilities, 145; and industry-specific policies, 33; and Japan, 6; and steel industry, 120, 121, 130; and transformer industry, 146
Dollar depreciation. *See* Exchange rates
Durable goods industries, 57

East North Central Region, 50, 55, 56, 64, 66
East South Central Region, 50, 56, 59, 64

Education, 5, 8, 224
Electric utilities: coal demand, 182, 186, 204, 206, 208; and corporate tax, 144, 148; investment, 133, 139–140, 141, 143–144; and nuclear energy, 204–206, 208; and oil prices, 206, 208; and transformer industry, 133, 134, 143–159
Electrical machinery industry, 39, 54, 73; and investment tax credits, 60, 64; *see also* Transformers
Eminent domain rights, 199–200
Employment, 7, 54; and imports, 80; and investment tax credits, 39, 47, 64, 65; and productivity, 216; regional, 53, 55, 60, 64, 65; and steel industry, 85, 105–106, 122, 219
Energy costs, 161; and capital stock, 185–186; and chemical industry, 162, 165–168, 172; and quality of capital, 165; regional, 49, 54, 55; and steel industry, 103–105, 110–111, 116–119
Environmental Protection Agency, 90
Environmental regulation: and capital stock, 177–179; and chemical industry, 162, 163–165, 172–173, 220; and coal industry, 198; and costs, 129; and productivity, 162, 163–165, 172–173; and steel industry, 87–88, 90, 92, 106, 107, 128, 131, 219
European Economic Community, 91, 92, 99
Evaluation of industrial policies, 6–8
Exchange rate, 21, 216, 217; and trade, 73, 80–83, 84
Export promotion, 31, 226; foreign, effects on United States, 67–84

Fabricated metal industry, 54, 64
Factor costs, 39, 92
Factor income, 73, 83
Fan, J., 182–183
Finland, 21
Fluidized bed combustion (FBC) coal technology, 197
France, 1, 3, 4, 225; coal, 189; computer development, 10; exports,

28; imports, 29 n.9; and U.S. industrial policy, 21
Furniture industry, 39

Galveston, 201
General industrial policies, 3, 5; and econometric modeling, 10–11; evaluation, 6–8; vs. industry-specific policies, 31–47; regional effects, 57–60
Griffin, J.M., 185
Gross national product: growth, 54; and imports, 73, 217; and industry-specific policies, 34–35, 39–42; and investment tax credits, 34–35, 39–42
Growth rates, 15, 17, 18, 28

Hamilton, Alexander, 68
Harbor construction, 200–201, 224
Heien, D., 175
High-technology industries, 3, 4, 12, 226; and industry-specific policies, 33; and investment tax credits, 42, 47, 60–64, 216; and regional effects, 50, 60–64

ICF model, 185
Ichimura, 68
Imports, 12, 67–84, 217–218; and employment, 80, 217; and exchange rate, 73; and gross national product, 73, 217; restriction, 98–99; and steel industry, 86, 90–91, 97–100, 113–114, 119, 122, 125–126, 127, 219
Industrial policy, definition, 2–6
Industry-specific policies, 3, 218–221; and econometric models, 9–10; evaluation, 6–8; vs. general industrial policies, 31–47; and gross national product, 34–35, 39–42; regional effects, 60–65
Inflation, 15, 17; and imports, 80; and investment tax credits, 42; and world economy, 28
Infrastructure development, 7, 224
Instrument transformers, 134
Instruments industry, 39, 64
Interest rate, 9, 11, 15–17, 32, 33; and industry-specific policies, 33;

and steel industry, 85, 110, 123–124, 130
Interstate Commerce Commission (ICC), 199
Investment: and electrical utilities, 133, 139–140, 141, 143–144; and steel industry, 12, 87, 106–108, 113–114, 123–124, 219
Investment incentives. *See* Corporate tax rate; Depreciation allowance; Investment tax credit
Investment tax credit, 35–42, 216; and automobile industry, 35, 39, 44; and basic industries, 42, 60, 65; and capital costs, 35–39, 64; and chemical industry, 35, 39, 60, 65, 161, 172, 220; and electric utilities, 145; and electrical machinery, 60, 64; and employment, 39, 47, 64, 65; and gross national product, 34–35, 39–42; and high-technology industry, 42, 47, 60–64, 216; and income, 39; and inflation, 42; and metals-using industries, 35, 42, 47, 60, 64, 211; and output, 39, 57, 59, 60, 64, 65; and productivity, 35, 39; regional effects, 57–65; and steel industry, 85, 111, 120, 121, 122, 130; and transformer industry, 146–148; and transportation industry, 73; and wages, 35, 39
Italy, 21, 28

Japan, 1, 2, 4, 68–69, 221–222; cartels, 10; coal, 189, 207; computer development, 10, 69; export policies, 68–70, 226; Ministry of International Trade and Industry, 5–6, 68, 221; and oil prices, 206; productivity, 28; steel industry, 6, 91, 92, 97, 98, 99, 112, 126, 130; trade, 28; and U.S. industrial policy, 21; wages, 126
Jorgenson, D., 9
Jorgenson Investment Function, 106–108, 114, 119, 137
Judge, G.G., 186–187, 189

Katell, S., 183
Kennedy administration, 211
Keynes, John M., 39
Klein, L.R., 1, 7, 221

Korea, 189
Kuhn–Tucker condition, 187

Labor: and capital ratio, 35, 39; and steel industry, 12, 89, 105–106, 109, 116, 119; training, 5, 224
Large, D.B., 185
Leather industry, 39
LINK, 11, 17–18, 215, 226
Locomotive industrial policy, 17, 21, 28, 216
Lumber industry, 65

Mansfield, E., 223
Manufacturing: and imports, 80; regional growth, 55–57; wages, 54
Mechanisms of industrial policy, 5–6
Metals-using industries, 12, 33; and investment tax credits, 35, 42, 44, 47, 60, 64, 211; regional effects, 50, 64–65
Middle Atlantic Region, 50, 55, 56, 57, 59, 64
Mining industry, 65
Mobile, Ala., 201
Monetary policy, 15–17; and steel industry, 123–124, 130
Montana, severance tax, 198, 199
Mountain Region, 50, 55, 56–57

Naylor, 8
Netherlands, 21
New England Region, 50, 55–56, 57, 60, 64
Newcomb, R.T., 182–183
Northern Great Plains coal, 195, 199, 200
Nuclear energy, 204–206, 208

Occupational safety and health regulation, 162, 164–165, 172, 178
Office of Technology Assessment, 90
Oil-exporting countries, 29
Oil prices, 15, 18; and electric utilities, 206, 208
Open-hearth furnaces, 87, 100–101, 103, 116
Organization for Economic Cooperation and Development (OECD), 18, 21
Output: and imports, 73–80, 83; and income, 54; and investment tax

credits, 39, 57, 59, 60, 64, 65; regional, 53, 54, 55–57, 60, 64, 65

Pacific Region, 55, 56, 60, 65
Perpetual inventory of capital stock, 169, 177–179
Pier capacity expansion, 201
Poland, coal production, 189, 202–204
Policy simulation methods, 8–11
Powder River Basin coal, 199–200
Power transformers. *See* Transformer industry
Price, 7; and productivity, 42; steel, 12, 85, 92, 111–112, 116–119, 122, 126, 127, 129, 219; transformers, 133, 135, 138–139, 143
Primary metals industry, 35–39, 65
Printing and publishing industry, 39, 65
Production function and models, 162–163, 172, 220
Productivity: and chemical industry, 163–165, 168–172, 220; and employment, 216; and environmental regulation, 162, 163–165, 172–173; and investment tax credit, 35, 39; in Japan, 28; and price, 42; and quality of capital, 161, 165–168; and quantity of capital, 161, 163–165; and research and development, 162, 168–173, 220, 222–223; and transformer industry, 133, 144, 151
Protectionism, 67, 68, 98–99, 226
Public-sector revenues, 7
Purpose of industrial policy, 4–5

Quotas, 125, 126, 130

Railroads, 199, 224
Reagan administration, 3, 54, 90, 198
Real income: and demand, 15, 39; growth, 54; and investment tax credits, 39; and output, 54; regional, 55
Recession, 15
Reclamation fees, 198, 208
Regional industry, 4, 12, 49–65, 216–217; basic industries, 50, 64; and capital costs, 49; coal,

Regional industry *(continued)*
189–195, 198–199, 208; and
corporate tax, 57, 59; and
employment, 53, 55, 60, 64, 65;
and energy costs, 49, 54, 55; and
high-technology industries, 50,
60–64; and industry-specific
policies, 60–65; and investment tax
credit, 57–65; and metals-using
industry, 50, 64–65; and output,
53, 54, 55–57, 60, 64, 65
Reich, R.B., 225
Research and development: and
chemical industry, 162, 168–172,
220; contracts, 69; and econometric
models, 10; government financing,
212, 223; and productivity, 162,
168–173, 220, 222–223
Robots, 224

Samuelson, P.A., 182, 186–188, 189
San Diego, 201
SASOL, 206
Sato, K., 175
Savannah, Ga., 201
Seattle, 201
Sectoral models. *See* Industry-specific
policies
Services industry, 4, 54, 222
Severance taxes, 198–199, 208
Shein, Y., 175
Shinohara, M., 68
Slurry pipelines, 199–200
South Africa, 189, 195, 197, 201,
202, 204, 206–207
South Atlantic Region, 50, 55, 56–57
Southeast Asia, 221–222
Spain, 189, 207
Steel industry, 12–13, 85–131, 213,
218–219; capacity utilization, 85,
87, 88–89, 97, 98, 99, 102–103,
109, 126; cash flow, 108,
112–113, 114, 121, 219, 225; and
corporate tax, 111, 124; demand,
12, 85, 88, 91, 92–97, 98, 99,
116; and depreciation allowance,
120, 121, 130; employment, 85,
105–106, 122, 219; energy and
materials, 103–105, 110–111,
116–119; and environmental
regulation, 87–88, 90, 92, 106,
107, 128, 131, 219; imports, 86,

90–91, 97–100, 113–114, 119,
122, 125–126, 127, 219; and
interest rates, 85, 110, 123–124,
130; investment, 12, 87, 106–108,
113–114, 123–124, 219; and
investment tax credits, 85, 111,
120, 121, 122, 130; in Japan, 6,
91, 92, 97, 98, 99, 112, 126, 130;
labor, 12, 89, 105–106, 109, 116,
119; and monetary policy,
123–124, 138; prices, 12, 85, 92,
111–112, 116–119, 122, 126, 127,
129, 219; profits, 89, 122; and
protectionism, 124–126, 130;
technologies, 87–88, 100–103;
validation of models, 113–119;
wages, 89, 92, 109, 114, 116,
126–128, 130, 219
Structure of industry, 221–222,
223–224
Subsidies, 6, 12
Subway cars, imports, 73
Supply-side economics and industrial
policies, 2, 3–4, 44–46, 215–216
Sweden, 21
Synthetic fuels, 197, 206, 208
Synthetic Fuels Corporation, 197

Takayama, T., 186–187, 189
Tariffs, 211; and econometric models,
9–10; and steel industry, 125–126,
130
Taxation incentives, 3, 31–32, 34–47;
and econometric modeling, 9, 17;
see also Corporate tax rate;
Depreciation allowance; Investment
tax credits
Tennessee–Tombigbee waterway, 199
Trade balance, 70, 73, 217
Transitions in industries, 4–5
Transformer industry, 13, 133–159;
capital expenditures and costs, 137,
140; capital stock, 136–137; and
corporate tax, 146–148; demand,
133, 135–136, 138, 141, 143, 144,
146–148; and depreciation
allowance, 146; and electrical
utilities, 133, 134, 143–159;
growth, 54; investment, 146–148;
labor productivity, 133, 144, 151;
man-hours worked, 136, 141, 146;
materials costs, 138, 143, 148;

Transformer industry *(continued)*
  payroll, 137, 143, 146; price, 133,
  135, 138–139, 143; shipments,
  136, 141, 143, 148; wage rate,
  137, 141, 148–151
Transportation: and coal industry,
  186, 187–188, 195, 199–202, 208;
  imports, 73; and investment tax
  credits, 60, 64
Trezise, P., 68
Trigger-price mechanism (TPM), 91,
  99
Turkey, 189

Unemployment. *See* Employment
United Kingdom, 4, 21, 189
United Nations Conference on Trade
  and Development (UNCTAD), 18
U.S. Army Corps of Engineers,
  200–201
U.S. International Trade Commission,
  69
U.S. Treasury, revenue costs of
  industrial policies, 32, 33–34, 44,
  216
User costs of capital. *See* Capital costs

Van Horn, A., 185

Voluntary restraint agreements
  (VRAs), 91, 98

Wages: and investment tax credits, 35,
  39; in Japan, 126; manufacturing,
  54; regional, 49, 53, 54, 55, 60; in
  steel industry, 89, 92, 109, 114,
  116, 126–128, 130, 219; in
  transformer industry, 137, 141,
  148–151
Water Pollution Act Amendments
  (1972), 164
Water Quality Act (1965), 164
Wescott, R., 204
West Germany, 1, 21, 28
West North Central Region, 50,
  56–57, 60, 65
West South Central Region, 50, 55,
  56–57, 59, 60, 64, 65
Wharton Annual and Industry Model,
  12, 32–33, 49, 53, 70, 133, 217
Wharton Census Region Model, 49,
  50–53
Wholesale industry, 54
Williams–Steiger Occupational Safety
  and Health Act (1970), 164, 178
Wilmington, Del., 201
Wyoming, 199

About the Contributors

F. Gerard Adams	University of Pennsylvania, Philadelphia, Pa.
Trevor Alleyne	University of Maryland, College Park, Md.
Christopher Bell	University of Pennsylvania, Philadelphia, Pa.
Andrea Bollino	Banca d'Italia, Rome, Italy
John del Roccili	Wharton Econometric Forecasting Associates, Inc., Philadelphia, Pa.
Vijaya G. Duggal	Widener College, Chester, Pa.
Shah Fardoust	United Nations, New York, New York
Lawrence R. Klein	University of Pennsylvania, Philadelphia, Pa.
Vladimir Kontorovich	University of Pennsylvania, Philadelphia, Pa.
Richard Koss	University of Pennsylvania, Philadelphia, Pa.
Priscilla Luce	Wharton Econometric Forecasting Associates, Inc., Philadelphia, Pa.
Brian Pinto	World Bank, Washington, D.C.
Menahem Prywes	OECD, Paris, France
Mikko Puhakka	University of Pennsylvania, Philadelphia, Pa.
Robert F. Westcott	Wharton Econometric Forecasting Associates, Inc., Philadelphia, Pa.

About the Editor

F. Gerard Adams received the doctorate from the University of Michigan. Since 1961, he has been at the University of Pennsylvania, where he is professor of economics and finance and director of the Economics Research Unit. He is also senior consultant of Wharton Econometric Forecasting Associates, Inc. Dr. Adams has served as a business economist in the petroleum industry and as a forecaster on the staff of the Council of Economic Advisers and the OECD. He is a consultant to numerous government agencies and business corporations. His work has ranged widely in the areas of macroeconometric model building and forecasting, energy economics, regional modeling, and international economics. He is coauthor of *An Econometric Analysis of International Trade* (1969), *Commodity Exports and Economic Development* (Lexington Books, 1982), *Modeling the Multiregional Economic System* (Lexington Books, 1980), and the companion to this volume, *Industrial Policies for Growth and Competitiveness: Volume I* (1983).